I0127883

Studia Fennica
Folkloristica 24

Oral Tradition and Book Culture

Edited by
Pertti Anttonen, Cecilia af Forselles and Kirsti Salmi-Niklander

Finnish Literature Society · SKS · Helsinki · 2018

STUDIA FENNICA FOLKLORISTICA 24

The publication has undergone a peer review.

VERTAISARVIOITU
KOLLEGIALT GRANSKAD
PEER-REVIEWED
www.tsv.fi/tunnus

© 2018 Pertti Anttonen, Cecilia af Forselles, Kirsti Salmi-Niklander and SKS
License CC-BY-NC-ND 4.0 International

A digital edition of a printed book first published in 2018 by the Finnish Literature Society.

Cover Design: Timo Numminen
EPUB: Tero Salmén

ISBN 978-951-858-007-5 (Print)
ISBN 978-951-858-033-4 (PDF)
ISBN 978-951-858-032-7 (EPUB)

ISSN 0085-6835 (Studia Fennica)
ISSN 1235-1946 (Studia Fennica Folkloristica)

DOI: http://dx.doi.org/10.21435/sff.24

A free open access version of the book is available at http://dx.doi.org/10.21435/sff.24 or by scanning this QR code with your mobile device.

BoD – Books on Demand, Norderstedt, Germany 2018

Contents

Pertti Anttonen
ⓘ http://orcid.org/0000-0003-4866-9910

Cecilia af Forselles

Kirsti Salmi-Niklander
ⓘ http://orcid.org/0000-0003-0552-1801

Introduction: Oral Tradition and Book Culture

In many academic environments, the study of oral traditions or folklore has traditionally excluded the influence of literature and other printed media on what is observed and documented as oral tradition. Oral traditions have been considered to diffuse and circulate only orally, and anything that informants (the "folk") have learned from printed sources has been regarded as "contamination" that would question the authenticity of the observed cultural performances as well as the collected materials. This has been evident, for example, in archival practices that have seen literary influences in archived texts as adulteration caused by careless collectors, who have added "embellishments" to that which has been faithfully recorded from "the mouth of the folk" (see e.g. Apo 2007). In the mid-20th century, the label of *fakelore* was coined to mark off anything learned from or distributed by books or other printed media as well as material composed by the informant him or herself as inauthentic (see e.g. Dorson 1950). Following Richard Dorson, Alan Dundes equates fakelore with "tailoring, fabrication, adulteration, manipulation and doctoring, and locates it in the combining of different versions and the production of composite texts, in the falsification of informant data, in the rewriting, embellishment and elaboration of oral materials, and in the imposing of literary criteria upon oral materials." (Anttonen 2014a, 70; see also Dundes 1985, 5, 8.) Besides fakelore, the term *booklore* has been used to distinguish "bookish" traces from the culture created and transmitted orally, from folklore. In addition to materials that draw on or originate from literary and/or printed sources, booklore also denotes orally transmitted lore that concerns and deals with literary and/or printed sources.

It has also been rather common to see oral traditions as a historical layer that preceded literature, constituting its generic system in an inchoate and primitive form. In order to provide an alternative perspective to this chronological relationship, the literary scholar Susan Stewart has argued that folkloristic genres, such as the epic, fable, proverb, fairy tale and ballad, are artefacts constructed by a literary culture. As such, they are projections of authenticity onto oral forms that are "antiqued", distressed, made old. Stewart emphasizes that "when oral forms are transformed into 'evidence' and 'artefacts,' they acquire all the characteristics of fragmentation, symbolic meaning, and literariness that are most valued by the literary culture." (Stewart 1991, 7; cited from Anttonen 2005, 55.) Despite – or in conceptual terms, because of – its long history of existence, oral tradition, or folklore, becomes a modern construct.

Oral tradition has become conceptually modern and literary also through its accessibility. On the one hand, as pointed out by Jack Zipes with reference to the Grimm Brothers and their fairy tales, literary representations are supposed to be "as close to the oral tradition as possible while incorporating stylistic, formal and substantial thematic changes to appeal to a growing middle-class audience" (Zipes 1987, 68). On the other hand, as discussed by Valdimar Hafstein, Romantics – meaning, we may infer, Romantic scholarship and book culture – elevated "bourgeois authors (…) to the rank of original geniuses and ratified their private ownership over their works, [while] they also coined concepts like 'folktales' and 'folksongs' to refer to texts supposedly circulating among common people, which, in contrast to novels and books of poetry, were recycled, unauthored, and not owned by anyone" (Hafstein 2014, 23). Oral tradition, or folklore, was "a constitutive outside of authorship", "nonauthored", or "antiauthored" (*Ibid.*, 22). In the world of copyrighted book culture, oral tradition was up for grabs – mainly for the sake of nation making in the Herderian sense, but also in other ways.

Indeed, in addition to historicizing oral tradition, literary culture has quoted, represented and drawn on oral tradition since the beginning of book culture. Romantic writers in particular got inspiration from oral and traditional sources. Many used old folk songs, tales and ballads as their sources without referring to the original recorded text. When the industrial change transformed society, literary culture cultivated new ideas about national heritage and a new aim of preserving old culture was born. Writers reflected on their encounters with tradition (Gilbert 2013, 105). Researching 18th-century antiquarianism deepens our knowledge about antiquarian initiatives and their substantial role in the preservation and documentation of oral traditions. When the focus is on later times in particular, the researcher has to take into consideration the wide nationalistic drive to reclaim cultural richness and personal connections to the collected traditions (cf. *Ibid.*, 108).

Despite the traditionally rigid lines drawn between oral and literary sources, there is a long-time scholarly interest in handwritten and printed materials within the study of oral traditions. In fact, old documents of, for example, ballads, often discovered and saved for posterity by accident or coincidence, have epitomized the essence of the antiquarian sentiment in folklore study (see Abrahams 1993). There is a long history regarding the study of handwritten manuscripts, field notes and other written documents, cheap and popular prints such as tracts, almanacs, broadsheets, scrapbooks, *Volksbücher* and *bibliothèque bleue*, as well as personal diaries, as both specimens of an oral-literary culture and as sources of information on oral traditions (see e.g. Burke 2009 [1978]; Hayes 1997; Fox 2000). Since the mid-1900s, the interest in printed materials has found parallels in the interest in the study of folklore in the age of technology and mass media (e.g. Bausinger 1990 [1961]; Dégh 1994; Dundes 1989). The denotation of folklore has been extended and expanded from "authentic" oral communication and transmission to reminiscence writing, print culture and, more recently, to the digital world on the internet and social media.

One of the key insights in the interest in printed materials within the study of oral traditions has concerned the idea of mutual interaction between literacy and orality. This interaction has been historically evident, for example, in printed materials meant to be read aloud. Moreover, folktales, popular legends, proverbs, ballads and other folksongs have moved back and forth between oral communication and various written forms of circulation. Oral traditions may also emerge from printed sources when these are read and transmitted through, for example, speech or song. Writing and printing require reading for their reception and use, and reading as a communicative act sets forth processes that often generate oral communication – and oral tradition.

Jack Goody pointed out in his classic work *The Domestication of the Savage Mind* (1977) how remarkable the interaction between oral and written culture has been for a very long time in human history and how the two-sided influence has marked our culture. Regarding folklore materials and print or book culture, a noteworthy source concentrating on the topic is by Kevin J. Hayes (1997). Recent research into post-Gutenberg manuscript media – miscellanies, separates, manuscript books and newspapers – has drawn new attention to the close connections between manuscript media and oral performance, social authorship and personal intimacy (see e.g. Love 1993; Ezell 1999; Chartier 2014, 61–63). The ethnographic-ideological orientation in the research of orality and literacy (Besnier 1995; Street 1993) has focused on hybrid oral-literate practices ("literacies"), challenging the Great Divide view on orality and literacy, theorized, among others, by Walter Ong (1982; cf. Goody 1987; Finnegan 1988).

In addition to mutual interaction, the relationship between orality and literacy has been studied and discussed as a question of representation. The line traditionally drawn at what constitutes influences from the world of print in the study of oral traditions is actually rather paradoxical, since oral traditions cannot be studied independently from the culture of writing – or the culture of reading, for that matter. Both writing and reading are fundamentally important in terms of providing access to oral traditions and the study of materials documenting oral traditions. Orality is studied through its written representations, not only when focusing on archival documents from past centuries and decades, but also when using sound recording devices. In text-centred research approaches, sound-recorded speech, regardless of whether it is classified as oral tradition or oral history, is most often analysed only after first transcribing it into text. Textual representations record and illustrate oral practices and products by employing various literary forms of language as well as literary conventions of documentation, handwriting, printing and print lay-outs. In text-centred approaches, oral tradition is accessed and preserved both as texts that serve as cultural references and as material representations of such references. Text-centred approaches can be contrasted with performance-centred approaches in which oral tradition – or verbal art in traditional formulations – is studied in the social contexts of its embodied production and circulation (see e.g. Bauman 1986; 2004; Briggs 1988).

One aspect in the question of textual representation of orality is a qualitative one: can a written text ever stand for or embody that which has been spoken? Folklore scholarship has a long tradition, at least since the days of Herder, in lamenting over the inability of written documents to represent orality in "high fidelity". A quite common sentiment is that something is lost in the process of documentation; a textual document of folklore does not live up to the real event from which the document was created. One might consider this as the search for authenticity (see Bendix 1997), but the difference is a fact that should direct scholarship into methodological questions in the representation of orality rather than into lamenting over the "loss of context". As put by Richard Bauman, "The texts we are accustomed to viewing as the raw materials of oral literature are merely the thin and partial record of deeply situated human behavior" (Bauman 1986, 2). The solution is not a "full record", as such a thing does not exist, but an analysis of the performance arenas which the text in question intertextually occupies and constructs – also across lines of oral and literary culture.

A new look into book culture

In recent years, a new interest has arisen to study and interpret the mutual interaction between oral and written culture; this especially concerns the links between oral tradition and book culture. Book culture not only means the use and dissemination of printed books but also the transmission and circulation of written texts, such as documents of oral tradition, for example, through the archive into public collections in book format. Much of folklore or oral tradition is made accessible for general reading audiences by publishing printed collections – by both scholars and collectors of folklore. Such circulation or recycling of oral traditions finds its context in both national and transnational histories of the book, printing and print circulation.

This is especially relevant in the case of the Finnish *Kalevala* epic, which is a literary rendition of oral poetry collected from illiterate Finnish-speaking singers in Eastern Finland and Russian Karelia. Ever since its publication in 1835, there have been heavy debates both in Finland and abroad concerning its authenticity (see Anttonen 2014a). Yet, regardless of its exact status as a representation of folk poetry, the *Kalevala* is an exemplary case of oral tradition in book culture: a collection of oral poetry in book format that can be reproduced, replicated, distributed and circulated in potentially unlimited number of reprints and editions. Being a book is essential to the *Kalevala*'s success both as a national epic and a representation of oral tradition.

Regarding book culture and its research, the questions that particularly interest the editors of the present volume include the following: How have printing and book publishing set terms for oral tradition scholarship transnationally and/or in given academic environments? How have the practices and social conventions of reading, as well as the composition of the reading public affected the circulation, study and representation of oral traditions? Which books and publishing projects have played a key role in this and how? How have editorial practices been significant for the constitution of the literary representation of oral genres? How have the written representations of oral traditions, as well as the roles of editors and publishers, introduced authorship to materials that are customarily regarded as anonymous and collective?

One starting point for our compilation of ongoing research into a volume on oral tradition and book culture was the Eighteenth Annual Conference of the Society for the History of Authorship, Reading and Publishing (SHARP) in Helsinki 2010, with the theme, "Book Culture from Below". The conference brought together scholars from different disciplines (including historians, ethnologists and folklore scholars) with a shared interest in the social history of literacy, or more specifically, the roles played by the written word in the everyday lives of people in the lower strata of society, i.e., those with little or no formal education.

The historian Martyn Lyons outlined in his opening keynote speech of the SHARP conference that the new trend is about "lower-class writers" or "the scribal culture of the subordinate classes" (Lyons 2013a; see also Lyons 2013b, 252–255). Lyons characterizes this as a new form of cultural and social history which differs from its intellectual ancestors, the Annales School and the British neo-Marxist social history, in focusing on the reading and writing practices of common people as individuals and as active agents in the shaping of their own lives. The new history from below re-evaluates individual experiences and treats people as agents in historical change, rather than as representatives of collective mentalities. According to Lyons, the new approach re-evaluates individual experience and focuses on personal and private voices and their mediation through various channels.

The new trend in the study of book culture has favoured interdisciplinary research and called for the re-evaluation of the basic terms of the field: authorship, reading, and publishing. Those who want to understand the force of written and published texts in society operate today in a dynamic cross section of different fields of study with many connections between folklore studies, ethnology and history. The common interest between book history and folklore studies is to understand how ideas, cultural meanings and oral tradition are converted into written culture, how they are transmitted through print, and how the exposure to writing and print has influenced human communication in different cultures.

The influence of printing and book culture on oral tradition can be heuristically distinguished from the spread of literacy across national populations, the increase of literary agency among less educated and previously illiterate social classes, and the history of textual interactions and exhanges between the (mostly) literary culture of the learned and the oral culture of the illiterate folk. The culture of the book has brought about new forms of communication as well as new forms of materiality in that communication. Books, manuscripts and related media constitute relevant aspects of vernacular literacy and communication.

The study of book culture has brought insightful analyses, for example, on materials produced by amateur writers and folklore collectors in the 19th and 20th centuries (see e.g. Kuismin & Driscoll 2013; Edlund, Ashplant & Kuismin 2016). For the classification of such materials, Lyons suggests the term "ordinary writings" (Lyons 2013b) to cover various autobiographical, fictional or political texts written by working-class and rural people. These texts have traditionally fallen outside the interest of folklore scholarship, but also outside of history research and literary history. The early folklorists were interested in the common people as intermediators of oral tradition, while their socio-political views, life experiences or expressions of creative writing were treated as "contaminating" factors (see Mikkola 2013). Still, many archives have collected and preserved texts dealing with these issues, and now they provide valuable sources for researchers. Especially in the Nordic countries, the numerous texts written by servants, crofters and members of the landless rural population are now being studied in many interdisciplinary research projects and networks. Issues of vernacular literacy practices are gaining more and more scholarly interest within research into oral traditions.

In the present volume, book culture is mainly dealt with in historical terms and book culture is taken as a practical synonym for book history. A few book historians, therefore, deserve special mention. The dynamic development of book history has been captured by Robert Darnton in his article entitled "What is the History of the Books" (1982). Darnton emphasizes that it should be possible to arrive at a firmer understanding of what books have meant to people. The position of book culture in folklore, and of folk motifs in books, shows that two-way influences were involved when oral traditions came into contact with printed texts and that books need to be studied in relation to other media. "The lines of research could lead to many directions, but they all should issue ultimately in a larger understanding of how printing has shaped man's attempts to make sense of the human condition" (Darnton 1982, 80). Darnton has explored the interaction of print, manuscript and oral media in his model of the communication circuit in 18th-century Paris (Darnton 1995, 189; 2000, 7–9). He emphasizes the creativity of this process: "It always involved discussion and sociability, so it was not simply a matter of messages transmitted down the line of diffusion to passive recipients but rather a process of assimilating information in groups – that is, the creation of collective consciousness or public opinion." (Darnton 2000, 26.)

Roger Chartier deals with the basic terms of book history in his book *The Author's Hand and the Printer's Mind* (2014), focusing on the complexities in the process of publication. He points out that even though writing has been considered an individual, solitary activity, publishing is always a collective activity. "The original and indestructible relationship" between the work and its author has been considered one of the distinctive features between written and oral communication (Chartier 2014, 12). Another distinctive feature of the book is its dual nature as a text and a material object. Today, however, these fundamentals are being questioned, as the digital revolution breaks up the traditional norms and practices for reading, writing and publishing. Chartier points to the "nostalgia for the lost orality" as the other aspect of the credit given to the written word (*Ibid.*, 21–22).

The focus on book history research extends from books to newspapers, documents, flyers, booklets, manuscripts and other, apparently marginal forms of manuscript and print culture. One of the recent examples of this research trend is Ellen Gruber Garvey's monograph *Writing with Scissors: American Scrapbooks from the Civil War to the Harlem Renaissance* (2013). Garvey focuses on marginal archival materials and scrapbooks, exploring their political and social contexts with multidisciplinary perspectives. Her work depicts the process of scrapbooking as "active reading that shifts the line between reading and writing" (Garvey 2013, 47). The reader has become an author.

Oral culture is also a topic of study in historical research. The historical study of oral culture explores the total field of oral communication, which was left outside the traditional folkloristic perspective. One of the path-breaking monographs in this field is Adam Fox's *Oral and Literate Culture in England, 1500–1700*. According to Fox, in 16th- and 17th-century England "the three media of speech, script and print infused and interacted in a myriad ways" (Fox 2000, 5), and even people who could not read "lived within an environment structured and fashioned by text" (*Ibid.*, 6). By the time the famous ballad *Chevy Chase* was first recorded as a transcription in mid-16th-century, it was "already the product of a long series of interactions between oral, manuscript, and print culture" (*Ibid.*, 2–3). According to Fox, it is "difficult to know whether to describe such a ballad as the product of oral, scribal, or print culture" (*Ibid.*, 5). In addition to arguing for a long history in the mutual interaction between oral and literary cultures in England, Fox points out that the growth of literacy did not destroy or weaken the power of oral communication; on the contrary, it provided new material and inspiration for the oral medium (*Ibid.*, 50).

Manuscript, print and oral tradition during the early modern and modern period

The present volume highlights some viewpoints and ongoing research in uncovering the diverse and complicated patterns of relationships and interaction between oral tradition and book culture. Some ideas behind their transmission are scrutinized and presented. Margaret Ezell's and Rikard Wingård's articles discuss the complex interplay of oral and written communication in the early modern period. **Margaret Ezell** has in her earlier work discussed the strategies of authorship and interaction of oral communication, script and print among Quaker women and upper-class writers in 17th- and 18th-century England. With the term "social authorship" (Ezell 1999), she has outlined the social sphere of writing residing in between public and private spheres – the term is useful in the study of communities and practices of reading and writing. In the present article, Ezell discusses the verbal strategies of mid-17th-century sectarian women, who reported their trials and interrogations in printed pamphlets and scribal media. As first-person narration, the accounts preserve elements of the original oral nature of the trials and "highlight the power of the extemporaneous utterance over the letter of the law".

On the basis of his doctoral dissertation, **Rikard Wingård** discusses Swedish early modern and 19th-century popular prints, *Volksbücher*, and their elements of oral culture in book culture. Some of these *Volksbücher* were published in 19th-century folktale collections, but their main link to oral culture was their *argumentum*, the summary of the contents of a story, as well as their peritexts (or paratexts), such as titles, introductory summaries and chapter headings. According to Wingård, the practice of using *argumentum* can be seen as a measure of oral notions of reception; the dominant response-inviting structures of *Volksbücher* support an assimilative type of reading, which is an early modern substitute to the reception of common sets and repertoires of stories in oral and traditional societies – knowing the story before one hears or reads it. Wingård also describes the tendency on the part of the publishers to gradually reduce *argumentum*.

The process of framing and defining oral genres has been closely intertwined with the ideological discussions in 18th- and 19th-century Europe. These discussions are reflected in articles written by Cecilia af Forselles and Yuri Cowan. **Cecilia af Forselles** investigates how newspapers were used to create interest in and understanding of new trends in history and literature, showing how the press was used in the initial phase to market and to make the oral tradition known to teachers and students at the university, as well as to a wider range of readers. By looking at the use of the early Finnish press in the late 18th century to promote academic interest in oral tradition and its literary qualities, af Forselles highlights how the press functioned from the outset as a pioneering medium for the learned in Finland in promoting new attitudes, in particular towards folklore, but also towards culture, language, literature, research and science in general. The scholars adapted their own way to document and interpret oral tradition, for example, by classifying it in the same way as naturalists did with nature. Some attention is also given to international intellectual trends that were, to some degree, also at work in Finland, reflecting, as it appears, universal conditions and scholarly interests and networks in existence among the clergy. Thus, by investigating newspaper writing in detail of one of the leading Finnish scholars, Henrik Gabriel Porthan, side by side with these universal conditions, af Forselles presents an idea of an early significant relationship between the press and oral tradition, the transformation of the spoken word into written text, and the nature of the interaction between the academic centre and the periphery in the context of oral tradition.

Yuri Cowan's main focus is on the ballad canon in the Victorian era. The ballad was defined by its oral delivery, but most extant ballad collections of the time stem largely from printed sources. The ballad on the printed page was treated as "the authentic artefact of British folk culture of oral composition and performance". Cowan analyses the arguments of the Victorian scholars on the "historiography of the everyday", which the ballads were supposed to reveal. Victorian scholars had a tense relationship with oral tradition and print: print was a necessity for the preservation of oral ballads, but print culture threatened and confused the popular culture of the past. Cowan concludes that Victorian scholars did not see the past as "an orderly evolution to a modern best of all possible worlds", but rather as a series of byways, diverse performative moments, abandoned experiments, and shared successes.

Folklore, ideology and archives

Book culture has a specific role in the creation of folklore collections, and folklore archives can be seen as specific forms of book culture. Traditionally, folklore collections – except for sound and photo archives – are written, mostly hand-written or typewritten, representations of oral tradition. Resonating closely with the theme of the present volume, Pertti Anttonen has discussed these issues in his article "Lost in Intersemiotic Translation? The Problem of Context in Folk Narratives in the Archive" (see Anttonen 2014b).

In the present volume, the questions of editing and curation are dealt with in conjunction with the creation of folklore collections on the basis of encounters with people from different backgrounds and literary skills, reflected especially in the articles by Kyrre Kverndokk, Kirsti Salmi-Niklander and Diarmuid Ó Giolláin. **Kyrre Kverndokk** discusses the epistemological basis for the production of folklore documents as texts, based on the establishment of the Norwegian Folklore Archives and debates related with its early phase. Some of these debates took place between Moltke Moe and Knut Liestøl, who represented centralized, academic and well-disciplined archival work, and Tov Flatin and Rikard Berge, who supported de-centralized autonomy of private folklore collections. The technology of transforming vernacular culture to folklore items was expressed in instruction books for folklore collectors. Collectors had a crucial role in the process of separation of folklore items from other kinds of cultural expressions and in the process of giving oral utterances a written shape. According to Kverndokk, fieldwork materials were presented as "herbarium specimens of what almost could be mistaken for being natural categories".

The interest in oral tradition emerged among Finnish university students during the 19th century as a result of new ideas, practices and lively debates. Students played a crucial role in collecting folklore and establishing folklore studies as an academic discipline. **Kirsti Salmi-Niklander** scrutinizes the activities in 19th-century provincial student organizations through the material produced by the student culture, analysing the interaction between printed, manuscript and oral media. Because of the unstable political situation in Europe after the revolutionary year of 1848, student activities were strictly controlled by the authorities. Publishing in print was difficult; therefore, students discussed and disseminated their ideas via manuscript media and oral performance. According to Salmi-Niklander, student organizations played a crucial role in the development of folklore archives and folklore scholarship, and served as arenas for the interaction among oral, manuscript and print media. Furthermore, from the oral-history perspective, the student culture produced materials on the writing of the group's history, and on the use of oral history materials in this process.

Ireland, too, provides an excellent example of the close interaction between oral, manuscript and print culture. Gaelic was established early as a written language, but the specific political situations in Ireland made the relationship of oral tradition, manuscript and print more complex than in many other countries in Western Europe. **Diarmuid Ó Giolláin** focuses on the close relationship that has existed between Gaelic oral and manuscript culture in Ireland, and as contrast to the mainly English-language print culture and literacy. Learned tradition and oral tradition as well as high and popular culture have interplayed in topics, themes and personages since the medieval times to the present, despite – or partially because – of adverse circumstances since the Anglo-Norman conquest in the 12th century, and especially since 16th and 17th centuries, when Protestant England strengthened its colonial control of the country. The interplay between oral and literary can also be seen in the concept of *béaloideas*, oral or unwritten tradition, which has been central in folklore and ethnology since the early 20th century, but has its origin in theology and the oral instructions of the Catholic Church. Ó Giolláin's article shows how Irish Gaelic book history was actually manuscript history and, as such, part of both oral and literary culture. In the 18th and 19th centuries, the Ossianic tradition of epic narratives and narrative poetry, unlike James Macpherson's primitivist claim of *Ossian*'s orality, lived on in both oral tradition and in an abundance of manuscripts that were read aloud in communal contexts, where also oral storytelling took place. Ó Giolláin also surveys 18th-century Gaelic literary poetry, which circulated in scribal culture and orally. The article further discusses how Gaelic learned culture came to inform an Anglo-Irish re-imagining of an Irish nation at the end of the 19th century.

The final article explores the question of textuality, writing and material-conceptual identities of texts. **Marija Dalbello** presents "micro-readings" of several texts. An example of non-literary letter writing, a literary letter-poem by Emily Dickinson, and a remediated modernist poem by Guillaume Apollinaire – all edited for a digital archive – are contrasted with contemporary artistic practices in conceptual drawings (by contemporary artist Molly Springfield), in which a work's artistic strategy is focused on revealing its materiality. Dalbello offers a reflection on writing as inextricable to creation through a fourfold distanciation of writing elaborated after Paul Ricoeur. The purpose of this reflection is to discuss texts and their actualization as belonging to the larger system of language in which texts are tied to speakers or writers as well as listeners or readers.

The present volume highlights varied and selected aspects of the expanding field of research into oral tradition and book culture. We take pride in presenting a collection of multifaceted approaches to this fascinating field of research. As editors of the collection, we sincerely hope that the articles will inspire further research and other publications on the topic. We want to express our compliments to the projects, institutions and individuals who have helped and supported us during the editing process.

These include the Finnish Literature Society, the Research Community "Cultural Meanings and Vernacular Genres" (CMVG) of Folklore Studies, University of Helsinki, and the Faculty of Arts at the University of Helsinki. Special thanks are due to Ms Seita Soininen for assistance during the final editing process. Kirsti Salmi-Niklander's research has been funded through the Academy of Finland fellowship for the project "Between voice and paper: authorial and narrative strategies in oral-literary traditions" (251289).

We appreciate the insightful comments of our peer reviewers, which helped us greatly improve the end result. We are thankful to the contributors for their articles as well as for their patience in the long editorial process. Last but not least, we would like to extend our sincere gratitude to the Finnish Literature Society for publishing the volume in its Studia Fennica series.

Helsinki & Joensuu, April 2018
Pertti Anttonen, Cecilia af Forselles & Kirsti Salmi-Niklander

References

Abrahams, Roger D. 1993. Phantoms of Romantic Nationalism in Folkloristics. *Journal of American Folklore* 106: 3–37.

Anttonen, Pertti J. 2005. *Tradition through Modernity: Postmodernism and the Nation-State in Folklore Scholarship.* Studia Fennica Folkloristica 15. Helsinki: Finnish Literature Society.

Anttonen, Pertti 2014a. The Kalevala and the Authenticity Debate. In János M. Bak, Patrick J. Geary & Gábor Klaniczay (eds), *Manufacturing a Past for the Present: Forgery and Authenticity in Medievalist Texts and Objects in Nineteenth-Century Europe.* Leiden: Brill, 56–80.

Anttonen, Pertti 2014b. Lost in Intersemiotic Translation? The Problem of Context in Folk Narratives in the Archive. *ARV – Nordic Yearbook of Folklore* 69: 153–170.

Apo, Satu 2007. The Relationship between Oral and Literary Tradition as a Challenge in Fairy-Tale Research: The Case of Finnish Folktales. *Marvels & Tales* 21 (1): 19–33.

Bauman, Richard 1986. *Story, Performance, and Event: Contextual Studies of Oral Narrative.* New York: Cambridge University Press.

Bauman, Richard 2004. *A World of Others' Words: Cross-Cultural Perspectives on Intertextuality.* Oxford: Blackwell Publishing.

Bausinger, Hermann 1990 [1961]. *Folk Culture in a World of Technology.* Translated by Elke Dettmer. Bloomington: Indiana University Press.

Bendix, Regina 1997. *In Search of Authenticity: The Formation of Folklore Studies.* Madison: University of Wisconsin Press.

Besnier, Niko 1995. *Literacy, Emotion and Authority: Reading and Writing on a Polynesian Atoll.* Cambridge: Cambridge University Press.

Briggs, Charles L. 1988. *Competence in Performance: The Creativity of Tradition in Mexicano Verbal Art.* Philadelphia: University of Pennsylvania Press.

Burke, Peter 2009 [1978]. *Popular Culture in Early Modern Europe.* Third edition. Farnham: Ashgate Publishing Company.

Chartier, Roger 2014. *The Author's Hand and the Printer's Mind: Transformations of the Written Word in Early Modern Europe.* Translated by Lydia G. Cochrane. Cambridge: Polity.

Darnton, Robert 1982. What is the History of Books? *Daedalus* 111 (3): 65–83.

Darnton, Robert 1995. *The Forbidden Best-Sellers of Pre-Revolutionary France.* New York: Norton.

Darnton, Robert 2000. An Early Information Society: News and the Media in Eighteenth-Century Paris. *The American Historical Review* 105 (1): 1–35.

Dégh, Linda 1994. *American Folklore and the Mass Media*. Bloomington: Indiana University Press.

Dorson, Richard M. 1950. Folklore and Fake Lore. *The American Mercury*, March 1950: 335–342.

Dundes, Alan 1985. Nationalistic Inferiority Complexes and the Fabrication of Fakelore: A Reconsideration of Ossian, the *Kinder- und Hausmärchen*, the *Kalevala*, and Paul Bunyan. *Journal of Folklore Research* 22 (1): 5–18.

Dundes, Alan 1989. *Folklore Matters*. Knoxville: University of Tennessee Press.

Edlund, Ann-Catrine, T.G. Ashplant & Anna Kuismin (eds) 2016. *Reading and Writing from Below: Exploring the Margins of Modernity*. Umeå: Umeå University & Royal Skyttean Society.

Ezell, Margaret 1999. *Social Authorship and the Advent of Print*. Baltimore: Johns Hopkins University Press.

Finnegan, Ruth 1988. *Literacy and Orality: Studies in the Technology of Communication*. Oxford: Basil Blackwell.

Fox, Adam 2000. *Oral and Literate Culture in England 1500–1700*. Oxford: Clarendon Press.

Garvey, Ellen Gruber 2013. *Writing with Scissors: American Scrapbooks from the Civil War to the Harlem Renaissance*. New York: Oxford University Press.

Gilbert, Suzanne 2013. Tradition and Scottish Romanticism. In Sarah Dunnigan & Suzanne Gilbert (eds), *The Edinburgh Companion to Scottish Traditional Literatures*. Edinburgh: Edinburgh University Press, 105–113.

Goody, Jack 1977. *The Domestication of the Savage Mind*. Cambridge: Cambridge University Press.

Goody, Jack 1987. *The Interface between the Written and the Oral*. Cambridge: Cambridge University Press.

Hafstein, Valdimar Tr. 2014. The Constant Muse: Copyright and Creative Agency. *Narrative Culture* 1 (1): 9–48.

Hayes, Kevin J. 1997. *Folklore and Book Culture*. Knoxville: University of Tennessee Press.

Kuismin, Anna & M.J. Driscoll (eds) 2013. *White Field, Black Seeds: Nordic Literacy Practices in the Long Nineteenth Century*. Helsinki: Finnish Literature Society.

Love, Harold 1993. *Scribal Publication in Seventeenth-Century England*. Oxford: Clarendon Press.

Lyons, Martyn 2013a. A New History from Below? The Writing Culture of European Peasants, c. 1850 – c. 1920. In Anna Kuismin & M.J. Driscoll (eds), *White Field, Black Seeds: Nordic Literacy Practices in the Long Nineteenth Century*. Helsinki: Finnish Literature Society, 14–29.

Lyons, Martyn 2013b. *The Writing Culture of Ordinary People in Europe, c. 1860–1920*. New York: Cambridge University Press.

Mikkola, Kati 2013. Self-Taught Collectors of Folklore and their Challenge to Archival Authority. In Anna Kuismin & M.J. Driscoll (eds), *White Field, Black Seeds: Nordic Literacy Practices in the Long Nineteenth Century*. Helsinki: Finnish Literature Society, 146–157.

Ong, Walter J. 1982. *Orality and Literacy: The Technologizing of the Word*. London: Methuen & Co.

Stewart, Susan 1991. Notes on Distressed Genres. *Journal of American Folklore* 104: 5–31.

Street, Brian V. 1993. Introduction: The New Literacy Studies. In Brian V. Street (ed.), *Cross-Cultural Approaches to Literacy*. Cambridge: Cambridge University Press, 1–21.

Zipes, Jack 1987. The Enchanted Forest of the Brothers Grimm: New Modes of Approaching the Grimms' Fairy Tales. *The Germanic Review: Literature, Culture, Theory* 62 (2): 66–74.

Margaret J.M. Ezell

"But the Lord said to me, 'Say Not guilty'": Recreating Courtroom Drama in Trial Accounts by 17th-Century English Sectarian Women

> He first demanded my name, and I told him; and he said, *Anna Trapnel, here is a Bill of Indictment to be read for you to give in your answer concerning*: then Justice Lobb said, *Read the Bill*: so it was read to me: and *Lobb* said, *Are you guilty, or not?* I had no word to say at the present; but the Lord said to me, *Say Not guilty, according to the form of the Bill*… (Trapnel 1654, 24.)

This was not the first time that the London ship-wright's daughter Anna Trapnel (fl. 1642–1660) had been in trouble with civil authorities. Trapnel, a member of a loosely defined radical sect that had arisen during the English Civil War called the Fifth Monarchists because of their belief that the end of the world was coming and that Christ was returning to reign over it, had created a public disturbance by falling in a trance during a trial at Whitehall in London. For days she continued in her trance, uttering prophecies foretelling the doom of Oliver Cromwell and the Protectorate and singing the praises of the imminent coming of Christ. As historians of this period have noted, Cromwell and his agents were alarmed by this woman whose public performances attracted and captivated crowds and also by the publications of her words taken down by on-lookers (Hinds 2000, xvii–xviii). Trapnel is one of the most colorful and most studied of the women prophets in the recent surge of interest in radical movements in the Civil War years, but she was not an isolated figure in her confrontations with civil authorities. There are numerous other published and handwritten accounts of women sectarians standing trial for their religious beliefs during this period.

Although the politics of the sectarian religious groups and the role of women within them has received increasing attention since the classic 20th-century studies by Keith Thomas, Elaine Hobby, and Phyllis Mack (Thomas 1958; Hobby 1989; Mack 1992), what has been left largely unexplored in their narratives is the dynamic oral nature of the event of the trial itself and how that is conveyed through a written medium. One important feature of these texts is that they are told in the first-person rather than being a record taken and published by a spectator or an officer of the court. As we will see, these first-person accounts of the women's trials highlight the power of the extemporaneous utterance over the letter of the law and attempt to evoke oral culture while preserving the record in print or in manuscripts in circulation.

Trials themselves, of course, are part of oral culture, a spoken performance during which life and death literally hang in the balance, depending on words spoken by all parties involved; as Laura Gowing has observed in her study of early modern women appearing in court as litigants, "justice in church courts depended on storytelling" (Gowing 1996, 41). As Fox and Woolf have highlighted "oral communication" is often a hybrid experience that can involve the written and printed. Instead of looking at the ways in which women in these trials created a rhetoric intended to be read, this essay will focus on the ways in which the published accounts of their trials attempted to preserve the elements of orality essential to the performance of their innocence through the spoken word (Fox & Woolf 2002, 12).

Trial narratives of early modern Englishwomen

There were numerous precedents of the publication of women on trial for their religion from the 16th and early 17th centuries, as well as conventions for the printing of trial narratives, including the use of dialogue format (Thomson 1965, 107–110; Watt 1997, 100). The most famous example, and one most widely known to 17th-century English Protestants, was no doubt that of Anne Askew (1520-1546), who died as a martyr for the Protestant faith. She left behind her own narrative of her examinations for heresy by Catholic church leaders; her account was retold repeatedly by several commentators, including John Foxe in his frequently republished *Acts and Monuments*, a central text in shaping later generations of English Protestantism and a text invoked by George Fox during his trial held with Margaret Fell's (Fell 1664, 23). There was even a popular ballad about her and her trials and examinations "I am a woman poore and blinde," which was sung throughout the 17th century, ensuring a widespread common familiarity of her as a woman on trial for her faith (Watt 2004).

The 17th-century women whose trials will be explored in this essay were charged with a variety of offences, ranging from witchcraft, to refusing to take an oath, pay tithes, and holding unlawful assemblies. What emerges when one compares these seemingly disparate narratives of conflict between the women and civil authorities, most often their social superiors, in spite of their differences in terms of location or specific event, are the ways in which the expectations of an oral culture shapes their written representation of themselves. The spoken word as opposed to a written text was an integral part of sectarian religious culture. Hinds has observed in the context of her analysis of the rhetorical strategies and the hybrid genres of 17th-century women's printed texts, many of the autobiographical writings are tied to the practice of giving public testimony before one's congregation: these, "conversion narratives," describe how one came to recognize sin and accept the teachings of that group before being received into it (Hinds 1996, 12–13). This public proclamation by an individual of their sins and shortcomings, as well as of the mercy and blessings from the Lord that they have experienced, was the gateway to membership in these groups.

Furthermore, there would have been an expectation by many of the women writing for publication that their texts, handwritten or printed, would be read aloud to groups of listeners (Ezell 1993, 141–145). For Quakers in particular, as Bauman has noted, at the heart their understanding of their faith is the "voice of God, God the speaker" (Bauman 1983, 24). Simultaneously with this valorization of public speaking, however, the sectarians were among the most prolific publishers of their times, turning to the press to persuade others of their innocence and good-will, as well as providing comfort and support to those believers facing persecution or suffering from religious doubts (Hobby 1989, 1–26; Ezell 1993, 149–158). In the case studies that follow, I will explore the tensions between using print to transmit what was originally an oral performance and the efforts made to preserve those elements of the oral moment in a different media, by women who believed in the authenticating power of the spoken word.

Trapnel's case has perhaps attracted more recent scholarly attention than the other women I shall discuss – Margaret Fell (1614–1702), Elizabeth Andrews (1628–1718), and Elizabeth Stirredge (1634–1706) – because she herself attracted attention during her lifetime, becoming an early type of celebrity figure through her performance of her mystic visions (Magro 2004, 417; Hinds 2004, 1–25; Warren 2010, 181–183). She was more extreme in her behavior and more aggressively confrontational with those in authority. In her trial in Cornwall in 1654, she was accused of "witchcraft, madness, whoredom, vagrancy, and seditious intent" (Davies 2004) whereas Fell was on trial primarily for refusing to swear an oath of loyalty and secondarily for permitting her house to be used to conduct illegal religious services. Trapnel was a young single woman, who vigorously defended her right to travel from London to Cornwall when questioned by the magistrates why she was there (Trapnel 1654, 26). In contrast, Fell, Andrews, and Stirredge were mature women with families and their physical presence in the courtroom, often accompanied by their children, most likely thus had a different resonance for those who were there to hear them.

Most of the existing historical studies have focused on the political issues underlying the conflict between these women and the male authority figures, while literary critics have examined the ways in which such women used the print publication of different genres of life writing to participate in public and political debates (Magro 2004; Gillespie 2004). As they point out, it was a common convention for both male and female prisoners brought before the court on issues relating to religious conformity to declare in their narratives that it was actually not them speaking, but the Lord speaking through them. Thus, as Magro and others have argued, they have a rhetorical defense to permit them as women to print their thoughts. This is clearly at work in these texts, but the emphasis on the women's desire for publication, whether print or scribal, may lead to a lack of appreciation of how the women were employing textual strategies to preserve an oral contest.

Anna Trapnel in the courtroom

Trapnel mixes first-person, present tense dialogue passages with descriptive narrative commentary about the events. She introduces multiple voices into the account, with the Lord's being one of several potent speakers. Before she goes to the Session House to have the indictment against her read, she records that she walked in a garden: "I was thinking what I should say before the Justices," but as she pondered, "I was taken off from my own thoughts quickly, through the words, *Take no heed what thou shalt say & being brought before them for the Lord Christ's sake, he will give thee words: dost thou know what they will ask thee? Therefore look to the Lord, who will give thee answers suitable to what shall be required of thee*" (Trapnel 1654, 23). And so, although she admits that she had already considered what she would say, "I had heard how the form of Bills run, and of that word *Not guilty*, according to the form of the Bill," she tells her reader she resolves not to speak unless prompted by God.

That she should speak in court and the necessity of her speaking eloquently and to the purpose is made clear when she describes the hostility of the crowd that watched her in the streets and who was present in the court. As she walked to the court house, "I had followed me abundance of all manner of people, men and women, boyes and girls, which crowded after me; and some pull'd me by the arms, and stared me in the face, making wry-faces at me, & saying *How do you now? How is it with you now?*" (Trapnel 1654, 23.) However, Trapnel describes herself as "never in such a blessed self-denying lambe-like frame of Spirit in my life; I had such lovely apprehension of Christ's sufferings." Inside the court, "I was a gazing-stock for all sorts of people," among whom she notes shrewdly was a clergyman who had brought the complaint accompanied by "the witch-trying-woman" who stared directly into her face (*Ibid.*, 24). She then gives a vivid account of the atmosphere of the courtroom, and how when asked how she would plead to the indictment, "I had no word to say at the present; but the Lord said to me, '*Say Not guilty, according to the form of the Bill,* so I spoke it as from the Lord'" which caused the justices to begin whispering among themselves. Trapnel explains to the reader that she had later learned that "the report was, That I would discover my self to be a witch when I came before the Justices, by having never a word to answer for my self; for it used to be so among the witches, they could not speak before the Magistrates, and so they said, it would be with me" (*Ibid.*, 25).

The format of the text then changes. Given the complexities of 17th-century book production, one might well wonder if indeed it was Trapnel or her publisher who changed to dialogue format and back to block narrative. As we do not have Trapnel's manuscripts for comparison, one can only point to the prevalence of the shift from block narrative to dialogue form and back again found in existing manuscripts, such as that by Agnes Beaumont in her account of her trial (Camden 1992). Regardless of who made the decision to change the type format, the presence of two distinct styles of communication on the page asks for a different response from the reader/listener and communicates more than the simple words on the page.

After the block of interpretive narrative, there follows a long dialogue section in which the individual Justices are identified by name, and her speeches are prefaced by "A.T."

> Then *Lobb* said, *Tender her the book which was written from something said at* White-Hall [Trapnel's prophetic utterances recorded in *The Cry of the Stone*]: so the book was reached out to me: and Justice *Lobb* said, *What say you to that book? Will you own it? Is it yours?*
>
> **A.T.** *I am not careful to answer you in that matter.*[1]
> Then they said, *She denies her book*. Then they whispered with those behind them. Then spake Justice *Lobb* again, and said, *Read a vision of the horns out of the book*: so that was read: then Justice *Lodd* said, *What say you to this? Is this yours?*
>
> **A.T.** *I am not careful to answer you in that matter, touching the whole book, as I told you before, so I say again: for what was spoken was at* White-Hall, *at a place of concourse of people, and neer a Counsel, I suppose wise enough to call me into question if I offended, and until them I appeal….Again, I said, I supposed they had not power to question me for that which was spoke in another county*: they said, *Yea, that they had*. Then the book was put by; and they again whispered. (Trapnel 1654, 25.)

Trapnel's narrative is thus mixed, offering a narrative block of description that is framed and glossed with hindsight, imposing an interpretation, which is then followed by a present tense dialogue which reenacts the oral event at its crisis moment, but leaves it to the hearer or reader to make a judgment. Trapnel does not assert her innocence to her reader – through the use of a dialogue format, she re-enacts the spoken scene itself that convinces the listener/reader of her innocence and her accusers' guilt.

She likewise records the effect of her words on the listeners. The Judges are clearly confused and surprised by her answers. When Justice Launse questions why she should come from London to Cornwall, she returns again to dialogue format:

> **Justice Launse**. *But pray tell us, what moved you to some such a journey?*
>
> **A.T.** *The Lord moved me, and gave me leave.*
>
> **Launse**. *But had you not some of extraordinary impulses of Spirit, that brought you down? Pray tell us what those were.*
>
> **A.T.** *When you are capable of extraordinary impulse of Spirit, I will tell you; but I suppose you are not in a capacity now*: for I saw how deridingly he spoke: and for answering his thus, he said, *I was one of a bold Spirit*; but he soon took me down; so himself said: but some said, it took them down: for the Lord carried me so to speak, and that they were in a hurry and confusion, and sometimes would speak all together… (Trapnel 1654, 26).

1 "Careful" in this sense suggests that she feels she need have no care or need to answer that question because it is an inappropriate question to ask her.

Her words animate the watchers in the court, causing one woman who was supposed to testify against her to flee the room and the justices to start speaking simultaneously. A soldier is ordered to be removed by the Justices as he "smiled to hear how the Lord carried me along in my speech; and justice *Selye* called to the Jailor to take him away, saying, *He laughed at the Court*" (*Ibid.*, 27). Trapnel acted quickly to prevent this, "then I said, *Scripture speaks of such who* make a man an offender for a word; *but you make a man an offender for a look.* They greatly bussled, as if they would have taken him away; but this was quickly squasht." The combination of representing Trapnel's speaking voice in dialogue form, which places the burden of interpretation on the listener or reader, and the reinforcement of its efficacy given the description of the responses of the listeners in court thus comes together to capture both the essential oral nature of her defense and the display of it on the page.

She leaves the court, having been bound over for trial. The justices "were willing to have no more discourse with me," after her display of verbal dexterity in response to their questions. The crowd who had been listening to her now responds to her very differently; having heard her testimony, "many strangers were very loving and careful to help me out of the croud: and the rude multitude said, *Sure this woman is no witch, for she speaks many good words, which the witches could not*" (Trapnel 1654, 28). On leaving the court, Trapnel reverts to past-tense descriptive narrative of her continuing journey, "and so I rode praying, all the first days Journey, til I came to *Foy-Town*" where she is respectfully greeted and "at length I spake to them in Scripture language." Her account of her subsequent imprisonment and her spiritual experiences there remain in this descriptive and interpretative style without the immediacy of the dialogue passages and requiring a different type of response from the reader.

Quaker women and courtroom performances: Margaret Fell

The issue of women speaking in court would have had an additional resonance with contemporary listeners and readers. On the one hand, silence supposedly might condemn Trapnel as a witch, while on the other, women speaking in public and preaching was considered transgressive and socially disruptive (Hinds 1996, 18–50). This aspect of women's public participation in religious and political events through speaking and moving a crowd characterizes the radical sects, none more so than the Quakers. Accounts of the hostile and even violent reaction to Quaker women's preaching are numerous: many were published individually while the writer was in prison, while others were circulated in manuscript. In 1753 such accounts were collected and published in two volumes by Joseph Besse, *A Collection of the Sufferings of the People called Quakers.* The terrifying ordeals chronicled in these works seemed to have not daunted women such as Priscilla Cotton and Mary Cole, the two housewives from Plymouth in Devon who were imprisoned when proselytizing in Exeter. They dictated a letter directed to

The Priests and People of England we Discharge our Consciences and Give them warning on the subject of women preaching and praying in public: "thou tellest the people Women must not speak in a church [but] the Scriptures do say, that all the Church prophesie one by one [I Cor. 14:31]" (Cotton & Cole 1655, np). When the men came to question the women, they were quickly routed by the women's words: "two of your Priests came to speak with us, and when they could not bear sound reproof and wholesome Doctrine, that did concern them, they railed on us with filthy speeches… and so ran from us."

Margaret Fell, one of the leaders of the early Quaker movement who would eventually marry its charismatic leader George Fox, was moved to write in 1666 *Womens speaking justified, proved and allowed of by the Scriptures, all such as speak by the spirit and power of the Lord Jesus.* In 1664, she and Fox had been imprisoned and brought to trial for a series of causes, including their refusing to take the required oath of loyalty to Charles II and also for her holding illegal worship services in her home. In her essay justifying women's public speech on matters of religion, Fell argues strongly that women's speech is essential in the world lest other speakers gain control over all religious discourse: "Let this Word of the Lord, which was from the beginning, stop the mouths of all that oppose Womens Speaking in the Power of the Lord; for he hath put enmity between the Woman and the Serpent; and if the Seed of the Woman speak not, the Seed of the Serpent speaks" (Fell 1666, 4). In her account of her appearances in court, Fell relies on the spoken word to obtain a true verdict for her. As with Trapnel's account of her trial, Fell also uses dialogue to highlight particular moments of her trial.

> Then one of the Justices that committed her, said, Mrs. *Fell* you may with a good Conscience. (if you cannot take the Oath) put in security that you may have no more meetings at your house.
>
> **M.F.** Wilt thou make that good, that I may with a safe Conscience make an engagement to forbear meetings, for fear of losing my Liberty and Estate[?]; wilt not thou and you all here judge of me that it was for saving my Estate and Liberty that I did it, and do I not in this deny my testimony; and would not this defile my Conscience [?]
>
> **Judge.** This is no answer, will you take the Oath? we must not spend time.
>
> **M.F.** I never took an Oath in my life, I have spent my days thus far, and I never took an Oath, I own Allegiance to the King as he is King of *England*, but Christ Jesus is King of my Conscience – Then the Clerk held out the Book and bid her pull off her Glove and lay her hand on the book.
>
> **M.F.** I never laid my hand on the book to swear in all my life, and I never was at this Assize before, I was bred and born in this County and have led my life in it, and I was never at an Assize before this time, and I bless the Lord that I am here this day upon this account, to bear testimony to the truth. (Fell 1664, 7).

Clearly, in Fell's mind, if she does not speak, the devil will; through her oral defense of herself, her trial became less of a test of faith and more of a stage on which to perform her innocence.

Unlike Trapnel who relies on the Lord to provide legal counsel, Fell, the widow of a well-to-do landowner (Kunze 2004), comes to her trial equipped with both spiritual and legal defenses. When she is brought before the bar, she is initially treated with a deference not shown to Trapnel, and an "order was given to the gaoler by the judge to set a stool and a cushion for her to sit upon" (Fell 1664, 1). She brought with her four of her daughters who stood beside their mother, but the Judge ordered that the children not "stand before the Bar" as if they were accused, but had them brought up near the judges to sit. The presiding judge was Sir Thomas Twisden, a noted justice of the King's Bench who would preside over the trials of John Bunyan and other prominent dissenters. He was noted for leniency with dissenters who did not otherwise disturb the peace, and also for directing his jurors to be alert to any possible corruption or oppression of the justices in the performance of their duties, and thus Fell was facing a more considerate judge than most (Halliday 2004).

As the Twisden explains "Mrs Fell you are committed by the Justices of the Peace for refusing to take the Oath of Obedience & I am commanded, or sent by the King to tender it to any that shall refuse it," Fell's response (as "M.F.") was to announce to the court in general that "I was set for from my own house & family but for what cause or transgression I do not known." The Judge then introduces an additional matter of concern, that "you keep multitudes of People at your house in a pretense of worshipping God; it may be you worship him in part," Twisden observes, "but we are not to dispute that." That, however, is precisely the point Fell is prepared to argue. Her response to this opening is to remind the entire court of Charles II's declaration of Breda prior to his being restored to the throne in 1660, in which he guaranteed to protect those of "tender conscience," and Fell quotes him pledge that "God forbid said he that I should hinder you of your Religion." Having established the King's own protection for her actions, she goes on to question the judge's assertion that there is a "law against unlawful meetings":

M.F. What law, have I broken for worshipping God in my own house?

Judges. The common law.

M.F. I thought you had proceeded by a Statute, then the sheriff whispered to him & mentioned the statute of the 35th of Eliz.

Judge. I could tell you of a Law but it is too penal for you for it might cost you, your life. (Fell 1664, 5.)

Having maneuvered Justice Twisden into citing legal precedent, Fell counters that "you are to consider this statue what it was made for & when, it was made for Papists, and the oath was Allegiance to King. Now let your Conscience judge, whether we be the people it was made for" (*Ibid.*, 6).

The success of this strategy was mixed, with sympathetic responses from the listeners in the court and some confusion on the part of the judges present. For the reader, however, the shift from descriptive narrative with interpretive glosses into direct dialogue replays the spoken drama of the court and again highlights the justness of Margaret Fell's position in contrast to that of those who enforce civil law. At one point, she turns directly to the jury and addresses them "Friends, I am here this day on account of my Conscience, and not for any evil or wrong done to any man but for obeying Christ's Doctrines and Command, who hath said in the Scripture, that God is a Spirit, and that his worship is in the Spirit & truth." She exhorts them, "Now you profess your selves to be Christians, and you own the Scriptures to be true, and for the obedience to the plain words of Scripture and for the testimony of my Conscience am I here, so I now appeal to the witness of God in all your consciences to Judge of me according to that" (Fell 1664, 6).

This appeal to the voice of conscience within over the external letter of the law is also an appeal to the power and the legitimacy of the spoken word over the written. Although Fell refers to the scriptures as being "the word of God" in the sense of what God has said, it is clear that she is evoking a higher understanding of justice than the written oath Twisden demands from her. As I have written elsewhere, the actions of sectarians of the 1650s and '60s in conflict with civil authorities through preaching or prophesying demonstrate how fluid the boundary was between oral, handwritten, and printed media (Ezell 2009, 69). Printed petitions were frequently viewed with suspicion – it seemed that anyone could put into print what they liked, but having to speak the words to the face of the person being petitioned was a different matter. Hinds has argued that printed prophetic writing in particular gained its validity for a reader because of is "pre-existing spoken versions," and its diffusion through multiple forms of media (Hinds 2000, xxiv).

Likewise, sectarians were vigorous in their rejection of ministers who simply prayed by the book and not from the spirit, that is, recited the formulaic words from texts such as the Book of Common Prayer rather than speaking in the spirit. Margaret Fell and others described such ministers as "false professors" who had university education, a formal ordination and title within the church hierarchy, yet lacked any true communion with God. This was the subject of several of Fell's early publications. In *A testimonie of the touch-stone, for all professions, and all forms, and gathered churches (as they call them), of what sort soever to try their ground and foundation by and a tryal by the Scriptures, who the false prophets are, which are in the world* (1656) and a broadside printed in 1659 *Concerning ministers made by the will of man* she contrasts the word of God that is "written in the heart" with the external authority invested in ministers and charges them "though ye professe a God and a Christ from Records without you, yet your possession and inheritance is the Devils Kingdome of sin. Let that of God in your consciences, which is pure, now examine and try you, and search you" (Fell 1656, 6, 12). "What ministery [sic] is that which is upheld by a Law given forth in mans will contrary to the Law of God, if it be not Antichristian?" she challenges, and urges true Christians to flee the artificial churches these ministers of texts have created (Fell 1659). The sectarians in general were profoundly resistant to distinguishing the clergy from the congregation on the basis of their formal education: as McDowell has explored, the attempt to restrict the clergy to elite educated males by the orthodox Churches was viewed by the sectarians as evidence of a hypocritical desire to amass worldly power and wealth (McDowell 2003, 62–65).

Quaker conflicts with secular society: Elizabeth Stirredge and Elizabeth Andrew

This connection between worldly power, wealth, and the written law in conflict with the oral profession of an internalized faith is seen clearly in the narratives of Elizabeth Stirredge and Elizabeth Andrews. Elizabeth Andrews (c. 1628–1718) wrote an account of her birth, education, and sufferings for the faith which was preserved in manuscript. In it, she recalls when she was a young woman how a neighbor of her family, Francis Newport, first earl of Bradford, attempted to persuade her conform to social customs such as curtsying before him by offering her £20, a considerable sum. As with Trapnel and Fell, Andrews also shifts from retrospective narration to dialogue, and the formatting of the page thus highlights the importance of her being willing to "stand boldly for the truth in that public house" (Booy 2004, 115–116). As she is waiting on him at the table, the earl asks,

> "Why do not you make me a curchy [curtsy] when you give me the glass?"
> My Answer was, "Before I knew how to do better, I did, which is well known to all that are here."
> Then he said to me, "Betty if you will make me a curchy, as I am a gentleman, and before all these gentlemen, I will give you 20 pounds."
> I said, "If I might have all Eyton Hall to do it yet I durst not do it, for all Honour belongeth to God...." (*Ibid.*, 116.)

She shifts again to this format when narrating an event after her marriage when the justices seize their goods for selling on Christmas day and for not paying "the Sunday shilling" or tithes. When she is brought before the justices, when she is called to the bar "I asked him whether it were lawful for excommunicated people to come into their assembly. He said 'No.' Then I said, 'By your own law I am now clear, they have excommunicated me, and taken away my goods, and now have me before me.'" The sympathetic justices declare that they cannot disobey the King's law, even though it is "hard" and she notes that "many more words we had, and those justices were ever after very loving to me, for great was my exercise in that country among great men" (Booy 2004, 117). The shift to the representation of their conversations through dialogue format again permits the text's reader/listener to be convinced by the very words from her mouth.

Elizabeth Stirredge (1634–1706) in the course of her spiritual autobiography, which was published in 1711 after her death likewise resorts to direct dialogue to recreate the oral moment of crisis in describing the conflicts she and her husband had with local constables. When the constables come demanding money, Elizabeth Stirredge and her husband refuse to pay, and the officers declare they will seize their goods, although one constable is reluctant. Consistent with the other examples, Stirredge again turns to direct dialogue to record the scene in which the innocence and justness of her and her husband's motives and behavior in contrast to that of the agents of the law is played out through their conversation.

> …the constable leaning his head down upon his hand, and with a heavy heart said, "It is against my conscience to take their goods from them."
> Then I said, "John, have a care of wrong thy consciences; for what could the Lord do more for thee than to place his good spirit in thy heart, to teach thee what thou shouldst do, and what thou shouldest leave undone?"
> He said, "I know not what to do in this matter; if paying the money once would do, I would do it, but it will not end so; but it will be thus, whilst you keep going to meeting; for the rulers have made such laws, that never was the like in any age."
> I said, "John, when thou hast wrong thy conscience, and brought a burthen upon thy spirit, it is not the rulers can remove it from thee. If though shouldst to the rulers, and say, 'I have done that which was against my conscience to do,' they may say as the rulers did to Judas, 'What is that to us, see thou to that.'" (Booy 2004, 123.)

Once again we see that it is through conversation – which she records in dialogue form – that Stirredge is able to affect the judges when she and her fellow Quakers who had been imprisoned for unlawful assembly are brought before the bar. The dialogue format here permits the reader to experience the shifting attitudes in the courtroom towards the speaker and it also again provides a stark contrast between the behavior of those on trial and the officers of the court.

> "Why that is a riot in law," said the bishop.
> Then I answered, "We are no rioters."
> Then the crier of the court shaked his white rod over my head, and said, "Be silent."
> I said, "No, we may not be silent, we are a sober people, and live a good life and conversation; we do unto all men, as we would be done by; I never wronged man, woman, nor child, nor I known none that I have ought against us, unless for the answer of good conscience; here are of our neighbours that can testify for us."
> The crier continued shaking his white rod over my head, crying, "Hush," and "be silent."
> Then one of the justices, a sober ancient man, said, "Let the woman alone to speak for herself, she speaketh truth, and reason, let more of them speak; you are many against them, and if they do not be suffered to speak for themselves, it is very hard." (Booy 2004, 143).

The bishop in this scene is clearly cast as the villain. With his relish for the finer points of the written law and twisting of legal language in order to increase the severity of the penalty that could be given, his law clearly is different from the scripture's command that Elizabeth Stirredge invokes, to do unto others as you would have done unto you. The court crier's attempt to shut her mouth through physical intimidation is also in stark contrast to the accused before the bar, who, as the sympathetic justice points out, have only their words spoken in court to defend them.

Conclusion

Adam Fox in his study of early modern English oral culture has stressed that during this period in particular there was a "dynamic process of reciprocal interactions and mutual infusion" of oral and print culture (Fox 2000, 410). It is clear in these narratives by 17th-century women telling the stories of their conflicts with civil authority figures that they are drawing on both the fundamentally oral culture of their group but also from print conventions for representing trials and persecution. Even while wielding the power of the printed word to bring their case before the widest possible reading audience, the women rely on the representation of speech at climatic moments of their conflicts. Male writers of trial and persecution narratives from this period of course also made use of dialogue format. The complex set of cultural anxieties about women's speech and public speech in particular, however, gives these women's stories power. Regardless of the social class of the woman speaking, they seek to validate their innocence, to strike out at the injustice of their accusers, and to communicate to their readers and listeners the voice that is at the heart of their spiritual lives.

References

Bauman, Richard 1983. *Let Your Words Be Few: Symbolism of Speaking and Silence Among Seventeenth-Century Quakers*. Cambridge: Cambridge University Press.

Besse, Joseph 1753. *A Collection of the Sufferings of the People Called Quakers*. 2 volumes. London: L. Hinde.

Booy, David (ed.) 2004. *Autobiographical Writings by Early Quaker Women*. Aldershot: Ashgate Publishing.

Camden, Vera (ed.) 1992. *The Narrative of the Persecutions of Agnes Beaumont*. East Lansing, MI: Colleagues Press.

Cotton, Priscilla & Mary Cole 1655. *To the Priests and People of England, we discharge our Consciences, and give them Warning*. London.

Davies, Stevie 2004. Trapnel, Anna (fl. 1642–1660), self-styled prophet. *Oxford Dictionary of National Biography*. Available from http://www.oxforddnb.com/view/10.1093/ref:odnb/9780198614128.001.0001/odnb-9780198614128-e-38075

Ezell, Margaret J.M. 1993. *Writing Women's Literary History*. Baltimore: Johns Hopkins University Press.

Ezell, Margaret J.M. 2009. Performance Texts: Arise Evans, Grace Carrie, and the Interplay of Oral and Handwritten Traditions During the Print Revolution. *ELH* 76 (1): 49–73.

Fell, Margaret 1656. *A testimonie of the touch-stone, for all professions, and all forms, and gathered churches (as they call them), of what sort soever to try their ground and foundation by and a tryal by the Scriptures, who the false prophets are, which are in the world*. London: Thomas Simmons.

Fell, Margaret 1659. *Concerning ministers made by the will of man*. London.

Fell, Margaret 1664. *The Examination and Tryall of Margaret Fell and George Fox*. London.

Fell, Margaret 1666. *Women's Speaking Justified*. London.

Fox, Adam 2000. *Oral and Literate Culture in England 1500–1700*. Oxford: Clarendon Press.

Fox, Adam & Daniel Woolf (eds) 2002. *The Spoken Word: Oral Culture in Britain 1500–1850*. Manchester: University of Manchester Press.

Gillespie, Katharine 2004. *Domesticity and Dissent in the Seventeenth Century: English Women's Writings and the Public Sphere*. Cambridge: Cambridge University Press.

Gowing, Laura 1996. *Domestic Dangers: Women, Words, and Sex in Early Modern London*. Oxford: Clarendon Press.

Halliday, Paul D. 2004. Twisden [formerly Twysden], Sir Thomas, first baronet (1602–1683), judge and politician. *Oxford Dictionary of National Biography*. Available from http://www.oxforddnb.com/view/10.1093/ref:odnb/9780198614128.001.0001/odnb-9780198614128-e-27930

Hinds, Hilary 1996. *God's Englishwomen: Seventeenth-Century Radical Writing and Feminist Criticism*. Manchester: University of Manchester Press.

Hinds, Hilary (ed.) 2000. *The Cry of a Stone by Anna Trapnel*. Tempe, AZ: Arizona Center for Medieval and Renaissance Studies.

Hinds, Hilary 2004. Sectarian Spaces: The Politics of Place and Gender in Seventeenth-Century Prophetic Writing. *Literature & History* 13 (2): 1–25.

Hobby, Elaine 1989. *Virtue of Necessity: English Women's Writing, 1649–88*. Ann Arbor, MI: University of Michigan Press.

Kunze, Bonnelyn Young 2004. Fell [née Askew], Margaret (1614–1702), Quaker leader. *Oxford Dictionary of National Biography*. Available from http://www.oxforddnb.com/view/10.1093/ref:odnb/9780198614128.001.0001/odnb-9780198614128-e-9260

Mack, Phyllis 1992. *Visionary Women: Ecstatic Prophecy in Seventeenth-Century England*. Los Angeles: University of California Press.

Magro, Maria 2004. Spiritual Autobiography and Radical Sectarian Women's Discourse: Anna Trapnel and the Bad Girls of the English Revolution. *The Journal of Medieval and Early Modern Studies* 34 (2): 405–438.

McDowell, Nicholas 2003. *The English Radical Imagination: Culture, Religion, and Revolution, 1630–1660*. Oxford: Oxford University Press.

Thomas, Keith 1958. Women and the Civil War Sects. *Past & Present* 13: 42–62.

Thomson, John A.F. 1965. *The Later Lollards 1414–1520*. Oxford: Oxford University Press.

Trapnel, Anna 1654. *Report and Plea, Or, a Narrative of her Journey from London into Cornwall*. London: Thomas Brewster.

Warren, Nancy Bradley 2010. *The Embodied Word: Female Spiritualties, Contested Orthodoxies, and English Religious Culture, 1350–1700*. Notre Dame: University of Notre Dame Press.

Watt, Diane 1997. *Secretaries of God: Women Prophets in Late Medieval and Early Modern England*. Woodbridge: Boydell & Brewer.

Watt, Diane 2004. Askew [married name Kyme], Anne (c. 1521–1546), writer and protestant martyr. *Oxford Dictionary of National Biography*. Available from http://www.oxforddnb.com/view/10.1093/ref:odnb/9780198614128.001.0001/odnb-9780198614128-e-798

Rikard Wingård
http://orcid.org/0000-0003-4709-3761

Argumentum as Oral Substitute and the Transformations of *Volksbuch* Peritexts

There are several different meanings of the Latin word *argumentum*, but in relation to literature it is often used to designate a summary of the contents of a story or part of a story. No conclusive study of *argumenta* in this sense seems to have been undertaken and research has so far been concentrated on the development of the prologue in plays, which has often contained an *argumentum* (e.g. Bower 1884; Mason 1949; Flügel 1969; Hirdt 1975; Schwitzgebel 1996; Bruster & Weiman 2004). What I aim to do is to show how the practice of using *argumenta* can be seen as a gauge of oral – in contrast to literate – notions of reception, and from this viewpoint discuss the transformation of *argumenta* in some early modern and 19th-century Swedish *Volksbücher*, notably *Fortunatus* and *Helen of Constantinople*.

First of all, what is a *Volksbuch*? *Volksbücher* [in Swedish *folkböcker*] may be said to be related to the English *chapbooks*, but the former term has a much more complicated and ideologically troublesome history. Although many were printed as chapbooks, the *Volksbuch* as a concept does not designate a common material or bibliographical background. On the contrary, as Anna Katharina Richter has argued, *Volksbücher*, or *Historienbücher* as she prefers to call them, may be said to consist of literary works constantly being transformed in different ways. They are identified by Richter by their "Dynamik, Varianz und Heterogenität oder Hybridität" ["dynamics, variation and heterogeneity or hybridity"] (Richter 2009, 11).

This definition, however, is too loose. Why do we need a general concept for literary works whose only common denominator is that they do not have anything in common? Instead, I have pinpointed the term by studying its reception history. What is to be found is that many of the works given the name of *Volksbücher* in the early 19th century, as a result of German romanticism, had been seen as a group of works with something in common since the end of the 15th century – although they had not been given a collective name. Again and again works like *Magelona*, *The Seven Wise Masters*, *Melusine*, *Til Eulenspiegel* were grouped together by scholars and intellectuals (and, to a certain extent, by the book producers themselves), mostly as examples of bad literature. In conclusion, the *Volksbuch* might be defined in terms of a concept of historical reception: *a corpus of (literary) works, largely consisting of fictive stories, which are incorporated in a specific tradition of reception, primarily of a critical kind.*[1] (Wingård 2011, 37–77.)

At the same time as the Church and the intellectual elite of early modern Europe were sceptical of the form, content and potential influence of *Volksbücher*, they were widely read and loved – from the late 15th and early 16th centuries by nobles and the elite themselves, and later on by burghers and commoners. In order to understand this discrepancy in the evaluation of the *Volksbücher*, it is useful to delineate between two contrasting ideal types of reading,[2] which, on the one hand, can be derived from an early modern context of mentality, religion, literacy, and orality, and on the other from the "response-inviting structures" (Iser 1974; 1978) of different *Volksbücher*. The first form of reading, named *the expansive type of reading*, is closely associated with those who were critical of the *Volksbücher*. For example, the 16th-century humanist Juan Luis Vives, in his critique of *Volksbücher* and fiction in general, emphasizes that a good story needs to respect the laws of nature; it should be verisimilar, have an intrinsic logic (*constantia*), and follow what is fitting (*decorum*). Most importantly, Vives argues that a good story should not reveal itself to the reader (or listener). Instead it should induce its reader to search for and reflect over its meaning, in other words to make the reader mimic a righteous Christian life, where the desire to seek God, the truth of his nature and work is worthwhile but cannot be fulfilled until after the moment of death when entering heaven. Similarly, for the fictional story to be acceptable, it can be surmised from Vives, the story ought not to explain itself to the reader until the very end – if at all. To figure out or come closer to the truth of the matter the Christian, in everyday life as well as when reading, should use what is already known, the experience gathered through history, to anticipate the future.[3] To make use of sorcery, oracles, divination, etc. is immoral and a way of cheating. (Wingård 2011, 79–187.)

---

1   In Sweden hymn books and catechisms have occasionally been called *Volksbücher*, because they were the first books available for common people to own and read. This, however, is a usage altogether unrelated to the romantic concept of *Volksbücher* discussed here.

2   They are ideal types in accordance with Max Weber's usage of the term: "[G]eneral concepts which do not describe the elements which the instances of a class of phenomena have in common in the empirical world, but the elements which they have in common in an imaginary world, a utopia. This utopian world is so constructed that what are 'characteristic' and 'significant' elements, existing in gradations in the empirical world, become common elements in the imaginary one. There they are shared by all relevant phenomena to the same degree." (Burger 1976, 123.)

3   In this way the reception theory of e.g. Wolfgang Iser (1974; 1978) could be seen as a typical Christian way of reading. For Iser reading is an unveiling process, where the reader interprets the already read in order to anticipate the coming, as well as interpreting the plot (*sjuzhet*) in order to reveal the story (*fabula*). This form of reception of the temporal and spatial is also put forth by narratologist Peter Brooks (1984), but neither he nor Iser makes the analogy with the Christian endeavor to search for the nature and plan of God and his creation. See Wingård 2011, 191–200, 218–220, for a detailed comparison between Iser, Brooks and Vives.

One of the main reasons for criticism directed against *Volksbücher* seems to be that they do not follow the ideals exemplified by Vives. In fact, they seem more apt to satisfy the second type of reading, what I have termed *the assimilative type*. It is a kind of reception predominantly practised in oral and traditional societies, where society shares a common set of stories forming a mythological whole. Whenever a story is told the audience knows it beforehand and the telling of the story is an enactment of a repetition that coincides with the original mythical event.[4] (Foley 1991; Eliade 1971; Havelock 1963.) The assimilative type of reception is, in its ideal form, *meaning-encompassing [meningsomslutande]* in that it places the recipient in a state of saturated meaning, where the (fictional) world is known in its entirety and nothing is unfamiliar (to the recipient's mind), whether in time or space. (Wingård 2011, *passim*.)

In traditional societies the shared body of knowledge is maintained by the stability of the society, which is what makes it traditional. As Foley puts it, conventional and traditional patterns of life and narration aim to create conventional and traditional meaning (Foley 1991, 6–8). Many historical developments, which might be termed modernizations, have exerted pressure on such conventional and traditional life patterns and makings of meaning, e.g. larger social structures, urbanization, centralization, individualization, increasing contact with foreign societies and cultures, and expansion of the flow of media and information. They are all processes potentially disrupting or shattering traditional, collective patterns, structures and conventions. To gradually lose a common repertoire of stories through the transformation of traditional into modern societies – or any other societal structures, whatever we may call them, built on the principle of change and ongoing development – does not, however, necessarily mean the loss of the need or desire for an assimilative type of reception.

The *Volksbücher* could be interpreted as filling such a need in early modern times; hence their popularity in contrast to the criticism of a literate, Christian elite. By a range of different means, intended or not, their dominant response-inviting structures support the assimilative type of reading and obstruct the expansive. This might be summarized as two meaning-encompassing forms of process: 1. a horizontal, syntagmatic direction where the opposing poles of past and future time move towards

---

4   However, it should not be surmised that the enactment of the story is identical from one time to another. As Foley (1991, 57) states: "[F]or the oral traditional element, whether employed in the oral performance or in an orally derived text, the referential field is, as we have seen, coextensive not with any single line, passage, or texts but rather with the tradition as a whole. Under these conditions there is no 'first' occurrence of a traditional structure nor any 'subsequent' usage; each instance of the phrase or scene is both ubiquitous and unique in that it commands a fixed referent, an inherent meaning, every time it appears, but without recourse to an earlier or later partner. The linear aspect of the texts has only limited importance here, since whatever has a beginning, middle, and end in itself also has a larger identity vis-à-vis the poetic tradition. Traditional elements can no more 'repeat themselves' than the multiform surface of a traditional tale can be frozen into a uniquely authoritative form."

each other by the power of the (assimilative type of) reader, helped by meaning-encompassing structures in the reading material, until, in the ideal case, they completely fuse into an eternal present, as comprehended by the reader; 2. a vertical, paradigmatic direction in which the one pole of "what is said", *sjuzhet*, signifier, etc., and the other of "what is meant", *fabula*, signified, etc., approach each other, and, in the ideal case, merge into an ahistorical space, isolated from reality, where everything, in the eyes of the reader, is revealed and called by its right name.[5] (Wingård 2011, 356–358.)

A simple example of a response-inviting structure with the potential to trigger the horizontal process might be foretellings on the part of the narrator or other characters in the story. An example of the vertical is a restrictive language with shallow descriptions of the events and objects depicted, which has low potential to interfere with the reader's previous experience; if, for example, the princess is described only as "fair", rather than "golden-haired, slender, with blue eyes and white hands", the reader can assimilate the princess's beauty to his or her own apprehension of beauty, instead of, as in the other case, being distanced from the story by being fond of brown-haired, fat princesses, and forced to expand his or her scope of experience in order to understand. Consequently, by using e.g. "non-realistic" forms of narration, stereotyped elements which can be known beforehand, and forebodings in the texts, the early modern *Volksbücher* considered in my study support the assimilative type of reading and help the reader towards encompassment of meaning, in a way resembling how traditional and oral cultures function.[6] (*Ibid., passim.*)

Volksbücher peritexts

One of the most prominent ways in which the early modern *Volksbücher* often aid the assimilative type of reading is through their peritexts[7] – especially titles, summaries and chapter headings. The titles can be quite

5 These types of reading, expansive and assimilative, should not be confused with what Rolf Engelsing has termed as extensive and intensive reading, which have more to do with the development of the book market and the general economic and social development during the late 18th century. In Engelsing's view, more books became available at that time to a growing reading public, which in turn changed the reading behavior from a constant, intensive, re-reading of a few works to an extensive, shallower consumption of a large and more varied corpus of works. (Engelsing 1974; Wingård 2011, 361–363.)

6 This is ideally the opposite of Iser's decription of the reading process where the reader is trying to establish consistency (create meaning), but the text is presenting "gaps" in the story, which obstructs the formation of stable meaning, and, to Iser's mind, preferably does so indefinitely. (Iser 1974, *passim*; 1978, *passim*.)

7 I use the term *peritext* rather than the more common *paratext*. The originator of these concepts, Gérard Genette, reserved the former for the texts found in immediate connection to the main text; in the case of a book it denotes e.g. the title page, foreword, author biography, index, footnotes and *impressum*. (Genette 1997, 4–5.) Paratext is used by Genette in a much wider sense: "in principle, every context serves as a paratext" (*Ibid.*, 8), which makes it more impractical to use.

extensive, as the following example shows, taken from an edition of *Fyra köpmän i främmande land* ["Four Merchants in a Foreign Country"] (1699):[8]

> *En skön och Lustig Historia, Om Fyra Köpmän som reeste uthi fremmande Land, och kommo till Gäst en gång uthi ett Härberge, och ibland annan Lustigheet begynte de at skämta något om sina Hustrur som de hwar uthi sin Stad hemma hade, och der igenom bleff emellan twenne uthfäst Wadh, hwarföre den som besweken bleff, wille låta Lijfwet affhända sin egen Hustru, men bleff doch underligen bewarat, och undkom honom owitterligen uthi fremmande Land, der hon bekände sig wara Mans Person, och kom til stoor Ähra och Myndigheet at hon bleff en Förste och Regent öfwer ett Konungarike, och fick omsider sin oförätt hämna låta, och kom til sin Mann igen medh Frögd och Glädie.*

> [*A lovely and amusing history of four merchants who travelled in a foreign country, and one time came as guests to an inn, and among other jovialities began to jest about their wives, which they each had in their respective home towns, and thereby a wager was made between two of them, and whoever lost would take the life of his own wife, but she [the wife of the man who eventually lost] was remarkably saved and escaped him [her husband] secretly in a foreign country, where she pretended to be a man, and gained great glory and reverence, so that she became a lord and ruler of a kingdom, and finally was able to avenge the wrongs done against her, and came to her husband again with joy and happiness.*]

Titles of this kind are very hard to ignore if one wishes to read in an expansive manner. They tend to spoil the reading as a research expedition towards an unknown end. But for a reader lacking a traditional common culture, a reader longing for such a connection to a larger whole, these introductory titles may serve as a substitute; when the reader enters the story he or she is familiar with it – to a certain degree.

The titles can of course be shorter and less informative.[9] Sometimes, however, in those cases a summary is added to the edition, placed before the main text, as, for instance, in the case of all Swedish 17th-century editions of *Apollonius of Tyre*. They all have simple titles, and attached to the beginning there is a versified summary that explains in detail the order of events to come.

Other types of peritextual elements, supportive of the assimilative type of reading, are chapter headings. These are very important, and during the 17th century they were found almost without exception in *Volksbücher* editions (of those studied they are missing only in the editions of *Apollonius of Tyre*). To give an example, the headings of the first three chapters of *Carsus and Moderus* (1683) reads (in English translation): "How Moderus was disgracefully beaten by his elder brother Carsus"; "How the father with

---

8   If not otherwise stated, all translations from Swedish to English are by the author.
9   John L. Flood (1980, vol. I, 69–70), argues that *Volksbuch* publishers "were careful not to kill the suspense" when composing the titles, and this might in many cases certainly be so. Carried to extremes, we have to be told the whole story before we are told the whole story in order to kill all suspense. What I am referring to is a matter of degree, and in those terms many *Volksbücher* titles are in different ways much more revealing regarding their contents compared to other types of contemporary and present-day fiction.

all his people searched for Moderus but did not find him"; "How Moderus, lying half-dead in the brushwood, was strangely carried by a lion to its den, and there laid down and kept in love". If the title or prologue gives the main structure of the story, the chapter headings continually give detailed information of the events in advance, and in this way the reader's need to figure out what will happen next is drastically diminished.

Informative titles and summaries are, of course, not confined to *Volksbücher* alone during the early modern period. The tradition of *argumentum* was strong, i.e. to supply the text with informative prologues, chapter headings and introductory summaries. Aristotle gave legitimacy to the practice: in his *Rhetoric* (III, chapter 14) he says that "[i]n prologues, and in epic poetry, a foretaste of the theme is given, intended to inform the hearers of it in advance instead of keeping their minds in suspense" (Aristotle 2010, 145).

During the 17th century we thus find *argumenta* in most types of literature – in epic poetry, drama, *Volksbücher* and novels. In his English translation of Ariosto's *Orlando Furioso*, John Harington (c. 1561–1612) explains in "An advertisement to the Reader [. . .]" that "(according to the Italian maner) I haue in a staffe of eight verses comprehended the contents of euery booke or canto, in the beginning thereof, which hath two good vses, one, to vnderstand the picture the perfecter, the other, to remember the storie the better" (Harington 1591, A[r]).[10] Harington makes an explicit case, so to speak, for the assimilative type of reading, the importance of the reader knowing the story *before* he or she starts reading it. The illustrations supplied also work to this end and collaborate with the *argumentum* in a sort of emblematic mode.

Another genre where *argumentum* frequently occurs is in the baroque or pastoral novel. As in the example of *Apollonius of Tyre* the reader too often gets a chapter-by-chapter summary at the beginning of the book. In contrast to the *Volksbücher*, however, the 17th-century novel is for its effect heavily reliant on hidden codes. The fictional characters and events in the novel usually stand for actual persons and events, or so it is supposed to be believed, and the reader of the novel is on a quest to reveal these hidden correspondences with the real world. The assimilative response-inviting structure constituted by the *argumentum* is hence weakened in favour of a response-inviting structure in accord with the expansive type of reading. What is notable about the *Volksbücher* is that they avoid revealing themselves as fiction, and, their dominant response-inviting structures taken together, might be considered as the most consistent type of literature designed for the assimilative type of reading during the early modern period. (Wingård 2011, 348–350.)

In the light of the above outline I will now look further ahead in time and examine diachronically what happens with the *argumenta* in *Volksbücher*. *Fortunatus* and *Helen of Constantinople* will be analysed regarding titles and chapter headings, and finally I will look at the few *Volksbuch* editions that were not published as cheap chapbooks during the 19th century.

10 Regarding other of Harington's ideas on typography and peritexts, see McKenzie 2002, 252, 254, 257–258.

Title transformations: An editorial history of Fortunatus

The earliest known version of *Fortunatus* is a German printed edition from 1509 (Gotzkowsky 1991, vol. I, 420, 423), but a Swedish version was not made until the 17th century. There are three early copies, A, B, and C, of the Swedish *Fortunatus* extant, each from different editions. A and B lack the title leaf, while C is complete. All three were possibly published not very far apart in time: A before 1651, B probably 1651, and C 1651.[11] For present purposes we leave the supposedly oldest one, A, aside, since it lacks not only the title leaf but the entire first sheet and a large part of the ending.

The newly found copy of *Fortunatus*, C, has a rather extensive title:

Een mechta lustigh Historia, Om FORTUNATO, Huru han, tå han myckin Nödh och stoor Lijffzfahra vthstått hade, och gick i tree dygn vthi en willan Skogh, bleff aff Jungfrun FORTUNA begåfwat medh en sådan lycksaligh Pung, vthi hwilken aldrigh trööt Penningar, medh hwilcken han igenom reeste många fremmande Land och Konungarijke, och omsijder Soldanen aff stoor Alkey medh list affhände en gammal vthsliten Hatt, medh hwilken han vthi itt Ögnableck kunde önska sigh hwart han wille, och huru hans twå Sönner effter hans dödh begge Klenodierne ärffde, och myckin Kortwijl ther medh bedrefwo.

[*A very amusing history of Fortunatus, how he, when he had outlived much distress and great danger for his life, and had walked for three days in a wild forest, by the maid Fortune was awarded such a blissful purse, out of which money never ceased to flow, with which he travelled through many foreign countries and kingdoms, and finally cunningly deprived the sultan of the great city of Cairo an old worn-out hat, with which he in an instant could wish himself wherever he wanted to go, and how after his death his two sons inherited both of the precious items, and had much fun with them.*]

It is noticeable that this long title, explaining the main features of the story, disappears in editions of the following century. In two undated 18th-century prints of *Fortunatus* (both "Tryckt på nytt" ["Printed anew"])[12] the title now is very much shorter and only reads, FORTUNATI HISTORIA, *Om Hans Pung och Önskehatt* ["The history of Fortunatus. Of his purse and wishing-cap"]. On the verso page of the title leaf of these latter editions, however, there is a preface inserted which focuses on the potential moral edification

11 On copy A, described by the Swedish bibliographer Isak Collijn as "before 1651?", his predecessor as national librarian, G.E. Klemming, has made a handwritten note that the priest and author Olaus Olai Sparrman (1640–1690) had a copy of 1651 but that this one is older. On copy B, not dated by Collijn, another hand has written that it has been part of a made-up volume belonging to the aforementioned Sparrman. Hence we might take a guess and say that this edition probably is from 1651. Copy C is on the title page dated 1651. For a further discussion of the relation between the copies and editions, see Wingård 2011, 29 n.

12 In the reference section they have been separated as a and b; which one is the older is difficult to say without further investigation, but it is probably a, which uses virgula (/) instead of comma, which b does; if this is the case, b seems to have been composed and printed with a as the original.

of the story and only has a very short introduction to the contents. To anticipate the reader's interpretation of the history seems here, for the editor (or editors), to have been of greater importance than to give a synopsis of the events.

Interestingly, the short title is found already in the preceding century in the oldest Danish edition available in a complete copy (probably from the 1670s): *En lystig Historie Om Fortunatus Pung Oc hans Ynske-Hat* ["An amusing history of Fortunatus' purse and his wishing-cap"]. This edition has also a complementary preface on the verso of the title leaf, but in contrast to our 18th-century *Fortunatus* it is almost entirely occupied with a summary of the events.[13] The Swedish edition B has a similar prefatory summary (starting at the recto of the second leaf) and is even more informative, and we might infer that the title of this edition was in the brief style of the Danish one. Instead of placing the *argumentum* in the title, as edition C does, it adds it as a preface.

In the C edition only the two last sentences of the preface are dedicated to some sort of edificial explanation of the story: "Hwar aff hwar och en, som någhot är angelägen, må tagha sigh Lärdom och Vndervijsning, at få een sådhan Pung och Önskehatt. Jagh låter migh åthnöya medh thet iagh hafwer, och GUDH migh wijdare förlänandes warder" ["Where of each and every one, that to some extent is eager to have such a purse and wishing-cap, may lend himself to erudition and instruction. I am happy with what I have, and what God further gives me"]. The tables are clearly turned in the 18th century, where it is the last two sentences that say something very vaguely about the contents of the story and everything above is about the moral teachings, or, more truly, a defence of the story as legitimate reading. What is interesting here is that the main text of the younger editions is mainly based on the 17th-century edition C, with some passages collected from B, but that the chapter headings are entirely taken from B. The editor/s, whoever that may have been, has had both 17th-century editions by his side (or any other two based on those) and selected the peritexts from the one with the supposedly simplest title, but rewritten the preface. Why, we may ask.

The answer is likely to be found in the considerable shift in official attitude against the *Volksbücher*, which takes place among the higher layers of society between the 17th and 18th centuries – from a relatively accepted literary form to a despised one, not proper for any person of position to read or display. (Wingård 2011, 79–98 and further references therein.) This development takes place at the same time as the book market broadens and *Volksbücher* start to be printed in cheaper ways, for people of less wealth. The aim of the chapbook publishers was, as has been shown by Henrik Horstbøll (2009) in a Danish context, to make the text fit on one to four sheets in octavo, i.e. 16 to 64 pages. Encompassing 8½ and 8 octavo sheets (editions a[14] and b respectively), the 18th-century editions of *Fortunatus* do not belong

---

13 *Danske folkebøger* 1927, vol. X, 4.

14 The copy that has been available is defect and the text stops short at page 128 at the next to last chapter. Comparing with the Danish (1670s) and Swedish edition B a half sheet could be expected for the copy to be complete.

to this latter category of inexpensive print. They were more probably aimed at a more sophisticated class of readers, with the means to afford average book prices.

Indicative of this is also the title, which uses the Latin form "FORTUNATI HISTORIA" and not a vernacular form – the Latin printed with roman type instead of the gothic used for German languages, as was the common practice. Two things point to the fact that this was a deviation, made by the editor, from the edition B. Firstly, the running heads on the verso pages of B say "Historia om Fortunatus", while the 18th-century edition a has "Fortunati Historia". We might assume that the former heads correspond to the title, as the latter does. Secondly, there is not one preceding Swedish, Danish or German edition that uses the genitive form *Fortunati historia*.[15] (*Danske folkebøger* 1927, vol. X, 275–284; Gotzkowsky 1991–1994, vol. I, 423–435, vol. II, 113–116.) The strong affiliation between the Danish print of the 1670s and B further strengthens the hypothesis that the latter had a title form akin to the former rather than to the 18th-century editions a and b.[16]

In conclusion, the 18th-century editor or editors have very possibly changed the title in order to better appeal to an educated group of book buyers. Their interest in this kind of literature was low and had to be stimulated, and, for the time being, the volume was too expensive to be bought by the poorer classes. The defensive preface emphasizing the morals to be learnt from the work is also symptomatic of a product that seeks to be bought by a reluctant audience.

What is noticeable, then, is, as we previously said, the choice of peritexts in order to get the attention of these new literate readers. The editor had two different forms of titles to choose from and picked the shorter one, making the alterations discussed. He could very well have printed the longer, which, in passing, already had a Latin form, "Historia, *Om* FORTUNATO", incorporated. But he did not. And he furthermore did not include the summarizing preface, but replaced it with another, much more unrevealing. He could have kept the old one and added his own to it (set in smaller type – the one used for the main text for instance – the verso of the title leaf would have accommodated it without any additional leaf needed). But he did not. The impression must be that the editor refrained from using an *argumentum* in the title and preface because he thought that this would have been a disadvantage in meeting the requirements of the potential buyers.

---

15 Some slight resemblance is to be found in one German edition, "Fortunati seckel vnd Wünschhütlein", (1540 or 1560) and one Danish, "Historie om Fortunati Pung och Ønske-Hat" (1706). (Gotzkowsky 1991, vol. I, 425; *Danske folkebøger* 1927, vol. X, 282.)

16 I do not share Bäckström's belief, repeated by R. Paulli, that *Fortunatus* has independent of each other been translated from German into Danish and Swedish. (Bäckström 1848, vol. II, 4; *Danske folkebøger* 1927, vol. X, xxxvii). Sample tests show that the Danish 1670s edition and the Swedish B follow each other very closely in wording and make the same deviations against the German original. Cf. e.g. *Fortunatus* B, 13 and 15, with Paulli's commentary to the Danish *Danske folkebøger* 1927 (vol. X, 245 18:18 and 246 20:24). Which one is based on the other, the Swedish on the Danish or the Danish on the Swedish, is for the moment hard to discern.

This is what is to be expected if assimilative and expansive types of reading are at play in a world more and more dominated by literate mentalities and modern ways of being.[17]

New headings or no headings: Helen of Constantinople *and the lethargy of printing*

Richter (2009) has, as previously mentioned, accentuated the open nature of *Volksbücher*, i.e. their willingness to lend themselves to all kinds of alterations.[18] They are never stable, but fluctuate in appearance and content depending on context. This is no doubt true, but seen from another perspective, especially if we focus on the 19th century, what is equally remarkable is that there actually were no changes made at all. Because it seems, as has been indicated elsewhere regarding Germany, that the ordinary procedure was to print from old copies without much editorial input. *Volksbücher* acted in many cases (at least in editions of the cheaper kind) only as a kind of second-choice literature, printed between bigger jobs, to a large extent only to keep up work. Publishers and printers just did not care very much about the form of these editions and chose the fastest way to get them onto the market, i.e. to print them in the manner they always had done. (Flood 1980, vol. I, 44–45, 50–51, vol. II, 272–273, 275). When changes do occur in their typographical or textual matter, we have reason to sit up and take notice.

A suitable exemplification of this is *Helen of Constantinople*, which became very popular in Sweden during the 18th and 19th centuries. In 1909 it was accounted for about sixty printed editions (Geete 1909, 288), and this may be more than in any other country.[19] In written form the story stretches back to the 13th century (*Danske folkebøger* 1920, vol. VIII, vii, xxii–xxv) and it was translated into Swedish from Danish for the first time in the second half of the 17th century – at least, the earliest edition known is from 1667 (mentioned in Möhlman 1769, 144). The oldest Swedish edition preserved in a copy is dated 1679 and has a rather short title: *Een Skiön och Sanfärdigh Historia, Om Den Tohlmodige Helena Aff Constantinopel Ganska liuflig at läsa* ["A lovely and true history of the patient Helen of Constantinople very pleasant to read"].

The title and the chapter headings of 1679 are in principle kept by succeeding Swedish editions, e.g. in 1699, in a late 18th-century edition[20], in editions of 1785 (Örebro: s. n.) and 1810 (Götheborg: Samuel Norberg). From 1824 there start to appear changes to the previous order. In an

---

17 The concept of literacy is here used in the sense outlined by Olson 1994. See also Wingård 2011, 131–152 for a summary and discussion.

18 To this end Richter, *inter alia*, presents a valuable analysis of the peritexts in the Danish and Swedish editions of *Apollonius of Tyre* (Richter 2009, 62–87).

19 *Danske folkebøger* 1920, vol. VIII, 207–229, lists 43 editions and it is not included at all in Gotzkowsky 1991–1994, volumes I–II. All known German editions seem to have been printed in the 18th century or later. (*Danske folkebøger* 1920, vol. VIII, xxvi.)

20 "Tryckt i år [Printed this year]"; according to a contemporary annotation on the title page possibly from 1772.

edition of that year (Stockholm: Johan Hörberg) the chapter headings have disappeared and some minor changes have been made to the main text. Hörberg's edition, which was published by J.G. Björnståhl, of whom we will talk later, was reproduced in 1828 by Elméns och Granbergs tryckeri [Elmén's and Granberg's print shop]. Elmén's and Granberg's press was also situated in Stockholm and the new proprietor, Ludvig Öberg, had probably without Björnståhl's permission printed from his edition.[21] Meanwhile, in Gothenburg, Samuel Norberg issued his second printing of *Helen of Constantinople* (1828) – with chapter headings – which was composed from his first, which was based on the 18th-century editions. In 1832 in the city of Jönköping two more editions of the story were published: the first by J.P. Lundström, from Hörberg's/Björnståhl's version, and the second by N.E. Lundström (J.P's younger brother), an abbreviated edition with revised chapter headings. J.P. Lundström republished his version in 1841, 1844 and 1848. In 1851 the print shop was sold to J.A. Björk, who together with his partner O.F. Bergman again published *Helen of Constantinople* in 1856 (Jönköping: J.A. Björk & Comp.), with Hörberg's/Björnståhl's version, via J.P. Lundström's, as original. From 1858 Bergman ran the print shop by himself and published a new edition in 1860, still from the same original. The same pattern is traceable for N.E. Lundström's edition, which became widely used not only within the firm, but also by printers in other places, e.g. in 1834 (Westervik: Carl. O. Ekblad), 1844 (Norrköping: Chr. Törneqvist) and again in 1844 (Sundswall: L. Blomdahl).[22] A simple stemmatic diagram of these editions would look like this:

Table 1. Three different Swedish traditions of printing *Helen of Constantinople*: I, with chapter headings from the first edition 1679. II, revised without chapter headings. III, revised differently from II with chapter headings different from I.

I	II	III
1699. S. l.: s. n.	1824. Stockholm: J. Hörberg	1832. Jönköping: N.E. Lundström
"Tryckt i år" (18th century, perhaps 1772)	1828. Stockholm: Elméns och Granbergs tryckeri	1834. Westervik: Carl O. Ekblad
1785. Örebro: s. n.	1832. Jönköping: J.P. Lundström	1844. Norrköping: Chr. Törnequist
1810. Götheborg: S. Norberg	1841. Jönköping: J.P. Lundström	1844. Sundswall: L. Blomdahl
1828. Götheborg: S. Norberg	1844. Jönköping: J.P. Lundström	
	1848. Jönköping: J.P. Lundström	
	1856. Jönköping: J.A Björk & Comp.	
	1860. Jönköping: O.F. Bergman	

21 The two contracting parties had earlier been cooperating (Björnståhl had his editions printed at the shop), but were at the time rivals (Bennich-Björkman 1988, 112, 119).

22 See also Bäckström 1848*, vol. II, 5–6, for a stemmatic comparison of editions of *Helen of Constantinople*.

The shortened text, and thus lower cost of production, should probably account for the greater popularity of N.E. Lundström's edition among publishers other than within the firm. N.E. Lundström reduced the pages to 20 in 8° compared to Hörberg's 32 and the older 18th and early 19th-century editions of about 40 to 50 pages – which, by the way, were still being printed, e.g. 1835 (Lund: Lundbergska tryckeriet) and 1864 (Karlshamn: E.G. Johansson). If N.E. Lundström had chosen not to include the chapter headings it is likely that they would not have appeared in any of the succeeding editions either.

This passive attitude among the printers, as is seen for instance at the press founded by J.P. Lundström, strengthens the assumption that when a transformation of the text or peritext really occurs it is done very intentionally. In the case of Hörberg/Björnståhl it seems as they discarded the headings to be able to force the otherwise rather unchanged text from the older editions into two octavo sheets – the text ends close to the bottom of the last page. In the case of N.E. Lundström it seems as he did everything to preserve the headings, and was ready to sacrifice the main text in order to keep them and still thin the print down to twenty pages. For Lundström, then, it is probable that he considered chapter headings to be so essential to the potential readers, or himself, that he could not do without them. He was still, possibly, selling to an audience that was reading in an assimilative type of way. Hörberg and Björnståhl, obviously, did not share this fear, and it might be a consequence of the fact that this edition was, as stated on the last page, to be sold at the latter gentleman's bookshop in Stockholm.

During the 1820s, Jacob Gustaf Björnståhl (1773–1837) specialized in chapbooks of different kinds and he acted both as publisher and retailer of books published by others. His publication of chapbooks reached its peak during the middle of the century and he seems to have been successful for a few years before his competitors caught up. The *Volksbücher* he published are distinguished by their well-crafted woodcuts (often cut uniquely for the edition) and, by chapbook standards, neat print. The bookshop was located near Stortorget ["The great square"], which was the center of commerce, and he could probably expect customers from a wide range of social backgrounds. We could safely assume that he knew his clientele, as he had been in the trade since the beginning of the century, starting off with an ambitious circulating library. As the edition of *Helen of Constantinople* indicates, Björnståhl was not a passive actor on the chapbook market. He had new stories translated and introduced, and he reworked old ones. (For the details on Björnståhl, see Bennich-Björkman 1988.)

Removing chapter headings seems to have been one of his strategies to satisfy the reading public. It is done not only in *Helen of Constantinople*, but also, for example, in *Carsus and Moderus* from the same year, 1824 (Stockholm: Marquardska boktryckeriet).[23] This latter edition shows much more explicitly a deliberate choice in removing the headings. The main text ends about two thirds the way down the penultimate page and the remaining

23 For other editions of this very popular work see Bäckström 1848*, vol. II, 12–13; Linnström 1883, vol. I, 629, 645–646, 648.

space is filled by an ornament. To fill the last page a large woodcut has been printed, picturing a man holding a pouch of gold, with a chest full of cups and plates standing next to him. The illustration can hardly be related to any event in the story and was probably inserted to fill the empty space as well as to give the consumer an additional treat. In this case there is consequently no evidence that the printer has been forced to exclude the chapter headings due to too little space, or to choose between cutting the text and the headings. To conjecture and repeat, Björnståhl intentionally edited away the chapter headings in order, to his mind, to better meet the expectations of Stockholm's reading public regarding a good book.

In contrast to Hörberg's/Björnståhl's edition, N.E. Lundström's cheaper print would probably be distributed by itinerant booksellers in the country-side. Jönköping was a small town (between 3500 and 4700 inhabitants during the 1830s) with two presses going, but no steady bookshop (Sandberg 2010, 31; Klemming & Nordin 1883, 492; Rinman 1951, 23). In 1844 J.P. Lundström, in a letter to Svenska bokförläggareföreningen [Swedish society of publishers], even advised against the establishing of one: "Denna del av Småland är glest peuplerad, och med undantag av 2ne härader, är folket här i Länet fattigt och platt icke läsgirigt, hvadan jag betviflar att en inlärd Bokhandlare nånsin finner god utkomst i Jönköping" ["This part of Småland is thinly populated, and with the exception of two hundreds, the people of this county are poor and have absolutely no appetite for reading, for which reason I doubt that an educated bookseller ever will find a good living in Jönköping"] (citation from Rinman 1951, 133). We may, in summary, assume that a more literate versus a more orally oriented readership could have played a role in the two different editorial choices.

Argumentum Ingratum: Editions for the educated

Another point of interest concerning the issues that presently occupy us is the 19th-century *Volksbücher* editions that were published with more ambitious, sometimes scholarly, aims. In the above we have only accounted for editions of *Helen of Constantinople* published in the traditional chapbook format, small volumes, cheaply produced and not intended to be bound with anything more than a simple stitching of the back. But during the 19th century *Volksbücher* were published in other ways too, where economy was not to such a large part a restraining influence on the textual presentation. In 1819 *Helen of Constantinople* was for example included in Lorenzo Hammarskölds and Johan Imnelius's anonymously published *Svenska folksagor* ["Swedish folktales"] together with the famous story of Melusine and an alleged local story named *Pelle Båtsman*. Hammarskjöld and Imnelius were inspired by A.W. Schlegel, Ludwig Tieck and Joseph von Görres, the originators of the romantic *Volksbuch* concept, and had the ambition to put the Swedish *Volksgeist* in print. (H[ammarsköl]d & I[mneliu]s 1819, vol. I, iii; Wingård 2011, 311, 64 n.). Their edition was printed in roman type and not in gothic, as was usual for prints aimed for the common people. It has the briefest, or most modern, of the title variants we have seen, *Den sköna och tålmodiga*

Helena Antonia af Constantinopel ["The fair and patient Helen Antonia of Constantinople"], and it bears no chapter headings or other introductory materials. As we have observed before, when the publications were aimed at a literate audience such features seem to disappear.

In a similar manner the literary historian Carl Julius Lénström published two volumes of folktales in 1839 and 1843, which included several *Volks-bücher*, e.g. *Helen of Constantinople, Melusine* and *Hildegard and Taland.* He claims to have intended them for young and old people, but from the preface it is clear that he was also aiming at the higher strata of society, regardless of age, which, as he states, has lost the healthy way of spending their leisure with the telling of tales in favour of soul-destructive drinking, card playing and news gossip. ([Lénström] 1839, vol. I, 3–8.) Whereas *Helen of Constantinople* in *Svenska folksagor* was, naturally, printed from the old editions, which all included chapter headings, Lénström used Hörberg's/ Björnståhl's slightly revised edition of 1824, where the chapter headings were not present from the beginning.[24] In spite of this, Lénström assumes a scholarly position and an asserted editorial role. He insists, for instance, that he will have everything published on purpose without modification, out of respect for older times and traditional folk culture (*Ibid.*, 7–8). He could nevertheless hardly be classed as a publisher printing for printing's sake, or out of some old habit. His choice of leaving out the chapter headings must be seen as a conscious decision.

This tendency is repeated in other works of literary ambition, like P.O. Bäckström's *Svenska folkböcker* ["Swedish *Volksbücher*"], volumes I– II, 1845–1848. Bäckström's intentions, he states, are not strictly scholarly – although he provides lots of information on the origins, variants and editions of the different histories – but to introduce the *Volksbücher* to the educated part of society. (Bäckström 1845, vol. I, vi.) He further claims that he has used the oldest available copies for his edition and has done nothing to "modernize" them, but "sökt så troget som möjligt, återgifva de svenska folkböckernes egenheter" ["tried, as faithfully as possible, to reproduce the peculiarities of the Swedish *Volksbücher*"] (*Ibid.*, vii). All the same, he has removed the long titles, summaries and chapter headings, which are such fundamental features of the earliest printed works. Either he found them unimportant or they were not compatible with his other aim, to show that the reading of *Volksbücher* "i sjelfva verket icke är så att förakta, som man vanligen föreställt sig" ["is not really to be as despised as one generally assumes"] (*Ibid.*, vi). Contemplating the pattern that emerges from the two previous collections discussed, the analysis of *Fortunatus*, and the case with J.G. Björnståhl's *Volksbuch* editions, the latter answer is a tempting one.

---

24 It cannot be ruled out that Hörberg/Björnståhl used *Svenska folksagor* as base for their edition of *Helen of Constantinople* (1824) and so were ignorant of the chapter headings of the earlier editions. However, as we showed, the elimination of chapter headings was a recurrent theme in Björnståhl's publications and therefore seems to have been a conscious choice also in the case of *Helen of Constantinople*. Hörberg/ Björnståhl furthermore uses a slightly different title: *Den Sköna och Tålmodiga Helena af Constantinopel, eller Lyckans Obeständighet.*

Conclusion

Having seen the close connection between *argumentum* and the assimilative type of reading it might be concluded that the disappearance of different forms of *argumentum* is, in some way, connected to an increasing group of readers reading in variants dominated by the contrasting expansive type. Where *Volksbücher* during the 17th and 18th centuries appear in literate environments, or at least less orally and traditionally dominated – be it the larger city or among the educated – we have, throughout our study, detected a tendency on the part of the publishers to reduce *argumentum*.

This is also compatible with our initial supposition that the *argumentum* may serve as an oral substitute, giving traditional readers a sense of belonging, a knowing-beforehand, in a world less and less constituted by collective and familiar structures. *Argumentum* might in this sense be viewed as bridging an oral culture into a book culture; a *longue durée*, the usefulness of which has gradually faded, as Westerners, in more and more systematic and centralized ways, have been made to live in, conform to, and appreciate the culture of modernity, in its economic, educational, religious, cultural and societal structures (see e.g. Elias 1939) and in this process have adopted other ways of reading, where the *argumentum* is no longer of any value as a link back to traditional forms of being.

Today the use of the *argumentum* is not widely spread anymore, as every reader of literature will notice. It is largely confined to a text on the back cover, which, in the case of fiction, is intended to stimulate the buyer's curiousness, rather than give a synopsis of the story – including the ending. The attempts to "modernize" the old *Volksbücher* by, amongst other things, transforming their peritexts were only successful for a while. Like *argumenta* they too vanished as the 20th century closed in and we entered the age of the detective novel.

References

Volksbuch editions

(Due to the large number of editions used, the reference list has been shortened to include only year, place and printer/publisher, when bibliographical information can be obtained from elsewhere. If nothing else is stated the reader is directed to the following bibliographical works: Bäckström 1845–1848, volumes I–II; Bäckström 1848*; Collijn 1942–1946, volumes I–II; Linnström 1883–1884, volumes I–II. If not included or otherwise unsatisfactorily recorded in these works, the full title of the edition is given after the work title and year of publication.)

Carsus och Moderus ["Carsus and Moderus"] 1683. *En Ny, Ynkeligh och ganska vnderligh Historia om twenne Bröder, CARSO och MODERO, Huruledes then ena then andra döda wille, och han på ett vnderligit sätt slapp. Hwilke författat är vthi 14. Capit. som på effterfölliande Bladen finnes til at läse.* S. l.: s. n.

– "Tryckt nu på nytt" (18th century). *En ganska Ynckelig och Tänckwärdig Historia, Om twenne Bröder Carso och Modero, Huruledes then ena then andra döda wille,*

och han på et underligit sät undankom. Hwilken Historia är författad uti 14 Capitel, dock ganska lustig at läsa. Härjämte och en annan theßlikes Historia Om Chariton, Hwilken på resan åt Jerusalem af Röfware fången och fängslad blef, och dock genom GUDs underliga Skickelse omsider lyckeligen befriad wardt. S. l.: s. n.
  − 1824. Marquardska boktryckeriet.

Fortunatus before 1651?. Title leaf is missing. See the edition "före 1651?" listed by Collijn 1942–1944, vol. I, 275.

  − 1651. *Een mechta lustigh* Historia, *Om* FORTUNATO, *Huru han, tå han myckin Nödh och stoor Lijffzfahra vthstått hade, och gick i tree dygn vthi en willan Skogh, bleff aff Jungfrun* FORTUNA *begåfwat medh en sådan lycksaligh Pung, vthi hwilken aldrigh trööt Penningar, medh hwilcken han igenom reeste många fremmande Land och Konungarijke, och omsijder Soldanen aff stoor Alkey medh list affhände en gammal vthsliten Hatt, medh hwilken han vthi itt Ögnableck kunde önska sigh hwart han wille, och huru hans twå Sönner effter hans dödh begge Klenodierne ärffde, och myckin Kortwijl ther medh bedrefwo. På nytt* reviderat, *medh åtskillige Figurer beprydd, ock itt stort Register öfwer alla Historier widh Ändan tilsatt.* S. l.: s. n.
  − 1651?. Title leaf is missing. See the last edition listed by Collijn 1942–1944, vol. I, 275.
  − 1670s?. Reprinted in *Danske Folkebøger fra 16. og 17. Aarhundrede* 1927, vol. X.
  − "Tryckt på nytt" (18th century) a. FORTUNATI HISTORIA. *Om Hans Pung och Önskehatt. I ledige stunder mycket lustig och behagelig at läsa; Hwilken nu efter mångens begiäran, är Tryckt på nytt.* S. l.: s. n.
  − "Tryckt på nytt" (18th century) b. See Bäckström 1848, vol. II, 4.

Fyra köpmän i främmande land ["Four Merchants in a Foreign Country"] 1699. S. l.: s. n. See under "Historia" in Collijn 1942–1944, vol. I, 390–391.

Helena av Konstantinopel ["Helen of Constantinople"] 1679. Stockholm: Henrich Keyser.
  − 1699. S. l.: s. n.
  − "Tryckt i år" (18th century). *En underlig och mycket sälsam Historia Om then Tolamodiga Helena Antonia af Constantinopel Hwar utinnan man kan beskåda Lyckones obeständiga Lopp; mycket behagelig at läsa, Här jemte är ock wid ändan infördt En kort Beskrifning och Wisa Om Paris och skjöna Helena af Grekeland, Samt hela Trojaniske y:nckeliga undergång och förstöring igenom then stora Trä-Hästen; Sammanfattat af the trowärdigste Scribenter.* S. l.: s. n.
  − 1785. Örebro: s. n.
  − 1810. Götheborg: Samuel Norberg.
  − 1824. Stockholm: Johan Hörberg.
  − 1828. Stockholm: Elméns och Granbergs tryckeri.
  − 1828. Götheborg: Samuel Norberg.
  − 1832. Jönköping: J.P. Lundström.
  − 1832. Jönköping: N.E. Lundström.
  − 1834. Westervik: Carl O. Ekblad.
  − 1835. Lund: Lundbergska tryckeriet.
  − 1841. Jönköping: J.P. Lundström.
  − 1844. Jönköping: J.P. Lundström.
  − 1844. Norrköping: Chr. Törnequist.
  − 1844. Sundswall: L. Blomdahl.
  − 1848. *Den Sköna och Tålmodiga Helena Antonia af Constantinopel, eller Lyckans Obeständighet.* Jönköping: J.P. Lundström.
  − 1856. *Den sköna och tålmodiga Helena Antonia af Constantinopel, eller Lyckans Obeständighet.* Jönköping: J.A. Björk & Comp.

- 1860. *Den sköna och tålmodiga Helena Antonia af Constantinopel, eller Lyckans Obeständighet.* Jönköping: O.F. Bergman.
- 1864. Karlshamn: E.G. Johansson.

Collections of Volksbücher

Bäckström, P.O.: See *Literature*.
Danske Folkebøger: See *Literature*.
H[ammarsköl]d, [Lorenzo] & [Johan] I[mneliu]s 1819. *Svenska folksagor.* Vol. I (no further volumes were published). Stockholm: Johan Imnelius.
[Lénström, Carl Julius] 1839–1843. *Folk-Sagor för Gamla och Unga.* Volumes I–II. Örebro: N.M. Lindhs boktryckeri.

Literature

Aristotle 2010. *Rhetoric.* Edited by W.D. Ross. Translated by W. Rhys Roberts. New York: Cosimo.
Bäckström, P.O. 1845–1848. *Svenska folkböcker: Sagor, legender och äfventyr.* Volumes I–II. Stockholm: A. Bohlins förlag.
Bäckström, P.O. 1848*. Öfversigt af svensk folkläsning från äldre till närvarande tid. In idem (separately paginated), *Svenska folkböcker: Sagor, legender och äfventyr.* Vol. II. Stockholm: A. Bohlins förlag.
Bennich-Björkman, Bo 1988. Jacob Gustaf Björnståhl: Sago- och viskung i Stockholm på 1820-talet. In Eric Johannesson & Sonja Svensson (eds), *Litteraturens vägar: Litteratursociologiska studier tillägnade Lars Furuland.* Hedemora: Gidlunds, 93–135.
Bower, G.S. 1884. *The Prologue and Epilogue in English Literature from Shakespeare to Dryden.* London: Kegan Paul.
Brooks, Peter 1992. *Reading for the Plot: Design and Intention in Narrative.* Cambridge: Harvard University Press.
Bruster, Douglas & Robert Weimann 2004. *Prologues to Shakespeare's Theatre: Performance and Liminality in Early Modern Drama.* London: Routledge.
Burger, Thomas 1976. *Max Weber's Theory of Concept Formation: History, Laws, and Ideal Types.* Durham, N.C: Duke University Press.
Collijn, Isak 1942–1946. *Sveriges bibliografi: 1600-talet: Bidrag till en bibliografisk förteckning.* Volumes I–II. Uppsala: Svenska litteratursällskapet.
Danske Folkebøger fra 16. og 17. Aarhundrede 1915–1936. Volumes I–XIV, edited by J.P. Jacobsen, Jørgen Olrik & R. Paulli. København: Gyldendalske boghandel.
Eliade, Mircea 1971. *The Myth of the Eternal Return, or Cosmos and History.* Translated by Willard R. Trask. Princeton: Princeton University Press.
Elias, Norbert 1939. *Über den Prozeß der Zivilisation: Sociogenetische und psychogenetische Untersuchungen.* Volumes I–II. Basel: Haus zum Falken.
Engelsing, Rolf 1974. *Der Bürger als Leser: Lesergeschichte in Deutschland 1500–1800.* Stuttgart: J.B. Metzler Verlag.
Flood, John L. 1980. *The Survival of German Volksbücher: Three Studies in Bibliography.* Volumes I–II. Diss., University of London.
Flügel, Christoph 1969. *Prolog und Epilog in den deutschen Dramen und Legenden des Mittelalters.* Zürich: Verlag P.G. Keller.
Foley, John Miles 1991. *Immanent Art: From Structure to Meaning in Traditional Oral Epic.* Bloomington: Indiana University Press.
Geete, K.R. 1909. Helena (l. Helena Antonia) af Konstantinopel. In Th. Westrin (ed.),

Nordisk familjebok: Konversationslexikon och realencyklopedi. Vol. XI. Stockholm: Nordisk familjeboks förlags aktiebolag.

Genette, Gérard 1997. *Paratexts: Thresholds of Interpretation.* Translated by Jane E. Lewin. Literature, Culture, Theory 20. Cambridge: Cambridge University Press.

Gotzkowsky, Bodo 1991–1994. *"Volksbücher": Prosaromane, Renaissancenovellen, Versdichtungen und Schwankbücher: Bibliographie der deutschen Drucke.* Volumes I–II. Bibliotheca Bibliographica Aureliana 125. Baden-Baden: Verlag Valentin Koerner.

Harington, John 1591. An advertisement to the Reader [. . .]. In Ludovico Ariosto, *Orlando Fvrioso in English Heroical Verse.* Translated by John Harington. London: Richard Field.

Havelock, Eric A. 1963. *Preface to Plato.* A History of the Greek Mind 1. Cambridge: Harvard University Press.

Hirdt, Willy 1975. *Studien zum epischen Prolog: Der Eingang in der erzählenden Versdichtung Italiens.* München: Vilhelm Fink Verlag.

Horstbøll, Henrik 2009. In octavo: Formater, form og indhold på det populære litterære marked i 1700-tallets Danmark. In Mats Malm, Barbro Ståhle Sjönell & Petra Söderlund (eds), *Bokens materialitet: Bokhistoria och bibliografi. Bidrag till en konferens anordnad av Nordiskt Nätverk för Editionsfilologer 14–16 september 2007.* Nordiskt Nätverk för Editionsfilologer, skrifter 8. Stockholm: Svenska vitterhetssamfundet, 197–223.

Iser, Wolfgang 1974. *The Implied Reader: Patterns of Communication in Prose Fiction from Bunyan to Beckett.* Baltimore: Johns Hopkins University Press.

Iser, Wolfgang 1978. *The Act of Reading: A Theory of Aesthetic Response.* London: Routledge.

Klemming, G.E. & J.G. Nordin 1883. *Svensk boktryckeri-historia, 1483–1883 med inledande allmän öfversigt.* Stockholm: P.A. Norstedts & söners förlag.

Linnström, Hjalmar 1883–1884. *Svenskt boklexikon åren 1830–1865.* Volumes I–II. Uppsala: Bokgillets förlag.

Mason, Eva 1949. *Prolog, Epilog und Zwischenrede im deutschen Schauspiel des Mittelalters.* Diss., University of Basel. Affoltern am Albis: J. Weiss.

McKenzie, D.F. 2002. Speech – Manuscript – Print. In D.F. McKenzie, *Making Meaning: "Printers of the Mind" and Other Essays.* Edited by Peter D. McDonald & Michael F. Suarez. S.J. Amherst: University of Massachussetts Press, 237–258.

Möhlman, Jacob 1769. *Förteckning på framledne bruks-patron, wälborne hr. Jac. Möhlmans ansenliga boksamling, som består af en myckenhet böcker och manuscripter i hwarjehanda språk och wetenskaper, til en stor del wäl conditionerade. Hwilka igenom auction: komma at försäljas den [?] julii 1769.* Stockholm: Lars Salvius.

Olson, David R. 1994. *The World on Paper: The Conceptual and Cognitive Implications of Reading and Writing.* Cambridge: Cambridge University Press.

Richter, Anna Katharina 2009. *Transmissionsgeschichten: Untersuchungen zur dänischen und swedischen Erzählprosa in der frühen Neuzeit.* Beiträge zur Nordischen Philologie 41. Diss., University of Zürich. Tübingen: A. Francke Verlag.

Rinman, Sven 1951. *Studier i svensk bokhandel: Svenska bokförläggareföreningen 1843–1887.* Diss., Stockholm University College. Stockholm: P.A. Norstedts & söners förlag.

Sandberg, Peter 2010. *Ett tidningshus i Jönköping: Ursprung, tillkomst, framväxt, 1861–2008.* Sylwan 19. Göteborg: NORDICOM-Sverige.

Schwitzgebel, Bärbel 1996. *Noch nicht genug der Vorrede: Zur Vorrede volkssprachiger Sammlungen von Exempeln, Fabeln, Sprichwörtern und Schwänken des 16. Jahrhunderts.* Tübingen: Max Niemeyer Verlag.

Wingård, Rikard 2011. *Att sluta från början: Tidigmodern läsning och folkbokens receptionsestetik.* Diss., University of Gothenburg. Bokenäset: Frondes.

Cecilia af Forselles

Oral Tradition and the Press: Interaction between Periphery and Academic Centre in 18th-Century Finland

In the late 18th century, some of the leading scholars at the Academy in Turku,[1] Finland, contributed to a major paradigm shift at their university. They oriented the academic interest towards patriotic goals and the study of local conditions, agriculture, economy and culture, including also some attention to vernacular life and culture. Members of the group included the internationally known explorer, botanist and first Finnish professor of economics Pehr Kalm (1716–1779); the professor of chemistry, scientist and economist Pehr Adrian Gadd (1727–1797); and the "father of Finnish history and folklore", the professor and newspaperman Henrik Gabriel Porthan (1739–1804).

All of these men had strong ties to the clergy either by birth or marriage, which has been rather overlooked by previous research. The role of the clergy in promoting the transmission of oral to written culture in Finland is in this article presented as crucial. My aim is to highlight that the shift of academic interest and focus on oral tradition strongly relied on the knowledge of and intimacy with the people and the local conditions of different parts of the country that the scholars and their students – many of whom were also sons of priests – shared. This orientation among scholars and the clergy enabled a new approach to history and literature. This approach recognized, revealed and re-evaluated the rich oral tradition, stories, verses and songs, which were still in those days to be found particularly in the Finnish-speaking vernacular culture, often in peripheral areas.

The central figure in the creation of the new interest in the Finnish language, oral tradition and the history of the Finnish people, and of a new perspective on literature and history, was Henrik Gabriel Porthan. He considered that oral tradition could reveal historical information about Finnish history and that Finnish oral poetry had literary qualities that had not been noticed before. He was also a scholarly pioneer who began using the press to promote academic and cultural goals and a wider interest in oral tradition in society.

---

1   The Academy in Turku [Regia academia Aboensis, Kungliga Akademien i Åbo] was a Swedish university in Finland, founded in 1640 during Swedish rule, which lasted until 1809. The city of Åbo is today better known by its Finnish name Turku.

Porthan was the founder and editor of the first newspaper in Finland, *Tidningar Utgifne av ett Sällskap i Åbo* (published 1771–1778 and 1782–1785). This paper was succeeded by *Åbo Nya Tidningar* (published 1789), to which Porthan also contributed as an important author. The language of both papers was Swedish, even though Latin had for decades been the dominant language of printed texts in Finland. Swedish and Finnish were the native languages, and although Swedish had by the end of the 18th century acquired the status of being the language of local administration, it had not yet become the language of the academic world. In an article published in 1773, Porthan emphasized that the Finnish language, which was used by the greater part of the people of Finland, was very well suited for poetry. Most of the literature available in Finland consisted of translations of well-known foreign authors of the day. Porthan's idea of Finnish as a language suitable for poetry and printed literature in a wider sense was striking and new, as were the examples of Finnish vernacular verses or songs that were printed in the paper.

In his article, Porthan wrote:

> The Finnish language is in this respect rather neglected, but possesses a firm natural position, whence its nature is soon grasped . . . [it] has in its common rune-songs much power and attractiveness. A few examples will likewise show that it is well suited to heroic poetry.[2] ("Om Finska Språkets skick til Stenstyl", *Tidningar Utgifne af ett Sällskap i Åbo*, 13 February 1773).

Porthan not only suggested a re-evaluation of the literary usefulness of the Finnish language, but also included examples of oral tradition in Finnish in print, in the paper and in the middle of the otherwise Swedish contents. The article was a strong public statement in favour of folk poetry and Finnish-language oral tradition, and has to be regarded as a declaration by the learned society, *Aurorasällskapet*, that published the paper. The society had undertaken a mission to promote the native languages, literature and poetry.

The scholars who in the late 18th century began to study, collect and publish works about oral tradition in fact introduced the Finnish-language oral tradition to other scholars and to the educated and literate groups in society, who did not all understand Finnish and who had not all come into contact with oral tradition. The academic publications on oral tradition and Porthan's writings about oral tradition in the press presented the Finnish oral tradition by means of Swedish translations.

Academic works about oral tradition did not reach a wide audience, nor did they rouse much interest (af Forselles 2011, 108), however, the purpose of this article is not to present the reception of these works, but to discuss the diverse links between oral tradition and book culture and, by using one

---

2   Translation into English by the author. In Swedish: "Det finska språket är härtils nog försummat; men äger en stadig naturlig ställning, hwaraf dess beskaffenhet snart inhämtas . . . [detta språket har] i sina wanliga Runor mycken styrka och behaglighet. Et och annat prof lägger ämväl å daga, at det är til heroiskt wersslag wäl fallit".

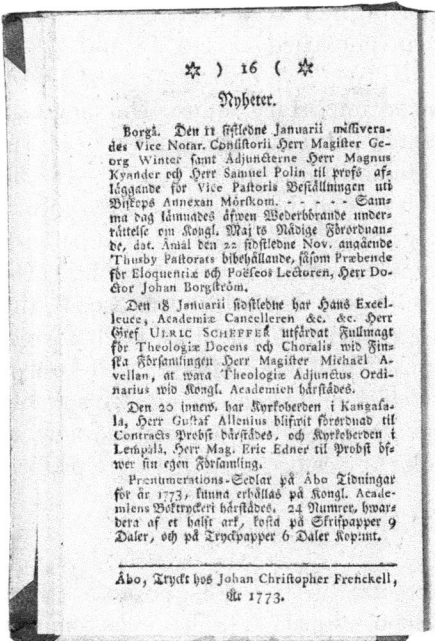

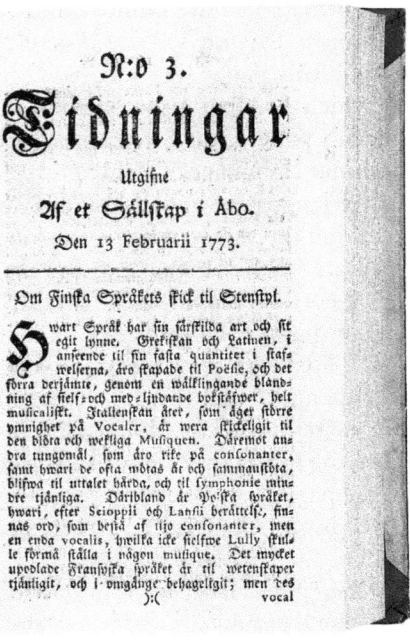

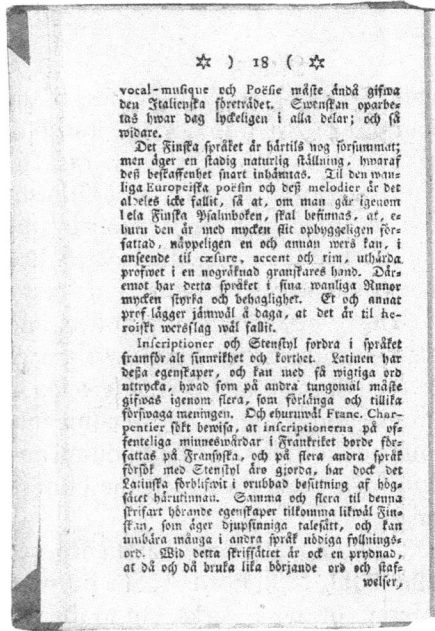

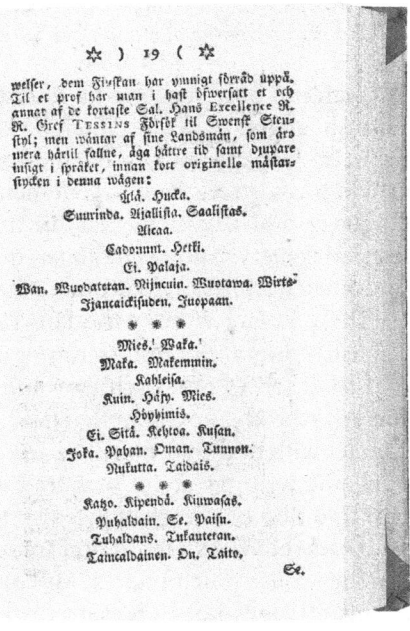

Tidningar utgifvne af ett sällskap i Åbo *[A newspaper published by a Society in Turku]*, 13 February 1773. The article Om Finska Språkets skick til Stenstyl *["The suitability of the Finnish language for poetry"] was a strong public statement in favour of folk poetry and Finnish-language oral tradition, and has to be regarded as a declaration by the learned society,* Aurorasällskapet, *which published the paper.*

crucial example, a press review, to reveal the importance of the press in this process. Written by Porthan, the review was published in a sequence of papers and was thus exceptionally extensive, which also indicates something about its impressiveness. The aim is to examine the actions that were taken and the conditions that prevailed in promoting interest in and marketing the new genre. In particular, I investigate how the newspaper was used to create interest in and understanding of new trends in history and literature, showing how the press was used in the initial phase to market and make the oral tradition known to university teachers and students, as well as to a wider range of readers.

The focus is on how already the first newspapers in the late 18th century functioned from the outset as a pioneering medium for the learned in Finland in promoting new attitudes in particular towards folklore, but also towards culture, language, literature, research and science in general. Some attention is also given to international intellectual trends that were, to some degree, also at work in Finland, reflecting, as it appears, universal conditions and scholarly interests and networks in existence among the clergy. Thus, by investigating one of Porthan's extensive writings in detail side by side with these universal conditions, we gain an idea of the relationship between the press and oral tradition, the transformation of the spoken word into written text and the nature of the interaction between the academic centre and the periphery in the matter of oral tradition.

The objective is to show how a paradigm shift was effected by means of the press in a way which made it possible for an interest in oral tradition to arise. I highlight how the press and academic channels of publishing were utilized to make oral tradition a part of the print culture and make it a focus for learned studies by the late 18th century in Finland at the Academy in Turku. I investigate what happened from an international viewpoint by presenting circumstances that were all but universal in the emerging re-evaluation of oral tradition. Regardless of any motives and ideas held by Finnish scholars, their activities fit well in an international context, which was based on a new *modi operandi*, trends and ideas among scholars.

The academic network and the paradigm shift

In the 18th century, a clearly expressed aim existed in Sweden, of which Finland was at that time a part: to support the idea and sense of locality and to raise interest in the conditions of local communities and home districts. In 1741, the Royal Academy of Sciences published an important work in support of these aims. Jacob Faggot (1699–1777), who was a prominent Swedish promoter of agriculture, published his influential text on the surveying and description of the fatherland, *Tankar om fäderneslandets känning och beskrifwande* ["Thoughts on the knowledge and description of the fatherland"] (Faggot 1741).

Faggot, who was the director of Svenska Lantmäterikontoret [The Swedish Royal Land Survey Office], delivered a heavy critique of the reading habits of the time. He noted that people read about the geography and economy of foreign countries and amused themselves with descriptions of places that foreign, even heathen poets and writers had made famous. Faggot's text clearly states that comparable information on one's own country was needed to counteract the growing interest in everything foreign. The overarching purpose in this utilitarian age was, however, to direct the interest towards an improvement of domestic affairs and towards an investigation of the possibilities of improving the economy and the living conditions of the people at home (*Ibid.*).[3]

In Finland, descriptions of the homeland published as academic dissertations contributed to a shift of language orientation in academic circles. Previously, academic dissertations had been published exclusively in Latin, but in the late 18th century a number of dissertations focusing on local conditions were published in Swedish. Because Latin was not widely spoken, these had a better chance of reaching more readers, especially outside the academic community. The homeland descriptions also cleared the way for an interest in vernacular culture, customs and traditions as well as oral tradition and folklore. The inclusion of studies of vernacular culture in the field of academic interest and knowledge is in this article presented as a precondition for the transmission of oral culture to book culture. The transmission can thus be regarded as a consequence of a larger scholarly paradigm shift.

Even though the Academy in Turku was not a scientific community in the sense we understand the term today, the pursuit of a higher scientific level of research was emerging. In this article, however, I use the term *paradigm shift* to describe a major change in the model for or pattern of conducting and presenting research at the university in Turku. This paradigm shift involved several academic disciplines, such as natural sciences, geography, economy, history and agriculture, and it included academically recognized scientific achievements that provided model problems and solutions for scholars in Finland. It also led to the development of new fields of research and disciplines, such as the study of oral tradition. Porthan clarified such questions, promoting the paradigm shift and urging academic studies to focus on oral tradition too, and he pushed for its acceptance in society by publishing texts about oral tradition in the newspapers.[4]

Porthan exercised a strong influence on academic life through the Aurora Society [*Aurorasällskapet*]. When the Aurora Society was founded in 1770, its main aim was to promote an interest in fiction, literature and academic studies. The society also strove to publish articles on the history, geography, language, economy and living conditions among various groups in society in different parts of the country. The society was firmly linked with the

3   These local descriptions have been comprehensively described and studied by Mattias Legnér in his 2004 dissertation *Fäderneslandets rätta beskrivning*.
4   The term "paradigm shift" is thus used according to certain principles introduced by Thomas S. Kuhn in his work on the structure of scientific revolutions (Kuhn 2009). I am aware, however, that scholarly praxis in the late 18th century limits a comprehensive use of Kuhn's principles.

Academy in its activities, and it offered an opportunity for the scholars of the Academy to debate and show their interest in patriotic questions and fiction, and to dine together.

The society also founded and published the newspaper *Tidningar Utgifne af et Sällskap i Åbo* to meet the need for a wider distribution of news about academic learning and science. Many leading scholars contributed to the paper as authors. Hence the paper maintained a high intellectual standard with varied topics discussed on its pages. In addition to the scholars Kalm and Gadd, Matthias Calonius (1737–1817) and Jacob Tengström (1755–1832) were among those who wrote for the paper. Although other topics, such as economic and geographical questions, were included, the focus was on literature and history-related materials, including news about academic and official life. The paper became a medium for presenting new orientations in the Academy (Tommila 2000, 16–17).[5]

Many newspapers in Europe, particularly in Germany, had taken as their mission to summarize academic studies and keep their readerships informed about current academic knowledge. The need for this lay in the expanding book production and changing concept of science and academic studies. Scholars no longer managed to find out about all innovations and studies that they could use in their own research. Somehow they had to get information about innovations, use them in their own work and discuss them openly. In this way, academic reputation was maintained at the time (Schneider 1999, 202).

The paradigm shift and the use of the press to promote it were possible because Porthan and other scholars shared an understanding of what the focus of research should be and how the results of their research should be presented. One of the primary conditions was the understanding of what was to be observed and scrutinized. This led to the mass production[6] of dissertations on local conditions at the Academy in Turku during the 18th century that radically changed the way in which society, the economy, geography, nature etc. were comprehended. Directives for the students about the kind of questions that were to be highlighted and described were published. Consequently, the dissertations were similarly structured and described similar facts, conditions and phenomena. In some of them, vernacular culture and the existence of oral tradition were also mentioned.

As early as 1754, the student Eric Castrén (1732–1787) wrote in his dissertation about the region of Kainuu/Kajanaland[7] in the east of Finland near the north of Ostrobothnia as follows:

> Some of the country folk are much given to creating and singing rune-songs, and as they are often funny, witty and profound they would be interesting to describe here, but these pages are supposed to contain something else. In pagan times,

5   For a general presentation of Porthan and central writings and sources about him see Tarkiainen 2012.
6   The use of the term "mass production" relates to over sixty descriptions of places clearly mentioned in the titles of dissertations.
7   Placename in Finnish/in Swedish.

many superstitions and curious customs became deep-rooted among the people and some remnants of these can [still] be found here and there in the country.[8] (Castrén 1754, 15).

Then, he continues to describe the possibility that giants lived in Kajaani[9] in olden days. In this instance, the author's attitude is very positive and he regrets not having the opportunity to describe in more detail the poetry and oral culture, which he obviously found interesting. Castrén, who came from Ostrobothnia and belonged to a renowned family of clergymen, later became rural dean and vicar in Kemi in northern Ostrobothnia, where he worked towards the economic improvement of the region.

Also, the presentation and interpretation of the results of the studies in the dissertations were quite homogeneous. As mentioned above, these dissertations favoured the use of Swedish instead of Latin and aimed at a wider circle of readers and use in society. Economic development and utility as well as the knowledge of Finland and its history were in focus, resulting in what was in many ways a changed view of society and a positive attitude also to folk poetry. The studies were conducted following a joint pattern, often relying on the information of the sons of clergymen as in the case of Castrén or, in some cases, sons of peasants, who often described in their dissertations their own districts or places of birth, which they knew well.[10] This already hints at the important role which the clergy played in the paradigm shift and for the interest for oral poetry. The Academy in Turku, as the only university in Finland, educated generations of students, many of whom became priests themselves according to this academic pattern and in this intellectual environment.

In this context, the press got an important mission: to inform the public of what was studied and going on at the Academy. It is, moreover, most obvious that the incorporation of material and writings about oral tradition was aimed to raise interest for the preservation and collection of oral poetry in Finnish and for the oral tradition studies at the Academy. The papers included, in addition to the varying literary material and oral poetry, many articles by known scholars and experts of the day about local conditions in Finland and about Finland's geography, flora and fauna.

The process of transmission of oral tradition into book culture took its initial steps when early in his academic life Porthan revealed his interest in oral poetry. During the years 1766–1778, he published in five volumes

8　Translation into English by the author. Swedish original: "En del af Allmogen är mycket fallen för Runors diktande och sjungande, som man här med flera sådane qwicka, och otroligen fintlige, samt sinnrika runor, hwilka de wid wissa tillfällen qwäda, kunde bestyrcka; så framt intet desse bladen til något annat wore ämnade. Uti Hedendomen hafwa ock åtsxillige widskeppelser och synnerlige plägseder inritat sig hos folket, af whilka någre öfwerlefwor ännu finnas här och där i landet."

9　Today a city in Kainuu.

10　The title page of a dissertation, or the page that follows the title page, often included information about the background of the student, such as his father's position as vicar or chaplain or his home district. Among the persons that Eric Castrén wanted to thank, he mentions mainly clergymen in Kajaani, one of whom was his cousin.

his own dissertation, *De Poesi Fennica*, comprising oral poetry that he had collected and information about classical poetry. His study of oral poetry was groundbreaking, as he used examples of Finnish oral poetry in print to explain and analyse the forms and patterns of Finnish oral poetry. Another major work, *Mythologia Fennica*, was produced in 1789 by the chaplain Christfrid Ganander, who had studied at the Academy in Turku. Porthan introduced this work to the general public by writing an exceptionally comprehensive review of it in the press. The review must be regarded as major manifestation of or act of promotion made by Porthan in favour of the transmission of oral tradition to written culture. That samples of oral tradition were printed in the press was an early crucial step in transferring poetry from oral versions to literary versions.

A new literary culture and the review of Mythologia Fennica

Mythologia Fennica was published by the Royal Academic Printing Office [Kongliga Academiska Boktryckeriet i Åbo] in 1789 and ran to 112 pages. Ganander had collected his materials from folk poems, spells, folklore and some written sources.[11] Porthan's review appeared in November 1789 in *Åbo Nya Tidningar*. By the standards of the time, the review was unusual, and not just in terms of its length. The review continued as a series in three subsequent issues and presented several extracts, citations and examples from the book in Finnish.

Porthan begins his introduction to the work by citing the title page as follows:

> *Mythologia Fennica*, or an explanation of the Nomina Propria Deastrorum, Idolorum, Locorum, Virorum etc., or false gods and goddesses, outstanding figures of antiquity, offerings and offering places, old traditions, giants, trolls, spirits of the forest, lakes and mountains, etc., which occur in the ancient Finnish magic rune-poems, origins, words, fairy tales, riddles etc. which are still in use and are mentioned in everyday speech to serve those who wish to thoroughly understand the Finnish language, and have a taste for Finnish history and poetry, collected and interpreted from old rune-poems. (*Åbo Nya Tidningar*, 12 November 1789).[12]

11 Mikael Agricola (1510–1557) was a clergyman who became the founder of literary Finnish. He translated the New Testament into Finnish and also produced a Finnish prayer book and hymns used in Finland's Lutheran Church. His list of Finnish heathen gods from early times published in 1551 belongs among the oldest literary sources of oral tradition and folk beliefs.

12 Translation by the author. "Mythologia Fennica, eller Förklaring öfver De Nomina Propria Deastrorum, Idolorum, Locorum, Virorum &c. eller Afgudar och Afgudinnor, Forntidens Märkelige Personer, Offer och Offer-Ställen, gamla Sedwänjor, Jättar, Troll, Skogs- Sjö- och Bergs-Rån m. m. Som förekomma i de äldre Finska Troll-Runor, Synnyt, Sanat, Sadut, Arwotuxet &c. samt än brukas och nämnas i dagligt tal; Til deras tjenst, som wela i grund förstå det Finska Språket, och hafwa smak för Finska Historien och *Poësin*, af Gamla Runor samlad och uttydd".

MYTHOLOGIA FENNICA,

ELLER

FÓRKLARING

ÖFVER

De NOMINA PROPRIA DEASTRORUM, IDOLORUM, LOCORUM, VIRORUM &c.

ELLER

AFGUDAR och AFGUDINNOR, FORNTIDENS MÅRKELIGE PERSONER, OFFER och OFFER-STäLLEN, GAMLA SEDVÅNJOR, JåTTAR, TROLL, SKOGS- SJÓ- och BERGS-RÅN m. m.

Som

Fórekomma i de *åldre Finfka Troll- Runor, Synnyt, Sanat, Sadut, Arwotuxet* &c. famt ån brukas och nåmnas i dagligt tal;

Til deras tjenft,

Som vela i grund förftå det Finfka Spräket, och hafva fmak för Finfka Hiftorien och Foë.in,

Af Gamla Runor famlad och uttydd

Af

CHRISTFRID GANANDER, Thomasfon

Philof. Mag. & Sacell.

ÅBO, Tryckt i FRENCKELLSKA Boktryckeriet 1789. På egen Bekoftnad.

Mythologia Fennica by Christfrid Ganander, Åbo (Turku) 1789.

Porthan introduces the author to the reader by mentioning that he is a Master of Philosophy and priest in Siikajoki parish in the Oulu/Uleåborg district in the north of Finland. According to Porthan, the author had been keenly occupied for more than thirty years in the study of the Finnish language and "his ancestors' wisdom". Porthan mentions that the author was working on a Finnish dictionary and that the *Mythologia Fennica* is compiled in alphabetical order and includes some Lappish entries. Porthan emphasizes additionally that Ganander had become a lover of antiquity.

Many of those who read the review spoke and understood little or no Finnish, and the paper seldom contained anything in Finnish. The presentation of the arrangement of the contents of the book emphasises that the poems in the *Mythologia Fennica* are in most cases presented both in the original Finnish language and in Swedish translation, which helped

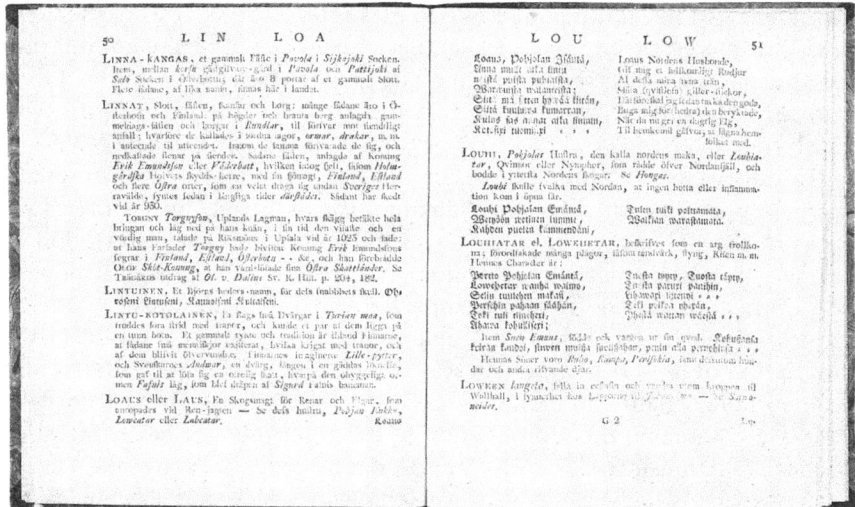

Mythologia Fennica was published as an encyclopedic dictionary with short listings, arranged alphabetically, and presenting mythological topics. The author, Christfrid Ganander, describes LOUHI as the housewife of the Northern lands, belonging to the women or nymphs who ruled at the Fell of the North [Nordanfjäll]. She has also, in other presentations, been described as the wicked witch of the North or queen of the land known as Pohjola [The North] in Finnish and Karelian mythology. LOUHITAR is by Ganander described in Mythologia Fennica as the wicked witch.

to arouse the reader's interest in the poems. This explains to some extent the length of the review. However, it is exceptional mainly because Porthan includes in it several of the poems from *Mythologia Fennica* which was a way to publish at least some of the most significant poems also in Finnish for a wider public than the book ever would reach.

Mythologia Fennica includes mainly explanations and presentations of mythological phenomena and figures, which are also extensively and thoroughly presented in the review. The long direct extracts presented in the review gave the readers of the newspaper a rare opportunity to understand and develop interest in the new antiquarian approach to Finnish history and poetry. The review contains the full descriptions, for example, of the horrible god or spirit Hiisi, who had power over wild animals. Hiisi's character, magic powers and different appearances as forest or mountain spirits are described, as well as different places called *Hiisi* or including *Hiisi* in their names. Some samples of poems containing information about Hiisi are also presented. Additionally, the review includes examples of different Finnish compound words beginning with *hiisi*, such as *hiienwäki* [the people in Hiisi's household] with a short description of his household (*Åbo Nya Tidningar*, 18 November 1789, 371–372).

Another entry and comprehensive description reproduced in the review is "Kalewan pojat" [the sons of Kalewa] which were, Porthan writes, described in the poems as twelve tremendously strong giants. Included is also the entry "Luonotaret" [fairies or spirits] who, as the poems relate, milked their own breasts in the smith god's forge to make three forms of iron. Included too is the interesting explanation that these fairies "are in reality nothing else than the natural effects of the iron-making process: because of this the Finns call them *Raudan-haltiat* [Iron fairies], the females, daughters or girls who give birth to the iron" (*Åbo Nya Tidningar*, 19 November 1789, 377–379).

In the last part of the review, the full description of one of the main characters in Finnish folklore, Wäinämöinen, is given, filling over four pages of the newspaper. In addition to the comprehensive description of Wäinämöinen's character and habitus, and the art of his magical powers and musical skills, the review compares Wäinämöinen's music with the music and musicians of the Greek epics. Finally, the review reproduces the description of how Wäinämöinen was able to touch everybody's heart and set the whole of nature in motion when he played his harp. The last words of the review state that the reproduction of the description of Wäinämöinen's magical and musical skills was important in order to show the reader a masterpiece, which challenged everything in Greek and Roman music (*Åbo Nya Tidningar*, 26 November 1789, 387–390). There is no doubt about the enthusiasm with which the review was written and which it aimed to transfer to the reader. It sought to arouse understanding of another kind of poetry than that which readers were acquainted with and usually read.

The comparison with the Greek and Roman epics shows that Porthan too shared the more subtle understanding scholars in the 18th century had of the European classical age itself. At this time, scholars began to see that the classical epic was built on the language of a more primitive pre-Homeric society. Although the Italian philosopher and historian Giovan Battista (Giambattista) Vico (1668–1744) and the Genevan philosopher Jean-Jacques Rousseau (1712–1778) had already questioned Homer's literacy, the learned in Britain, and especially in Scotland, did not publish texts arguing for sophisticated oral societies until 1760 (see Ó Giolláin in this volume). In Finland, Porthan's texts followed some years later in the 1770s and 1780s. As with the interest in Scottish Gaelic poetry shown by James Macpherson (1736–1796), resulting in his controversial publication of the *Ossian* verses, the Finnish case for orality derived both from specific local developments and from a more general European intellectual trend.

When writing his review, Porthan acted as a scholar in a modern way, using new media and ways to promote knowledge about academic studies. Reviews had fast become an international trend, which also promoted the academic community and its procedures with the 18th century experiencing a complex and widespread transformation in the production, consumption and distribution of print. The rapidly evolving journals and newspapers in Europe developed new ways of writing and marketing texts, and of using them. Many newspapers were established and new groups of readers were emerging. The growing trend of literary criticism and book reviews in the press was essential for the promotion of different kinds of new literature (cf. Raven 2001, 1–34 and Forster 2001, 170–190).

Porthan's activity as editor and author in the early established papers illustrates how the press adopted and transmitted the new literary culture in Finland and how it was used to promote new attitudes in the literary

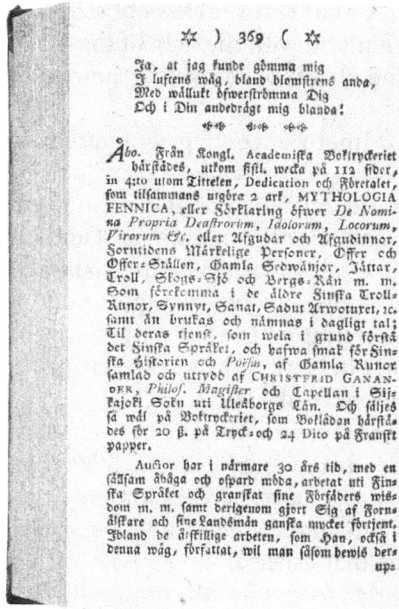

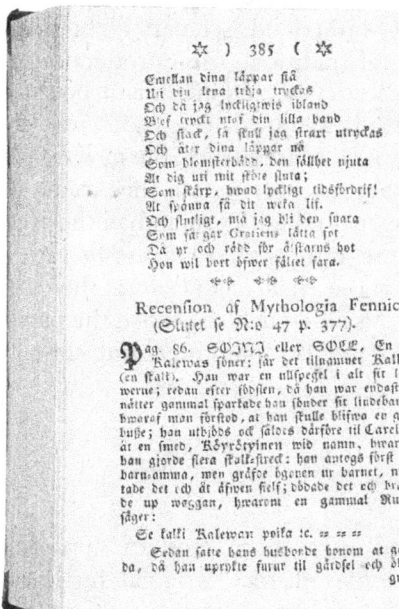

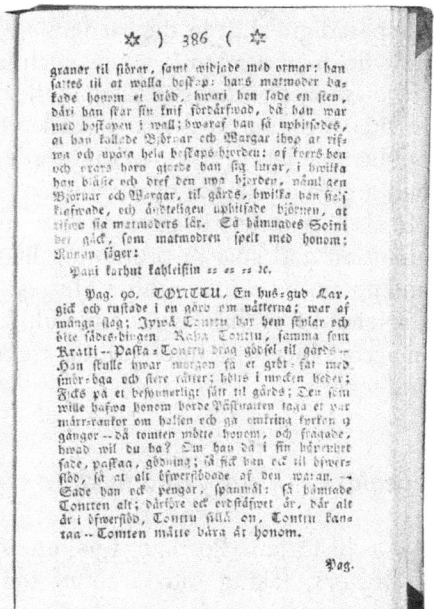

The review of Mythologia Fennica *in the newspaper* Åbo Nya Tidningar, *12 and 26 November 1789. The explanations and presentations of mythological phenomena and figures in* Mythologia Fennica *are extensively and thoroughly presented in the review, giving the readers of the newspaper a new and rare opportunity to get knowledge of the Finnish mythological world and oral tradition. The explanation of the Finnish word* TONTTU *[gnome] as a spirit or god of the house who restores the farm at night is chosen to illustrate the contents of the book.*

field as well as in scholarly undertakings. A market for reviews of scholarly works too took its first steps explicitly in Finland with the help of the newly established newspapers. Criticism became a way of marketing new ideas and research fields.

Book historians have emphasized the importance of paying attention to early literary criticism. In Michael Gavin's view, reviews contribute to describing how books interact with the world, reflecting on the institutional contexts of book production, and try to account for the intentions of authors and responses (Gavin 2012, 43). "This makes old criticism an indispensable archive of evidence for book history, but it also involves doing something like a history of ideas. Understanding its implication in all these arenas, and doing our best to keep them simultaneously in view, is the key to getting the most we can from criticism in our histories of books" (*Ibid.*, 61).

Porthan's writings on oral tradition in the press implied the new scholarly project of presenting and evaluating academic publications. We know Porthan's and the Aurora Society's goals and have here examined some newspaper texts that express what Porthan intended and wanted the readers to think or get interested in. It is obvious that especially the review of the *Mythologia Fennica* is an example of the early processes of the modernization and professionalization of academic life in Finland.

The review is also an example of how the press was used to follow through the paradigm shift in the academic world in Finland. Scholars highlighted new fields of academic study, such as oral tradition. The introduction of reviews was an interesting step in the intellectual history in Finland, because in this way the press made academic studies known to a wider reading public than just scholars of the Academy. As a consequence, the new trends had a greater chance of making an impact not only within the Academy, but also on society in general. As a newspaper editor, Porthan had the high ambition and goal of promoting literature and offering readers literature and poems by native authors. His review of the *Mythologia Fennica* shows in a splendid way that he not only fulfilled this aim, but also shaped the paper in accordance with international trends of the time both regarding content and form.

Scholars of history and folklore

As a historian, Porthan was interested in a more modern approach to history, taking into account the people's history, original historical documentation and a wider range of topics, instead of the earlier court histories and the focus on the kings, wars and "big history" (Tommila 2000, 17–19; af Forselles 2010, 108). Although Porthan was formally a professor of Latin literature, or officially of eloquence, he considered, as we have seen, that his field also included literature stretching from folk poetry to early romanticism. Porthan's publications reveal his concept of oral tradition as orally transmitted texts, which vary in performance but keep their main contents unchanged. He was well acquainted with the textual criticism of the classical period, and he sought to apply this to the Finnish rune-poems.

He warned the collectors of oral poetry against correcting and improving the rune-poems. (Hakamies 2010, 61.)

Christfrid Ganander had already as a student become interested in Porthan's patriotic ideas and he became a collector and scholar of oral poetry. He is an early example of a clergyman making a significant contribution as a scholar and folklore collector. In addition to *Mythologia Fennica*, he also published a collection of riddles in 1783 and a book of tales in 1784. He compiled a work on the origin, way of life and language of the Gypsies in 1780 and two books on medicine. He also worked on an extensive, unpublished Finnish–Swedish–Latin dictionary. He was, moreover, a published poet. He was also interested in archaeology and in 1782 published in the paper *Tidningar Utgifne af et Sällskap i Åbo* an article about cairns and barrows in the parish of Laihela in Ostrobothnia. During the same decade he also wrote other articles on similar topics in the same paper.

Porthan's and Ganander's scholarly orientation, aspirations, works and writings also mirrored the antiquarian interest of the day, and the changes in the study, interest, perception and reshaping of history. As elsewhere in Europe, the interest in history was growing in Finland. The study of court protocols and estate inventory deeds shows that a surprisingly plentiful amount of historical literature was also read. Like fiction and poetry, historical works were thought to foster individual thinking and interpretations of culture and society in general, and were in this respect also important vehicles for introducing new ideas to society. Historical writing was rejuvenated during the 18th century in many ways, and its impact on society grew. Historical works functioned as mentors for the readers' different political, ideological and cultural choices and identity. They helped to create not a fixed and imagined, but an interpretive society that paid attention to the telling of its own story (af Forselles 2010, 105–106; Hallberg 2003, 126).

In general, the era's interest in history manifested itself as an interest in one's own local history and past. Historians were no longer interested only in the political, military and royal history of great men, but began to focus also on the people's past. In Finland, in the field of history Porthan is also regarded as a reformer who elevated historical study and teaching to a new level. One of the main reasons why Porthan and Ganander turned their attention to oral tradition and folk poetry was in the hope of uncovering clues regarding the past of the Finnish people (af Forselles 2010, 108).

The relationship between Ganander and Porthan was not always harmonious, but it has usually been described as a relationship between teacher and pupil, mentor and adept. To what degree Porthan influenced or dictated Ganander's work is not a question discussed in this article, but it is evident that their cooperation illustrates how the scholarly network within the clergy operated to promote publishing and marketing of printed texts about oral tradition and how the initial steps were taken to transform oral culture into book culture in Finland.

To what degree were they aware of and influenced by international trends in history and literature favouring the collection and publishing of oral culture? We know that Porthan visited Germany and the University of

Göttingen in 1779 and that he came into contact with German academic and intellectual life, as well as new ideas. There are contradictory opinions among Finnish scholars as to the extent and ways Porthan was influenced by new ideas and trends during his visit to Germany. Some emphasize that he was throughout a scholar of the Enlightenment and was not influenced by the romantic trend to idealize primitive cultures, whereas others suggest that he was to some extent influenced by romanticism. It has also been claimed that he was clearly influenced by early romanticism and that his interest in oral tradition was due in large part to James Macpherson's *The Poems of Ossian* (Hakamies 2008, 60). It has been suggested that while he was an old-fashioned patriot at the beginning of his career, the visit to Göttingen and his acquaintance with German academic trends changed his views completely (Klinge 1989, 62).

Both Porthan and Ganander have, however, in recent research been characterised as representatives of the 18th-century mythological interpretation, who primarily understood the *Kalevala* epic as mythological. It has been emphasised, especially concerning Ganander, that he was a rationalist of the Enlightenment, who presented the contents of the poems as the results of primitive imagination or metaphors or allegories which were to be classified in categories and subcategories in the way the great naturalist Linné did with the plant kingdom. Ganander's encyclopaedic knowledge and interest in classification did not, however, exclude opinions about the nature of mythology. By relating it to ancient Greek mythology, Christian texts and Nordic sagas, he became the first to study Finnish mythology from a comparative perspective (Siikala 2012, 33–34; Hautala 1984, IX–X; Kajanto 1984).

After his visit to Germany, Porthan's interest in Finnish folklore became unstoppable, and he produced other pioneering studies side by side with his work as a newspaper editor and author as well as an inspiring university teacher. He published a study on the origin of the ancient Finns and their beliefs, *De superstitione veterum Fennorum theoretica et practica* (1782), and another about Finnish charms, *De fama magiae Fennis attributa* (1789), and, *inter alia*, studies about Finnish-Uralic languages, proverbs and dialects. He became as a scholar interested in oral tradition in Finland, efficiently developed it as a scholarly topic and promoted a wider interest in it. Moreover, his activities were based on circumstances that were not unique to Finland but were found elsewhere too.

The clergy and oral tradition

The clergy was one group among whom the early newspapers in Finland found interested readers outside the academic circles. The clergy already had a keen and special interest in the papers because they included a section at the end with news about appointments and arrangements among the clergy throughout Finland. Moreover, scholars among the clergy contributed with articles or, as in the case of Ganander, both wrote articles themselves and got their publications reviewed in the paper.

The clergymen's knowledge of local conditions and, to varying degrees, of the Finnish language, along with the patriotic interest boosted by the press, made them useful in the paradigm shift in the academic community. Students who studied at the Academy in Turku and published works and dissertations on the conditions in their home districts constituted a special group that acted in the spirit of the Enlightenment, supervised by and grouped around groundbreaking academic teachers such as Porthan. They had as their first conviction a keen interest in improving the conditions of the home district, rather than giving priority to theological topics. The assumption here is that it was within this academic circle, climate or orientation that the interest in folk poetry could also arise.

Here, the scholars' background and network among the clergy is emphasized as a contributing factor, which helps to explain why Porthan and Ganander came to have such a pioneering role in the study and promotion of oral tradition in Finland. However, the clergy also had a special role in their understanding of oral performance and the literary qualities of poetry. The shift in academic interest towards a new understanding and interpretation of history, literature and oral tradition was mainly conducted by scholars who relied on their knowledge of church sermons or their own sermons and were thus familiar with oral performance as a medium of communication.

At the university, the economic descriptions and dissertations on local conditions, nature, agriculture and occupations of the home districts, including vernacular ways of life, were produced to a significant degree by members of the clergy, or prospective clergymen and the sons of clergymen, many of whom went on to become clergymen themselves. A browse through the 18th-century dissertations at the Academy in Turku shows that many of the students who compiled their dissertations describing local conditions were, like many other students, sons of priests.

Both Porthan and Ganander belonged to families of clergymen with interests in their home districts and local conditions, the education and enlightenment of the people and the Finnish language. Porthan's father was a vicar at Viitasaari, but Porthan was raised by his maternal uncle Gustaf Juslenius, who was the vicar at Kruunupyy/Kronoby in Ostrobothnia. His and Porthan's mother's father was Daniel Juslenius (1676–1752), who is known as the first fennophile. He inspired Porthan to take an interest in Finnish culture and matters. Daniel Juslenius was professor in theology, Hebrew and Greek at the Academy in Turku. He promoted an interest in Finnish culture and history by publishing works with fantastic theories and depictions of the glorious past of the Finnish people. He produced the still fascinating description of Turku, *Aboa Vetus et Nova* (1700), and another work, *Vindiciae Fennorum* "The Defence of the Finns". Another prominent clergyman who influenced Porthan towards a Finnish patriotic interest was the bishop of Turku, Carl Fredrick Mennander (1712–1786), who also at one time was a professor at the Academy and also promoted descriptions of home districts as dissertations compiled as economic descriptions of places in Finland.

Ganander's parents also belonged to the clergy. Ganander was the son of a chaplain in northern Ostrobothnia, Thomas Ganander. After the death of his father, Ganander was taken care of by his mother's family and his grandfather, Henrik Hidén, who was a chaplain in the south of Ostrobothnia. Ganander himself worked as a chaplain in Ostrobothnia all his life, but he was in continuous contact with Porthan. Ganander had a lifelong interest in the Finnish language and oral tradition and from this point of view it is interesting to compare him and Porthan with the Scottish Highland clergy with similar interests. Donald E. Meek has highlighted the extent to which the clergy stood at the boundaries of oral and literary traditions in the Scottish Highlands. He explores the manner in which literate clergymen governed and shaped the Gaelic culture from the Middle Ages to the 19th century by acting as bridge-builders between oral and literary traditions (Meek 2002, 84). The observation that the clergy of the Highlands and Islands stood at the intersection of oral and literary tradition beyond the ecclesiastical sphere in the same way as is observed in this paper is interesting. The clergy was appreciative of the rich variety of traditional creative genres attested within the communities they served, and they themselves were in a way also oral creators when performing sermons in their churches. The clergy were thus aware in their daily work that written prose was not the only medium for communication. Songs and oral performance were a significant part of their own working practices and effective methods for inculcating higher values among the members of their community (cf. *Ibid.*, 109).

Like Scotland, Finland too seems to owe the survival of and interest in the oldest vernacular songs and tales to the Protestant Church. It is easy to assume that some of those who were interested in oral tradition were moderate clergymen and that, as in the Scottish Highlands, they made a much more significant contribution to recording secular oral material than they did to writing original scholarly works on theology (cf. Meek 2002, 111). Also, the clergy's (partial) knowledge of Finnish contributed to the development of Finnish culture on oral and literary levels in the same way as it did in the Highlands through the Gaelic-speaking clergymen. They had to use the day-to-day Finnish of their community in their daily work.

Both Porthan and Ganander had knowledge of Finnish. Ganander in particular operated as an educated clergyman all his life on one side of the boundary, in the domain of literacy, while, on the other, he depended on oral means for communication with the people. For the preservation of at least some of the old oral tradition, we also have in Finland to thank scholars, priests and priests' sons like Porthan and Ganander (cf. *Ibid.*, 112).

Yet another interesting comparison with the Gaelic-speaking clergy's activities in the Highlands is that Finnish-speaking clergymen, like their counterparts in the Scottish Highlands, apparently freed and widened their range of interest beyond mere translations of the Finnish rune-poems. Meek concludes:

> Those with an eye for creativity, who also happened to be placed in a context conducive to literary enterprise (usually in the Lowland cities or in the colonies), became the principal bridge-builders between orality and literacy, and also between orality and print. Pulpit oratory was traditionally and pre-eminently the domain of the clergy, and it may well been enhanced and ennobled as an oral art

by the impact of Ossianic debate. It is certainly clear that when ministers' original Gaelic sermons and views on style and language did reach the printing press, they brought much-needed stylistic sparkle and liveliness to a prose tradition which was in danger of succumbing to the tight corsetry of external imitation (Meek 2002, 112).

The clergy developed an understanding of the power of orality and they affirmed the importance of vernacular language, and helped to develop its impact on printed texts and literature (*Ibid.*).

Porthan's and Ganander's case for orality or efforts to include oral tradition in the literary culture reveals the role that the clergy played in Finland in the transmission of oral tradition into book culture, of oral versions into literary versions in the form not only of academic publications, but also of written samples in the press. Their activity fits well in an international pattern of scholarly development and circumstances with clergymen as significant agents. Their use of the press to promote a wider interest in the Finnish language, literature and folk poetry as well as studies of oral tradition was an effective step, which broadened the knowledge of *Mythologia Fennica* and the study of oral tradition in the academic community among the clergy and other educated groups in society as well as in society in general.

Although *Mythologia Fennica* was advertised along with other books in several papers with information on where it was sold, outside the academic community fewer are likely to have bought and read it than read about it in Porthan's extended press review. It is interesting to note that, for example, for the small southern coastal fortified town of Helsinki, we find no information in estate inventory deeds or auction protocols of ownership of *Mythologia Fennica*, whereas for the main northern coastal commercial town Oulu we know of at least four owners. The chamberlain Erik Tulindberg sold a copy of *Mythologia Fennica* in 1794 to the merchant Simon Axelsson, and ten years later the military chamberlain Justus Dobbins's copy went to a Mr Krank in an auction (The Henrik Database, Books and their owners in Finland up to 1809).

The auction protocols illustrate the ownership some years later than when the book was originally purchased and there is of course no information available through the protocols of all book ownership at the time. However, the ownership noted in the protocols shows that there was at least some interest in wider society in *Mythologia Fennica*. This was most probably increased by the publicity *Mythologia Fennica* got from Porthan's review and the advertisements in the press, even in the north, far away from the academic centre in the south.

Language, culture and development of scholarly behaviour

What happened among Finnish scholars was related to the wider international revolution of ideas about language, history and culture. The reassessment of oral tradition among European scholars, which began in the middle of the 18th century, was, as we have seen, an outcome of a re-evaluation of societies without writing. The intellectual culture of the Enlightenment put forward the idea that a "primitive" society could be organized with a political culture based on common values and that these societies could have a poetical creativity and mind that even excelled the literary resources of the European states of the day. The main distinction between literate *civilization* and pre-literate *barbarity* gave way to a modern appreciation of oral tradition as a poetical expression and expression of social organization (Hudson 2002, 240–241). Porthan's review of *Mythologia Fennica* can be regarded as one step in this direction.

The new ways of conceiving language that emerged in Europe in the middle of 18th century radiated to some degree as far as Finland. When Porthan began to recognize the special powers of speech and oral culture and their special characteristics, the idea of the written and the spoken languages as two media operating according to different principles, won ground. Internationally, scholars had accepted the argument of modern linguistics on the fluid and adaptable nature of speech opposed to the greater fixity of writing. In literature, a new emphasis was put on the capability of oral resources to express passions, intonation and gestures, which writing lacked. European scholars also began to stress that written texts had a pervasive influence on language. Societies without writing could develop a language and speech in its purest form, unchanged by writing (*Ibid.,* 244–246).

The European re-evaluation of oral language and culture also affected scholars in Finland. The reaction against the fixed writing culture at the Academy in Turku and publication in Latin went hand in hand with the new scholarly aspirations, which included an interest in oral culture and native languages. Whereas the interest in oral culture was also promoted in Europe through the critique of European society by the Enlightenment ideology, this was not the case in Finland. However, the early interest in oral poetry in Finland led by Porthan more or less consciously prepared the ground for such ideas as the idealization of folk culture and oral tradition in Finland. Later, however, this had implications for Finnish culture and politics at large.

Regardless of Porthan's intentions, his concept of oral culture corre-sponded well to new ideas among European scholars about language and history. Porthan shared the then groundbreaking idea of oral and written literature as being of equal importance. The international scholarly context in which Porthan's activity has to be viewed contained and was grounded in the change in the intellectual climate in Finland. This meant that in a society marked by religiosity and biblical interpretation, it was possible for even clergymen to carry out studies of oral and sometimes indeed pagan tradition.

Some significant trends in Europe influenced the way literature was regarded and oral poetry appreciated. Passion and expressions of strong emotion as an important characteristic of poetry was one major trend. How much this influenced Porthan and Ganander is, however, unclear. Porthan did refer in his review positively to the special value of Finnish used in oral poetry and of the strong musical expression and magic of the runes in *Mythologia Fennica*, but Finnish researchers are nevertheless divided in their interpretations of how much he was influenced by the European re-evaluation of literature and appreciation of strong feelings in literature.

The Enlightenment philosophers' conclusion that primitive people were capable of expressing strong passions better than civilized people and that primitive languages were therefore more poetic had far-reaching effects. Oral poetry came to be seen as particularly passionate and metaphorical. Many researchers (Meek, Hudson, Bennett, Dunbar) emphasize today that authors and others who favoured the idea of the poetic potential of oral and primitive cultures in Britain came from the periphery of British civilization or had significant experiences of it. In the periphery, the authors were critical of literate culture and interested in the idea that non-literate people's poetry could even be superior (cf. Hudson 2002, 248–250). In particular, the romantic writers', such as Walter Scott, experience of the Borders or periphery, rather than formal schooling, is regarded as having the strongest influence on their writings (Bennett 2013, 7).

In Scotland, however, the pioneers of collecting folk narratives in manuscript and recorded forms already came from the periphery. Martin Martin, who compiled his pioneering work *Description of the Western Isles of Scotland* (c. 1695) with its information of the narrative traditions of this area, was a native of Bealach, near Duntulm, Skye. Robert Chambers, who was born in the rural country town of Peebles in the Borders at the turn of the 19th century, published the groundbreaking works *the Popular Rhymes of Scotland* (1826) and *Scottish Jets and Anecdotes* (1832). In addition, the folklorist Hugh Miller, who published *Scenes and Legends of the North of Scotland* (1835), was born in Cromarty in the Highland area of Scotland (Lyle, Bold & Russel 2013, 19).

In his description of vernacular Gaelic tradition, Robert Dunbar states that very limited collecting of the massive vernacular oral tradition was done before the 18th century but also he emphasizes the central role of clergymen and their geographical bonds for the establishment of an enduring pattern for the collection of oral tradition. The two most important Gaelic collections in the 18th century were compiled by the vicars, Rev. Ewen MacDiarmid and Rev. James MacLagan, both natives of Perthshire in the geographical heart of Scotland (Dunbar 2013, 53).

Although Porthan and Ganander are not regarded as romantics, they – much in the same way as the early Gaelic oral tradition compilers – in a way represented the periphery in relation to academic centres or the capital Stockholm. Their belonging to those clerical families who served in remote areas in the North where the oral tradition or other folk culture of elder times had prevailed remarkably well suggests that their places of birth gave them a unique field of experience that not all educated people at that time shared. Although the place perhaps cannot be regarded as a determining factor for the development for their interest in oral tradition, it certainly gave them through, amongst other things, their understanding of the Finnish language and local culture a good basis for their studies and authorship.

Essential in trying to place Porthan in an international context is, however, the new temporalized view of orality and literacy. The influential work of William Warburton (1698–1779), *The Divine Legation of Moses*

(1738), promoted an understanding that writing developed long after speech (Hudson 2002, 251). In consequence, the existence of oral culture was perceived as evidence of an ancient culture, and this was important for European scholars looking for their own past. One of Porthan's motives in his interest in oral tradition was his aim as a historian to look for and find documentation of a rich historical past in the oral tradition.

Some of the assumptions of Robert Wood (1717–1771) in *An Essay on the Original Genius and Writing of Homer* (1769) correspond to some degree with Porthan's interest in and idea of oral poetry. Wood did not base his opinion on historical evidence, but stated that only a tradition without letters could have produced poetry like Homer's *Odyssey* and *Iliad*. The genius of Homer derived from passionate and spontaneous primitive speech uninfluenced by stiff writing. At the end of the 18th century, the German scholar Friedrich August Wolf (1759–1824) presented a historical investigation of language and poetry in ancient Greece, which even questioned the existence of Homer as a single individual. This notion of a bardic tradition, which composed and transmitted the epic, inspired later research into oral tradition. Although scholars became aware of orality as a separate mode of expression they nevertheless interpreted orality as a literary concept (Hudson 2002, 251–252). This was obviously also Porthan's assumption when he took the Finnish oral folk poems as examples of how suitable the Finnish language was as a literate language.

Additionally, besides the literary appreciation of primitivism, naturalness, passion and bardic tradition in poetry, the 18th century developed an understanding of the history of language that was based on the assumption that passions, and not reason, inspired the first languages among primitive people. Primitive language was seen as more poetic than modern European languages, which had lost in passion what they had gained in clarity and reason. The bold metaphorical style and language of the Old Testament was reinterpreted as representing an essentially oral culture. Poetic declamation, not writing, was the primary source for authority and memory. The identification of oral poetry with passionate and metaphorical language made it possible to reinterpret even sacred texts. The Enlightenment era examined pagan texts and oral culture in the light of contemporary developments in history, linguistics, philosophy and poetics. (*Ibid.*, 248–249). This altered international scholarly context made it culturally acceptable to study oral tradition including even pagan tradition as an academic topic even by scholars belonging to the clergy in Finland.

We have seen that, as in the Scottish Highlands, many of those in Finland who led the way towards re-evaluating oral culture came from the periphery of their own culture. As in the Highlands, the oral culture in Finland had survived on the periphery to some extent and some scholars and authors were interested in experimenting with the idea that non-literate cultures could in some respects be interesting or superior (cf. Hudson 2002, 250). It is, however, obvious that in Finland the interaction between the clerical periphery and the academic centre was successfully carried out on the basis of several interacting factors, with the press as an important medium.

In Finland, the early interest in oral tradition in addition contributed to changing and developing scholarly activity and academic occupations. Porthan's review of the *Mythologia Fennica* was an important step in this development and the progress of academic life in general in Finland. This also shows how the press, and reviews in particular, was introduced as part of academic life and behaviour. The review made the study of oral tradition known among scholars and other educated groups in various parts of Finland. It inspired other collectors and scholars of oral poetry and it evaluated and emphasized the importance of the published work. Moreover, it was an important step towards the transmission of oral tradition into book culture as well as a professionalization of scholarly activity and a shift of the academic paradigm in Finland in a wider sense.

References

Internet sources

The Henrik Database. Books and their owners in Finland up to 1809, Finnish Literature Society. Available from http://dbgw.finlit.fi/henrik/henrik_english.php

Newspapers

Tidningar Utgifne af ett Sällskap i Åbo. Om Finska Språkets skick til Stenstyl. (13 February 1773), N:o 3: 18–20.
Åbo Nya Tidningar. Recension af Mythologia Fennica. (12 November 1789), N:o 46. Tryckt hos Kgl. Acad. Boktr. Mag. J.C. Frenckell: 369–374.
Åbo Nya Tidningar. Recension af Mythologia Fennica. (Fortsättning se N:o 46, 369). (19 November 1789), N:o 47. Tryckt hos Kgl. Acad. Boktr. Mag. J.C. Frenckell: 377–381.
Åbo Nya Tidningar. Recension af Mythologia Fennica. (Fortsättning se N:o 47, 377). (26 November 1789), N:o 48 Tryckt hos Kgl. Acad. Boktr. Mag. J.C. Frenckell: 385–390.
The National Library of Finland. Digital Collections. Newspapers. https://digi.kansalliskirjasto.fi/sanomalehti/search?set_language=en

Literature

Bennett, Margaret 2013. The Roots of Living Tradition. In Sarah Dunnigan & Suzanne Gilbert (eds), *The Edinburgh Companion to Scottish Traditional Literatures*. Edinburgh: Edinburgh University Press, 7–13.
Castrén, Eric 1754. *Historisk och oeconomisk beskrifning öfwer Cajanaborgslän . . . under oeconomiae professorens . . . Pehr Kalms inseende, för magister krantsens erhållande . . .* Åbo: Kongl. boktr. Jacob Merckell.
Dunbar, Robert 2013. Vernacular Gaelic Tradition. In Sarah Dunnigen & Suzanne Gilbert (eds), *The Edinburgh Companion to Scottish Traditional Literatures*. Edinburgh: Edinburgh University Press, 51–62.

Faggot, Jacob 1741. *Tankar om fäderneslandets känning och beskrifwande*. Kungl. vetenskapsakademiens handlingar, vol. 2. Stockholm.

af Forselles, Cecilia 2011. Individualistic Reading Culture. Fiction, Historical Works and Travel Accounts as Literary Genres Enhancing the Development of the Inner Self. In Cecilia af Forselles & Tuija Laine (eds), *The Emergence of Finnish Book and Reading Culture in the 1700s*. Studia Fennica Litteraria 5. Helsinki: Finnish Literature Society, 95–119.

Forster, Antonia 2001. Review Journals and the Reading Public. In Isabel Rivers (ed.), *Books and Their Readers in Eighteenth-Century England: New Essays*. London: Leicester University Press, 170–190.

Ganander, Christfrid 1984 [1789]. *Mythologia Fennica, eller förklaring öfver de nomina propria deastrorum, idolorum, locorum, virorum &c. eller afgudar och afgudinnor, forntidens märkelige personer, offer och offerställen, gamla sedvänjor, jättar, troll, skogs- sjö- och bergs-rån m.m. som förekomma i de äldre finska troll-runor, synnyt, sanat, sadut, arwotuxet &c. samt än brukas och nämnas i dagligt tal; Til dess tjenst, som vela i grund förstå det finska språket, och hava smak för finska historien och poesin, af gamla runor samlad och uttydd*. Facsimile. Helsinki: Finnish Literature Society.

Gavin, Michael 2012. Writing Print Cultures Past: Literary Criticism and Book History. *Book History* 15: 26–47.

Hakamies, Pekka 2008. Henrik Gabriel Porthan kansanrunouden kerääjänä ja tutkijana. *AURAICA, Scripta a Societate Porthan edita* 1: 59–65.

Hallberg, Peter 2003. History writing and the idea of 'the public' in eighteenth-century Sweden: Olof Dalin's history of the realm. *Studies on Voltaire and the Eighteenth Century* 12: 123–171.

Hautala, Jouko 1954. *Suomalainen kansanrunoudentutkimus*. Helsinki: Finnish Literature Society.

Hautala, Jouko 1984. Christfrid Ganander ja hänen Mythologia Fennicansa. In Christfrid Ganander, *Mythologia Fennica…* Facsimile. Helsinki: Finnish Literature Society, V–X.

Honko, Lauri 2000. Porthan suomalaisen runouden ja mytologian tutkijana. In Juha Manninen (ed.), *Porthanin monet kasvot. Kirjoituksia humanistisen tieteen monitaiturista*. Historiallinen Arkisto 114. Helsinki: Finnish Literature Society, 87–99.

Hudson, Nicolas 2002. Constructing oral tradition: the origins of the concept in Enlightenment intellectual culture. In Adam Fox & Daniel Woolf (eds), *The Spoken Word: Oral Culture in Britain, 1500–1850*. Manchester: Manchester University Press, 240–255.

Kajanto, Iiro 1984. *Porthan and Classical Scholarship. A Study of Classical Influences in Eighteenth-Century Finland*. Humaniora 225. Helsinki: Finnish Academy of Science and Letters.

Klinge, Matti 1989. *Mikä mies Porthan oli?* Tietolipas 116. Helsinki: Finnish Literature Society.

Kuhn, Thomas 2009. *De vetenskapliga revolutionernas struktur*. Andra utökade upplagan. Stockholm: Thales.

Legnér, Mattias 2004. *Fäderneslandets rätta beskrivning: Mötet mellan antikvarisk forskning och ekonomisk nyttokult i 1700-talets Sverige*. Helsinki: The Society of Swedish Literature in Finland.

Lyle, Emily, Valentina Bold & Ian Russell 2013. Genre. In Sarah Dunnigan & Suzanne Gilbert (eds), *The Edinburgh Companion to Scottish Traditional Literatures*. Edinburgh: Edinburgh University Press, 14–25.

Manninen, Juha (ed.) 2000. *Porthanin monet kasvot. Kirjoituksia humanistisen tieteen monitaiturista*. Historiallinen Arkisto 114. Helsinki: Finnish Literature Society.

Meek, Donald E. 2002. The Pulpit and the Pen: Clergy, Orality and Print in the Scottish Gaelic World. In Adam Fox & Daniel Woolf (eds), *The Spoken Word: Oral Culture in Britain 1500–1850*. Manchester: Manchester University Press, 84–118.

Pentikäinen, Juha & Juha Gustafson 1995. Kristfrid Ganander. In Pentti Pulakka (ed.), *Keskipohjalaisia elämäkertoja*. Kokkola: Keskipohjanmaa-säätiö.

Raven, James 2001. The book trades. In Isabel Rivers (ed.), *Books and their Readers in Eighteenth-Century England: New Essays*. London: Leicester University Press, 1–34.

Schneider, Ute 1999. Literaturkritische Zeitschriften. In Ernst Fischer, Wilhelm Haefs & York-Gothart Mix (eds), *Von Almanach bis Zeitung. Ein Handbuch der Medien in Deutschland 1700–1800*. Munich: C.H. Beck, 191–206.

Siikala, Anna-Leena 2012. *Itämerensuomalaisten mytologia*. Suomalaisen Kirjallisuuden Seuran Toimituksia 1388. Helsinki: Finnish Literature Society.

Tarkiainen Kari 2012. *Porthan, Henrik Gabriel (1739–1804) historiantutkija, kaunopuheisuuden professori, kanslianeuvos*. Kansallisbiblografia. Available from https://www.kansallisbiografia.fi/kb/artikkeli/2599/

Tommila, Päiviö 2000. Suomen ensimmäinen lehtimies. In Juha Manninen (ed.), *Porthanin monet kasvot. Kirjoituksia humanistisen tieteen monitaiturista*. Historiallinen Arkisto 114. Helsinki: Finnish Literature Society, 15–23.

Yuri Cowan

Orality, Authenticity, and the Historiography of the Everyday: The Ballad in Victorian Scholarship and Print Culture

The narrative ballad is a form of song defined by its oral delivery, but it is a paradox of its dissemination that most extant ballad collections – both those for popular consumption and those intended as works of scholarship – stem largely from printed sources. This is particularly true of those that became part of the ballad canon in the Victorian era, when the ballad was particularly loved and respected by a mainstream reading audience that thought of it as an artefact of the popular oral culture of the past. Most of the ballad collections of that era were in fact compiled at second or third hand from the canons that had already been established by Thomas Percy, Walter Scott, and others. And yet the paratexts of those collections (introductions extolling the roots of the ballad in improvisation and song, frontispieces showing eager medieval audiences raptly listening to a harper) unanimously pay homage to the ballad as an oral performance. There is little doubt that the editors and readers of those collections shared an assumption that the ballad as it appeared on the printed page was the authentic artefact of a British folk culture of oral composition and performance.

Drawing on the history of editorial and epitextual performances by editors and scholars from Percy through to Frederick Furnivall, John W. Hales, and Francis James Child, as well as on the claims and assumptions made by 18th- and 19th-century editors regarding the authenticity, poetic value, and cultural significance of ballad oral composition, this article will examine the causes and consequences of this Victorian infatuation with ballad literature. Although the written word had historically held more authority than the fleeting performance or utterance, editors such as Samuel Carter Hall, William Allingham, and Furnivall now used the topos of oral composition variously to justify a patriotic reading of the ballads, to provide an excuse to edit for literary merit, and to argue for the ballads as a body of documentary evidence conveying authentic detail regarding the everyday life of the past (what Francis Gummere would later call the "journalistic ballad"). Scholarly and mass-market ballad anthologies alike drew on both printed and oral versions, but always placed a premium upon the oral composition of the ballads, relying paradoxically upon the ballads' perceived status as genuine creations of the "folk" to lend authority to editorial intervention.

We have quite a bit of scholarship on how the antiquarians and classicists of the 18th century saw the relation between orality and print. The 19th century has been less thoroughly covered in the secondary literature, but Victorian scholars too engaged with the implications of oral composition for the printed form of ballad texts. In that period, editors may have been less enamoured of the idea that ballad anthologies should capture "pure" oral performances, at least in part because many of them were editing for a broader public that was particularly a reading audience. And yet they too were often eager to exploit the notion of oral performance. There were several reasons for this. First, because the place of performance was often envisioned as being in the home or at work – and there likeliest in a rural setting which was viewed as conservative and closer to the folkways of the pre-industrial past – Victorian scholarship felt that the ballads could reveal something about the everyday lives of past men and women. This historiography of the everyday played out not only in an understanding of the roles of song and entertainment in everyday life, but also in the matter of ballads themselves, which was thought to reveal a rough but honest morality (Hall 1842, ii) as well as many of the customs, usages, and material culture surrounding marriage, death, conflict, and friendship. Second, the fact of the ballad's oral performance was itself picturesque and appealed to a sense of nostalgia. In the paratexts to ballad collections throughout the century, the pattern emerges of a frontispiece showing a singer in a domestic setting, paired with an introduction that makes a claim for the patriotic or "folk" nature of the ballads. Finally, this evocation of an oral performance for the ballad reinforced the relationship between individual genius (the composer of the ballad) and the collective, which under this model made subtle adjustments to the ballad text in performance. These adjustments were recorded not only in the performances which ballad scholars had seen and sometimes recorded in the field, but especially in the more permanent forms of text, either as manuscript or as print.

Elsewhere I have distinguished between Victorian ballad collections from fieldwork and ballad "anthologies" extracted at second or third hand for popular consumption (Cowan & Demoor 2012). It is important to recognize that the former were painstaking, usually localized efforts with a limited reach of publication; the most successful ballad anthologies – the ones most reprinted, the ones printed in the largest numbers, those which Victorian reading audiences with enough money were buying (the lower classes were still accessing the broadside ballad, which is another subject entirely) – were drawn from printed sources. One great paradox of the post-Romantic reception of the ballad, as William St. Clair has noted (2004, 346), was that it was framing a print tradition as an oral one. Among other things, we need to ask: how precisely did Victorian scholarship view the oral nature of the ballad and its relationship to print, and how did that perception filter down into the multiple apparatuses that framed Victorian ballad collections for the reading public? The editors of the most popular collections, after all, relied heavily on conversations between scholars such as Ritson and Percy, Scott and Hogg, Furnivall and Hales, and Child and his international network–conversations that had taken place largely in the print world of

19th-century literary and periodical culture. I hope that my discussion here of the Victorian understanding of the ballads' relation to oral culture can begin in part to answer the important challenge posed by Mary Ellen Brown in her important and thoughtful 2006 article "The Ballads' Progress," which considers the cultural status of the ballad from its first appearance as an object of literary importance on up to the present day:

> While the collective framing narratives might be called the literary history of the popular ballad, it is clear that this literary history itself needs to be re-examined and critiqued; while its pronouncements and assumptions may have no basis in fact, they have yet influenced the generic definitions of the ballad. In other words, the framing narratives have helped to form generic ideas about the ballad which may well reflect a particular cultural context. While "true" to that time and place, the ideas may well be dead wrong, or incomplete at best. (Brown 2006, 119).

Among the most prominent of these "collective framing narratives" was that of the ballad's oral provenance, either to claim the ballad as a popular entertainment for ordinary people or to draw attention to its status as a public performance. This oral status of the ballad was reiterated in various forms in 19th-century ballad scholarship and commentary. Philip Sidney's pronouncement that "I never heard the old song of Percy and Douglas that I heard not my heart moved more than with a trumpet, and yet it is sung but by some blind crowder, with no rougher voice than rude style," for instance, finds itself invoked in multiple defences of the ballad's canonical status, while nearly every ballad collection of the 19th century is possessed of a frontispiece that shows a minstrel performing before an appreciative public or private audience (as, for instance, the frontispiece to Samuel Carter Hall's lavish 1842 collection, or George Barnett Smith's from 1881).

Walter Ong suggests that the Romantic movement marks "the beginning of the end of the old orality-grounded rhetoric" (Ong 2002 [1982], 158). What then is the consequence for the Victorian period – the first industrial era of print – that accordingly formed the transitional period? Surely their attitude towards orality (manifested as what Ong calls "typographic bias" or, conversely, as the development of folklore studies as a special discipline) must have affected their theories of how ballads were understood to have been created. In relation to the era's increasing consciousness of high and low culture, the ballad offered a site where what we might now call a "highbrow" reading audience could embrace the productions of an apparently low culture; the antiquarians had tested it and proclaimed it safe, and the Romantic poets had made it interesting. Thus the romanticization of the minstrel figure (McLane 2008) or the multiple instances of a declaiming or singing bard that we find in the frontispieces of the many ballad collections published throughout the century at considerable remove from the ballads' putative origins in oral culture (Cowan & Demoor 2012). There was still a sense that oral composition took place in a special space; almost immediately as orality began to feel like a distant reality it became worthy of study. And yet how did the Victorians think that oral composition was carried out in practice? In a way their views are hard for us to recover without resorting to our own intellectual biases and understandings of how oral composition worked and works. 19th-century scholars and editors were, after all, writing before Milman Parry and Albert Lord. To understand their theories of the relationship between orality and print culture, we need to return to the textual, antiquarian, and classical scholarship of the 18th century.

Textual performances: Between print and oral culture

Classical scholarship was from the very beginning a program of textual recovery, dealing as it did with works that had long been communicated through the often-fragmentary or incomplete manuscript word. It has been said that the prestige of the classics was based on the authority of letters as apparently fixed forms; but the real source of this apparent relationship between prestige, literacy, and the authoritative text was already more complicated than that. At any rate, the late 18th century marks the moment when cracks began to appear in the veneer of authority that the written word had lent extant classical literature. Hudson describes Robert Wood's *Essay on the Original Genius and Writings of Homer* (1769) as being "the first sustained argument that Homer belonged to an 'oral tradition.'" (Hudson 2002, 251). Wood, says Hudson, "portrayed the peculiar beauties of Homer not as the fruits of literate refinement but of untrammelled [sic] nature." (*Ibid.*).[1] This sort of phrasing participates not only in the Romantic discourses on orality described by Maureen McLane (and which would later be reiterated by Victorian editors such as Hales), but also strikingly within the discourse of the divide between orality and print, or "nature" and "refinement." Indeed, it is reminiscent of the 18th-century school of criticism surrounding Shakespeare that suggested he was, in Ben Jonson's words, "the child of nature". Given Shakespeare's own roots in performance, the relationship of Jonson's characterization to an implicit theory of orality is not so far-fetched as it might first appear. Perhaps we might take this theory further, and suggest that for the 18th century and especially the Romantic

---

1   Ong 2002 [1982], 19: "The nineteenth century saw the development of the Homeric theories of the so-called Analysts, initiated by Friedrich August Wolf (1759–1824), in his 1795 *Prolegomena*. The Analysts saw the texts of the *Iliad* and the *Odyssey* as combinations of earlier poems or fragments, and set out to determine by analysis what the bits were and how they had been layered together. But, as Adam Parry notes, (1971, xiv–xvii), the Analysts assumed that the bits being put together were simply texts, no alternative having suggested itself to their minds."

> Or, as Adam Parry puts it in his introduction to his father's notes (ix–lxii),
> The dominant movement of this period of scholarship was that of the Analysts, that is, of those who, in one way or another, saw our texts of the *Iliad* and *Odyssey* as combinations of earlier poems or fragments of poems. Their theories all rested on one assumption, an assumption which, because it was so fundamental, was never clearly stated by any of them. This was that there existed, previous to Homer, an 'original' text, or 'original' texts, of the Homeric epics, which either were written, or were possessed of the fixed form which only a written text can provide (xiv).

era, orality represented a mode of composition that was not mechanical, but organic. Again drawing on Shakespeare as an example, and considering the multiple conflicting testimonials to his precise words, of which Victorian scholars like Furnivall (who very intentionally spelled the author's name "Shakspere") were quite aware, it is possible that even in print composition had long been considered a social practice rather than the work of an individual improvising composer or author.

Penny Fielding, in *Writing and Orality: Nationality, Culture, and Nineteenth-Century Scottish Fiction*, argues that literacy was a point of cultural capital, especially in Scotland, which "was promoting a version of orality which was in the hands – or the pens – of highly self-consciously [sic] literary figures" (Fielding 1996, 46). A work like Scott's *Minstrelsy*, she argues, enacted "the uneasy splitting-off of the written from the spoken" (*Ibid.*, 47). Quite apart from this, however, 19th-century editors began to theorize the importance of maintaining as precisely as possible the form of the ballads as they had earlier been collected, whether written down or printed. Folkloric collecting in the centuries before audio recording after all had to manifest its findings in the only medium available to it, which was necessarily textual, although it manifested itself in diverse forms, from the informal written collection that would later be known as the Percy Folio MS, to the more systematic records of Motherwell, to the printed broadside collections compiled by bibliophiles and enthusiasts. The material permanence of print or manuscript relative to the spoken word was a matter of record and not necessarily at all times a value judgment.

The Victorian editor-scholars were in their element when dealing with the extant relics of this social practice; they were first-rate organizers, cataloguers, and editors of the profuse documents of the past. Their editorial theory had assimilated from manuscript studies the notion that ballads had been formed from numerous versions, so the editors did not feel the need always to be precisely faithful to their badly-spelled and sometimes seemingly arhythmical sources, especially when they were being re-edited for popular consumption. Different 19th-century editors approached this issue in slightly different ways, however, alternately printing them as parallel-text editions, eclectic texts, or composite texts. Their editing practices may even be said to represent similar approaches to the way in which collectors have seen oral texts, sometimes as representing singular performances in their respective historical moments and sometimes as representing performances with the influence and cultural weight of past performances upon them. It is important to remember that, in an age before the mechanical reproduction of sound, the printed or scribal text was the only available method of capturing the moment of performance (if, indeed, the voice recording itself can truly be considered a faithful reproduction). We must at least consider the possibility that even ballad editors who were engaged in recension-like pursuit of an authentic or best version (though not, of course, when they were amalgamating different versions) felt that they were reconstructing or preserving authentic performances in the best medium available to them.

Authorial intention was not much of an obstacle for Victorian editorial theory when it came to the ballads, although many editors felt the need to grapple with it, if only to elevate the bard or minstrel to the status of a cultural icon comparable to the celebrity author of the print-obsessed 19th century. From the 1803 review of Scott's *Minstrelsy of the Scottish Border* in the *Monthly Review* that repeatedly lamented the lack of names of authors for the ballads (Anonymous 1803, 25), through Robert Chambers's theory that Lady Wardlaw was the 17th-century author of ballads such as "Sir Patrick Spens" (cited in Brown 2006, 122), on up to George Barnett Smith's (1881) edition that organized the ballads along with literary attempts at the form only in alphabetical order by title, the 19th-century discourse becomes increasingly at ease with the anonymity of the creators of the ballads. This was partly because the editor had taken over the public custody of the ballad text and, as have I argued elsewhere (Cowan & Demoor 2012), was exploiting the apparent anonymity of the canonical ballads to underscore his own taste in compiling the "best" versions of the "best" ballads. But it also bespeaks an intellectual milieu that was becoming used to the idea that composition for oral performance was somehow distinct from writing for a literate audience. Thus it is possible to suggest that even as orality according to Ong's definition was retreating from public notice, and even (or especially) as the profession of print authorship was growing more celebrated, 19th-century scholarship and popular understanding grew more and more comfortable with the notion that not every fine or memorable poem or song need be traced to a single talented minstrel composer. As we shall see, even when such an authorial presence was invoked, the presence of previous performers, collectors, editors, and printers served to undermine it. No doubt this realization was a relief to editors confronted with the bewildering variety of ballad versions.

The idea of the single author, then, often had to give way to a vision of something like a collective enterprise working on the ballad corpus, refining it, shaping it, and re-presenting it to suit the historical moment. What Brown has described as the homogenous "folk society of early antiquarian dreams" (Brown 2006, 120) was not only a social, anthropological, or national space, it was also a textual space, where different hands contributed at different times to the received text of a song. Thus it would be possible to live in what Ong would call a typographically biased culture, and yet still subscribe to a theory that celebrated the more organic and improvisatory nature of oral composition. Indeed, it might be an important point to make here that the Victorians are generally little concerned with the formal or formulaic aspects of oral culture; for them a more important factor was the way in which it revealed the history of everyday life. It was left to the later work of [Vladimir] Propp, [Antti] Aarne and [Stith] Thompson, and Parry himself to approach folklore and the visible relics of preliteracy with an eye to unraveling their structural features. This historiography of the everyday relied on the documents of the past for its evocation of the ordinary lives and entertainment of past generations. But those documents were partial, and as soon as they entered the realm of preservation in paper and ink they began to split into multiple versions and splintered perspectives on songs that everyone thought they knew. Even as everyday life began to be better documented, the very profusion of those documents threatened the attempt to define it.

It turned out, then, that although there are in fact very few moments in history when ballad scholarship has consciously privileged print over the oral, print was still a necessity for the preservation of old song, yet print culture simultaneously served, threatened, and confused the custodians of the popular culture of the past. To give one well-known example, James Hogg's mother objected to his collecting the ballads in print, saying famously that "there was never ane o' my songs prentit till ye prentit them yoursell, an' ye hae spoilt them a'thegither. They war made for singing, an' no for reading; and they're nouther right spelled nor right setten down" (Hogg 1972, 62). Her complaint has been frequently cited in ballad scholarship. And yet throughout the 19th century her words appear most often in a spirit of nostalgia rather than in an effort to parse their true import. Hogg's mother is pointing out the inaccuracies attendant upon the editing and printing process as much she argues for inherent definitiveness in the oral performance (the latter, as we shall see, was the basic assumption of ballad scholarship for editors such as Child).

Paula McDowell similarly positions the 18th-century discourse on ballads as somewhat less biased in favour of print than we might expect, noting that for instance Thomas Percy, "Like Ong, [...], modeled historic communications developments as in some ways *de*volutionary. In his scenario, ancient minstrels and their successors, modern balladmongers, are not participants in one continuous artistic tradition; rather, the institutionalization of the commercial press contributed to the 'extinct[ion]' of an earlier (and superior) cultural practice based on voice" (McDowell 2010, 36), although elsewhere she notes by way of contrast Percy's elitist positioning of the minstrel and Joseph Ritson's suggestion that the printed ballad was the primary location where popular song could be preserved. It is hard to say whether Percy for instance truly thought of the earlier practice of oral composition as "superior" to written composition, although he certainly valued it. He seems at least to have taken for granted the civilizing function of print. In his "Essay on the Ancient English Minstrels" that opens the first volume of the *Reliques*, he suggests that

> When the Saxons were converted to christianity, in proportion as letters prevailed among them, [...] poetry was no longer a peculiar profession. The Poet and the Minstrel became two persons. Poetry was cultivated by men of letters indiscriminately, and many of the most popular rhimes were composed amidst the leisure and retirement of monasteries. But the Minstrels continued a distinct order of men, and got their livelihood by singing verses to the harp, at the houses of the great. [...] And indeed tho' some of them only recited the compositions of others, many of them still composed songs themselves, and all of them could probably invent a few stanzas on occasion. I have no doubt but most of the old heroic ballads in this collection were composed by this order of men. [...] From the amazing variations, which occur in different copies of these old pieces, it is evident they made no scruple to alter each other's productions, and the reciter added or omitted whole stanzas, according to his own fancy or convenience. (Percy 1765, vol. 1, xv–xvi).

Percy's words here are striking in that they frankly avow his reliance on "copies of these old pieces" for the recognition of the mutability of ballad texts over time. Mary Ellen Brown suggests that Percy's "discourses on the pre-history of English literature gave the ballads an author, the minstrels ('literature' must have author and thereby a period location), and the objects themselves pride of place, privileging the manuscript over orality as source" (Brown 2006, 116). And yet in this passage Percy seems rather to display a more equable sense of an interrelation between oral performance and textual preservation; after all, he seems to be concluding that the alterations, which come first in the process of "recitation," are manifested in textual form.

The Victorian ballad scholars never doubted that the ballads partook of a popular oral tradition; their discourse is shot through with the rhetoric of oral performance and adaptation. And yet for them the ballads' histories were still textual in form, even if in performance they were thought of as sung. The typographical bias we find in Percy is necessarily implicit in Victorian ballad collections – after all, whichever version an editor like Allingham would choose as somehow best or definitive, he would ultimately always be choosing from among textual versions and not copying from oral recitation – and yet there is a strong sense of nostalgia for an apparently preliterate culture. This they inherited from the Romantic scholarship of William Motherwell, Walter Scott, and James Hogg. Motherwell's dedication to collecting from oral sources was the first systematic self-conscious attempt to do so. Scott, as collector of both print and oral tradition, was entrenched in antiquarian notions of authentic ancient texts as representing the authentic historical lives of the folk. Hogg was in the same vein an antiquarian, although he differed in being dissatisfied with his contemporaries, including even his friend Scott, for treating oral testimony as unreliable when it came to the editing of ballads (see Gilbert 2009). Indeed, as his literary works, including the famous *Confessions of a Justified Sinner*, show, Hogg had a laudable suspicion of the written record. Textual fidelity to speech, then, was tenuous, but it was all that 19th-century scholarship had if it wished to preserve its favourite examples of the fluid ballad tradition.

Furnivall and Hales: Establishing the Percy Folio MS

In a similar vein, that great 19th-century project of lexicographical scholarship the *New [Oxford] English Dictionary on Historical Principles* necessarily relied for its evidence on the textual tradition and not on preserved oral examples of dialect and usage, as the British Library, mimicking earlier 20th-century large-scale attempts at the preservation of spoken English, has recently attempted to do with its Evolving English exhibition and archive[2]. The establishment in 1864 of the Early English Text Society (EETS), with its inclusive mandate to recover, edit and publish as many of the texts of medieval and Early Modern English as possible, was intended to provide a quarry for the gems, semiprecious stones, and gravel of English speech

2   http://www.bl.uk/evolvingenglish/mapabout.html

and usage. The driving force behind the society, as behind so many other Victorian societies devoted to the preservation and editing of past texts, was the indefatigable Frederick James Furnivall. The EETS's broad mandate to publish the ordinary textual artefacts of the past – from wills and dietaries to guild statutes and romances – was intended to reveal the popular culture of the past in all its diversity and with its power, quirks, and failings intact.

It was in the context of this kind of textual and philological scholarship that Furnivall and his fellow editor John Hales set out to establish and print the text of the famous manuscript that Thomas Percy had rescued from oblivion and which had formed the basis for his *Reliques of Ancient English Poetry* one hundred years before. The fact that Hales and Furnivall thought that it was at all important to set the record straight with regard to Percy's "original" texts was itself significant. This push to publish the Percy Folio MS was in part encouraged by Francis James Child, working at Harvard University across the Atlantic, who, as Mary Ellen Brown writes in "Child's Ballads and the Broadside Conundrum," felt the importance of getting as far back behind the printed versions as possible. In Furnivall's "Forewords" [sic] to the edition, he begins by pointing out that Child was the one who insisted that the book should be published as a "foundation document of English balladry, the basis of that structure which Percy raised, so fair to the eyes of all English-speaking men throughout the world" (Hales & Furnivall 1867, vol. 1, ix). Furnivall's praise, however, is not exactly unstinting, since he makes it clear that the intention of the volume is also to make up for the ways in which Percy had in the texts of the *Reliques* misrepresented the actual contents of his folio manuscript. It was certainly true that Percy had interfered substantially with the texts of the ballads as they were received, and the diligence of an editor, even one as notoriously hasty as Furnivall, was welcome in recovering for a modern antiquarian audience the unique 17th-century versions that the Percy Folio MS preserved. But the three-volume *Bishop Percy's Folio Manuscript* was fuelled by more than just the desire to set the editorial record straight (as Furnivall says in his introduction, "to tell the truth, and tell the whole truth, of a text or MS. is an editor's first duty," *Ibid.*, xx). It may even be more than an attempt to seek a primal text, an authentic oral performance encoded in a relatively reliable but still incompletely authentic manuscript form that later was reshaped out of recognition by print[3]. As the editorial paratexts, and the introductions in particular, show, the edition was intended to reposition the historical manuscript itself, in its own time and place, as an artefact both of its composition and its reception.

In their introductions, Hales and Furnivall describe the physical form of the manuscript and write its history in terms of a process of reception and re-creation, working to evoke the worldview equally of the composing minstrel, of the antiquarian preserver of the songs, and of Percy himself. So in his "Forewords" Furnivall describes at length the various challenges

---

3   It is possible that Child's geographical isolation from the residual insular spaces of oral performance led him to assume still more reliability for the oral than many of his contemporaries in Great Britain did.

posed by Joseph Ritson, that fierce advocate of textual fidelity, to Percy, and takes it for granted that Ritson was correct to make those challenges. It was not enough, however, that the publication of Hales and Furnivall's print edition of the Percy Folio MS was intended to right the wrongs of Percy's transgressions against the manuscript. It was important to them that they reflect on the reasons Percy had for interpolating modern ballads, and for cleaning up the most graphic episodes, such as the rape in "Glasgerion." As the title of Hales's essay on "The Revival of Ballad Poetry in the Eighteenth Century" suggests, they were engaged in historicizing the social and textual situation of the ballads at various times – their scholarship was intended to recover moments of reception that were not necessarily the vaguely medieval or Early Modern period with which we often assume the Victorians associated the ballad.

So, for instance, Hales in his introduction situates the *Reliques* as a production of the polite 18th century. Like Furnivall and Child, he considers the modern pieces added by Percy to be a problematic intervention. He has very little positive to say about them:

> [...] Such were the pieces whose elegance was to make atonement to the readers of a century ago, for the barbarousness of the other components of the *Reliques*.

> This barbarousness was further mitigated by an application of a polishing process to the ballads themselves. Percy performed the offices of a sort of tireman for them. He dressed and adorned them to go into polite society. To how great an extent he labored in their service, is now at last manifested by the publication of the Folio. (Hales & Furnivall, vol. 1, 1867, xxiv).

The *Reliques* in Hales's view – and in that of any proponent of the primacy of orality over print in this branch of popular culture – were "dressed and adorned," augmented, polished, and made to rub elbows with ahistorical imitations of a later date. And yet all this does not mean that Hales felt that the style of the ballads was a non-issue. In spite of his and Furnivall's apparent dedication to publishing and preserving the ballads in the Percy Folio MS in as faithful a state as they could, Hales himself in his introductions is critical of the style of many of the ballads. In introducing the ballad of "Hugh Spencer" ("It is no considerable addition to English literature. It gives, with average dullness, a ridiculously bragging account of the achievements of one Sir Hugh Spencer at the court of France, whither he was dispatched as ambassador"), he resorts to suggesting the lowness of the song's originator as the source of the poem: "What a vulgar Philistine was this ballad-monger!" (Hales & Furnivall 1867, vol. 2, 290). Elsewhere, Hales suggests that the composition process may possibly have involved perfecting original narratives, as when he writes of "Eglamore" that "The minstrel who wrote, or rather translated, this piece, if a minstrel he was, as verses 1227–9 might suggest, told an old tale freshly" (*Ibid.*, 339). Although Hales worked hard to maintain an editorial equanimity in the face of the diversity of textual versions that confronted him, his sense of taste, which had been shaped in a literary rather than an oral milieu, never deserted him.

For all his criticism of Percy's interventions, in Hales's view they agreed on the individual creativity of the minstrel (or, in less complimentary moments, of a "ballad monger" like the implied author of "Hugh Spencer" above). But they could not precisely trace his identity, nor even his occupation; they had to adjust their theories to accommodate the anonymous everyday voices of past songsters. This accounts for Hales's apparent reversal at the end of the essay, when he moves from critiquing Percy for his editorial and creative interventions to asserting that the ballads, in whatever form they survive and are published, and whoever their unknown authors are, are important in the history of *taste*. Hales's introduction culminates with the story of Walter Scott's first encounter with the *Reliques*; the description of Scott lost in rapture "beneath a huge plantanas tree" is emphatically the encounter of a reader with a book ("nor do I believe I ever read a book half so frequently or with half the enthusiasm" Hales & Furnivall 1867, vol. 2, xxxi). This is not entirely at odds with Hales's criticism of Percy for having performed a similar domestication of the ballad. The assertion of editorial or readerly taste in relation to the ballad was a common theme throughout the 19th century. It was more than just a residue of Percy's and Scott's own assertions that the ballad, though a product of a barbarous age, was an important part of the education of a modern chivalrous sensibility. Other editors (such as William Allingham, as recently as 1864) had even gone so far as to equate editorial interventions on the grounds of literary merit with the borrowings that occur in oral performance. For Hales, spontaneous, or at least relatively spontaneous, oral composition was an act that could result in a song that partook of the same aesthetic virtues as a poem in print.

But Percy, by way of contrast, may not have tried very hard to distinguish between written and oral composition. Nor was he perhaps even very conscious of the transition between song and manuscript. As he explains, "To atone for the rudeness of the more obsolete poems, each volume concludes with a few modern attempts *in the same kind of writing*" (Percy 1765, vol. 1, x, my emphasis). Percy's language is careless, and forgets the sung dimensions of the ballads; but it is possible as well that he saw written composition as working on the same principles as oral. For Hale, Percy's words indicate Percy's less-than-whole-hearted reverence for the ballads; but they may also suggest that Percy was engaging with the ballads on what he thought was equal ground: that of text. Percy's language when describing the state of his ballads and MS is on the one hand literary (marking for instance their "rudeness" here) and, on the other, equally often material ("these old writings have, as might be expected, been handed down to us with less care, than any other writings in the world," *Ibid.*, xii). Implicitly, Percy was compensating for apparent deficiencies of rhythm and metre and language by suggesting carelessness on the part of the transcriber, as well as on that of the composer. The notoriously fragmentary state of the manuscript was for Percy indicative of carelessness of preservation as well as of the roughness of the ballad composer's talent.

Francis James Child and the pressures of print

In his 1867 essay, then, John Hales opposes the "spontaneity" of the ballad to the "polish" that for him defines the taste of the Enlightenment. This is distinctive language that suggests an opposition of nonce oral improvisation to the putative careful revision inherent in printed forms. Rather than replicate the "typographic bias" described by Ong, Hales gushes over the ballads' positive attributes: as he describes it, "in the midst of conventionalisms and artificialities, Simplicity and Truth asserted themselves" (Hales & Furnivall 1867, vol. 2, xviii). This is the Victorian manifestation of that shift to resistance against "typographic bias" that would culminate in the more measured conclusions of Ong and of his tutor Marshall McLuhan. However, Victorian scholarship, for all its desire to valorise oral tradition as honest, aesthetically pleasing, and revelatory of popular history, could not entirely relinquish its base in the printed or manuscript word. When Hales evokes the ballad corpus as being made up of "songs dear to the hearts of the common people – songs whose power was sometimes confessed by the higher classes, but not so thoroughly appreciated as to induce them to exert themselves for their preservation" (*Ibid.*, vii), he is not so much replicating Ong's typographical bias as he is acknowledging the virtues of print as a preservative.

Indeed, one wonders if in the ages before it was possible to record voices it was at all possible to have such a positive reflection on the value of oral culture as Ong gives us. The longing for stability, permanence, and preservation of utterance is understandable; the intimate linking of such preservation with the "higher classes" that Hales makes here, is also significant. But the witnesses for the ballad corpus that print provided were diverse, fragmentary, and quite at odds with the orderly and convincing world of type. It is significant and ironic, but perhaps unsurprising, that Hales's portrayal of the "Simplicity and Truth" of an apparently oral tradition coincides so closely [data of publication] with the apex of the first great age of the industrialization of print. Nicholas Hudson notes in a similar vein with reference to the previous century that "as European society became *more* literate, it gained an ever sharper awareness of oral cultures and their special characteristics" (Hudson 2002, 241), and with exponentially increased literacy the process would only continue to accelerate.

This undercurrent of reaction against print was not only based on an elevation of the oral as closer to the pure originary source of the sung ballad, but also founded on a spirit of suspicion very like that articulated by Hales above for the more grubby and anarchic milieu of the balladmonger. Certainly Francis James Child, compiler of the most thorough 19th-century collection of ballads, saw the broadside ballads as being inferior to those that circulated in oral tradition (according to McDowell 2010, 54). This was another reversal of Ong's "typographic bias," though one that was at times equally problematic. As Mary Ellen Brown (2010, 70) puts it in her article "Child's Ballads and the Broadside Conundrum," "When [Child] used the word 'popular' in the title of his critical edition, he meant 'traditionary,' that is, material that was old, circulating orally, and variable." As she points out, in many cases broadsides were the oldest texts that Child had, and yet he was sometimes still loath to include them. Thus, in spite of the fact that his was necessarily a textual project, Child instinctively overcompensated for the typographical bias that he had perceived in his own literary milieu. This was partly due to his Romantic sense of nostalgia and partly to what Brown notes as his roots in the "comparative philological tradition of the Brothers Grimm" (Brown 2006, 116).

Child's print database of ballads was not an insignificant project, comprising as it did not only the famous massive and eventually posthumous ten-volume set of *The English and Scottish Popular Ballads* (1882–1898), but also its precursor, the eight smaller volumes of *The English and Scottish Ballads* (1857–1858) for the Little, Brown British Poets series. Child's magnum opus, for all that it may have left out so many extant broadside versions, was an exercise in completism, including multiple versions of each ballad. Like the diversity of texts published by the Early English Text Society, and having in common with it that desire to provide a corpus for the exercise of comparative philology, Child's ballad collection embodied a significant material outlay in paper, ink, and the other costs attendant on publishing such a major work of comparative scholarship. Although not what we would now term "crowd-sourced" (as the much larger EETS's series were), *The English and Scottish Popular Ballads* gathered together the efforts of multiple collectors and editors from the previous hundred and fifty years of ballad scholarship. The fifteen different versions of Child ballad number 12, "Lord Rendal," for instance, stem from sources as various as the Hales and Furnivall printed edition of the Percy Folio MS, Scott's *Minstrelsy of the Scottish Border*, Motherwell's diligent collecting, other printed editions such as those of James Orchard Halliwell, and diverse sources collected from recitation by local amateurs and by Child himself.

It is as though Child, by collecting as many diverse versions in one place as possible (a kind of Smithsonian Folkways Collection carried out when print was the only medium for preserving the performance) was attempting to reassure himself of the simultaneous individual diversity and social homogeneity of the culture which had given rise to the ballads. As he writes in his entry on "Ballad Poetry" for *Johnson's New Universal Cyclopaedia*,

> The primitive ballad, then, is popular not in the sense of something arising from and suited to the lower orders of a people. As yet, no sharp distinction of high and low exists in respect to knowledge, desires, and tastes. An increased civilization, and especially the introduction of book-culture, gradually gives rise to such a division; the poetry of art appears; the popular poetry is no longer relished by a portion of the people, and is abandoned to an uncultivated or not over-cultivated class – a constantly diminishing number. (Child 1881, 365).

The popular or everyday ballad culture of the past, then, for Child had been at first evenly spread among classes, and it was the advance of literacy itself that had tended to create cultural elites and to upset the balance between individual and shared enjoyment. But this same evolving situation had, according to him, also an effect on the material form in which the ballad text was preserved, in terms of its consistency with older forms, in terms of its polish, and in terms of its relationship to both archaic and contemporary language:

> Next it must be observed that ballads which have been handed down by long-repeated tradition have always departed considerably from their original form. If the transmission has been purely through the mouths of unlearned people, there is less probability of wilful change, but once in the hands of professional singers, there is no amount of change which they may not undergo. Last of all comes the modern editor, whose so-called improvements are more to be feared than the mischances of a thousand years [...] In all cases the language drifts insensibly from ancient forms, though not at the same rate with the language of every-day life (Child 1881, 367).

This is a remarkable passage of Child's encyclopaedia entry on the ballad, since it evokes the philological connection that Furnivall and others had assumed between linguistic history and its manifestations over time in text and in performance, and makes explicit the importance of the ballad – marked here as existing in a space participating both in oral and in print culture – for documenting that connection. The agents of that documentation are in Child's view various, and they all have an effect on the extant forms of the ballad. Note for instance that for Child the uneducated repeater of a ballad is the most reliable or at least the most conservative, while the more educated the custodian of a ballad is, the more likely he or she is to make "improvements." The sort of editor Child has in mind here is someone like the poet William Allingham, who in the introduction to his 1864 collection remarked that "The ballads owe no little of their merit to the countless riddlings, siftings, shiftings, omissions, and additions of innumerable reciters. The lucky changes hold, the stupid ones fall aside" (Allingham 1864, viii), thereby complacently justifying his own eclectic editing practice.

Child, then, was a sort of latter-day Joseph Ritson, admonishing editors to edit as little as possible in order to maintain the philological and cultural integrity of the ballad. The material form of the ballad's preservation was at the heart of this enterprise, conveying as it did the most precise impression of the moment of oral performance – a problematic notion, of course, since even now neither an audio nor even a video recording can be said to convey more than a single perspective on that moment, as anyone can attest who has seen shaky cameraphone video on youtube of a concert he or she has attended, or sifted through the diverse audience recordings, each using different microphone technology and each from a different part of the auditorium, that document a single given Grateful Dead concert. And if, returning to the diverse manuscript and type witnesses to a ballad like "Lord Rendal" (or "Lord Rowlande," or "Lord Donald," or "Willy Doo", or "my little wee croudlin doo" – all, according to Child, legitimate alternative versions of the same title), we reconsider Child's project and that of the EETS, we find they have a lot in common with the performance archives and databases of our own era preserved in, for instance, the Internet Archive or, looking back seventy or eighty years, in the Mass Observation Project.

We also find, unsurprisingly, that their witnesses are bewilderingly various, and that they cannot be made entirely to support Child's utopian theory of editorial fidelity to the moment of performance, whatever kind or amount of documentation might be made possible by technology.

Michael J. Bell, who argues persuasively for the validity and indeed the importance of Child's article entry on ballads in *Johnson's New Universal Cyclopaedia*, makes explicit the ways in which textual diversity, canonical aesthetic value, and historical significance are all linked in Child's expression of his theories in the entry. In Bell's view, Child felt that

> ballads are popular in the strict use of the word; they are the products of a people who deeply share the same worldview until it is broken by print, Protestantism, and science. What had been the property of all was left to those peasants untouched by the moral and intellectual revolutions that ended the high Middle Ages and the Renaissance and brought on the modern era. What is interesting is that Child wants to guarantee that his audience will acknowledge only certain texts as legitimate and only certain experiences as productive of popular poetry. (Bell 1988, 292).

We have already seen how complex the idea of a "legitimate" ballad text was and is; what is interesting here is how the difficulty of pinning down the best of those texts is linked to the influence of print and technology. Once again it appears that at the very same time as scholars, with their increased forensic skills and increased possibilities of dissemination, were able to exercise more and more control over the printed ballad canon, they began to value the oral as being more authentic, which in turn made them realize just how diverse and uncontrollable that canon was. Popular culture, come to the fore again, had had its revenge, undermining the scholars' efforts to pin it down.

The multiple forms of the popular ballad

The Edwardian poet Henry Newbolt, in a 1915 article for *The English Review*, sought to overwrite this individuality of text and concomitant textual instability with a national narrative. Drawing on the ballad scholar Francis Gummere, but with a view of authorial creativity shaped by the world of the celebrity author and by the apparent immutability of the print version, Newbolt sought to reassure the readers of *The English Review* that the received texts of the British ballad canon were the result of the workings of a benevolent evolutionary spirit:

> [T]hough a poem cannot be made by a committee working simultaneously, it may be made by a whole people working upon it in succession; and it will then represent or express not the obscure and forgotten individual who first roughed it out, but the view of life of the community which instinctively changed it to its own likeness.

The ballads, then, after all, are not so wholly impersonal as some have thought them; by choice, by rejection, and by addition they have been made to set forth a personal view, and this they do as consistently as if they were all the compositions of a single author. The view is the view of a nation and not of an individual, but it does mingle regret and desire, it does re-create the world for us (Newbolt 1915, 465).

Newbolt, remembered as the poet of empire for works such as "Vitaï Lampada," suggests here a misty invisible hand at work, that of "the community," which works in "instinctive" ways. This is not the oral culture that we now understand from the work of Milman Parry and Walter Ong, made up of individual performers who often simultaneously recreate different versions of what is more or less the same song, using a shared hoard of words and phrases. Rather, Newbolt, like Allingham and others before him, imagines a sequential process, one that involves songs layering atop one another and improving, leading inevitably to a final best text. As Mary Ellen Brown wryly puts it,

> The beauty of all such totalizing theories is their global supposition, the answering of the unanswerable questions for all times: the ballads are a closed account; they were created in an earlier time and place where society was homogeneous – the folk society of early antiquarian dreams, the premodern haven (Brown 2006, 120).

And yet Newbolt in summarizing current thinking on the ballad for his mainstream reading audience seems to have missed some of the most important currents of 19th-century scholarship with regard to the ballads' manifestations in print and oral culture. As we have seen, writers such as Child had been troubled in far more productive ways when they were confronted by the diversity of ballad versions. The 19th-century desire to recover and to preserve as many documents as possible of the ordinary popular culture of the past suggests that, in contrast to what Brown says here, scholars such as Child, Hales, and Furnivall hoped to portray the ballad as an evocative document of unseen moments of past history, rather than to preserve its best exemplars in single authoritative forms. Here, too, their recognition of the diversity of these documents of popular entertainment may help us to understand how, historically, these scholars saw the everyday life of the past: not as an orderly evolution to a modern best of all possible worlds, but as a halting series of interesting byways followed, creative experiments abandoned, and shared successes passed on. All such attempts were worthy of documentation, no matter their aesthetic success by contemporary standards of literary merit.

Raphael Samuel poses an historiographical question in "Grand Narratives" that may be apposite here: "Does a more pluralist understanding of the present entail abandoning any unified view of the national past, and indeed, as some anti-racists argue, make any idea of a national past offensive? Does the abandonment of evolutionary schemes of development, and the discredit attaching to notions of historical 'destiny,' mean that the only safe subject to study is 'moments'?" (Samuel 1990, 124). This is a political problem of historiography posed in a modern manner, but Victorian scholars were themselves interested in the ways in which the "moments" that Samuel evokes were attested to by the episodes of passion, conflict, and ordinary everyday ritual found in ballad narratives and in the diverse documents recovered and published by the Early English Text Society. Victorian scholars certainly came to the study of such moments from the view of the past that we see in Brown's evocation of "the homogeneous folk society of early antiquarian dreams." But they also recognized the vicissitudes of history and the textual variations that pulled the ballad canon away from being a unified celebration of a homogeneous national past. When Child agonized over the question of what constituted the best form of each of the ballads he studied, he was grappling with precisely this question of pluralism and perfectionism. The answer lay in the diversity of the very documents they were studying. The texts of the ballads were multiple witnesses to the popular culture of the past, not well reducible to a single canon comprising the best versions of each narrative. On the contrary, the record shows that the 19th-century ballad editors contributed most to our understanding of the history of popular culture when they imagined historical everyday life as being made up of diverse performative moments, and harnessed the era's considerable print resources to preserve the ballad corpus in all its profusion, with all its flaws and inconsistencies intact.

References

Allingham, William 1864. *The Ballad Book: A Selection of the Choicest British Ballads.* London: Macmillan.

Anonymous 1803. Review of Walter Scott. Minstrelsy of the Scottish Border. *The Monthly Review* 42: 21–33.

Bell, Michael J. 1988. 'No Borders to the Ballad Maker's Art': Francis James Child and the Politics of the People. *Western Folklore* 47 (4): 285–307.

Brown, Mary Ellen 2006. Placed, Replaced, or Misplaced?: The Ballads' Progress. *The Eighteenth Century* 47 (2): 115–129.

Brown, Mary Ellen 2010. Child's Ballads and the Broadside Conundrum. In Patricia Fumerton, Anita Guerrini & Kris McAbee (eds), *Ballads and Broadsides in Britain, 1500–1800.* Farnham: Ashgate, 57–74.

Child, Francis James 1857–1858. *The English and Scottish Ballads.* The British Poets series. 8 volumes. Boston: Little, Brown & Co.

Child, Francis James 1881. Ballad Poetry. In *Johnson's New Universal Cyclopaedia.* Vol. 1 of 4. New York: A.J. Johnson, 365–368.

Child, Francis James 1882–1898. *The English and Scottish Popular Ballads.* 10 volumes. Boston: Houghton, Mifflin & Co.

Cowan, Yuri & Marysa Demoor 2012. Scott's Minstrelsy and Victorian Ballad Anthologies: Authorship, Editing, and Authority. *Zeitschrift für Anglistik und Amerikanistik* 60 (1): 47–63.

Fielding, Penny 1996. *Writing and Orality: Nationality, Culture and Nineteenth-Century Scottish Fiction.* Oxford: Oxford University Press.

Gilbert, Suzanne 2009. James Hogg and the Authority of Tradition. In Sharon Alker & Holly Faith Nelson (eds), *James Hogg and the Literary Marketplace: Scottish Romanticism and the Working-Class Author.* Surrey: Ashgate, 93–109.

Groom, Nick 1999. *The Making of Percy's Reliques*. Oxford: Clarendon Press.

Hales, John W. & Frederick J. Furnivall (eds) 1867. *Bishop Percy's Folio Manuscript*. 3 volumes. London: N. Trübner & Co.

Hall, Samuel Carter (ed.) 1842. *The Book of British Ballads*. London: Jeremiah How.

Hogg, James 1972. *Memoirs of the Author's Life and Familiar Anecdotes of Sir Walter Scott*. Edited by Douglas S. Mack. Edinburgh: Scottish Academic Press.

Hudson, Nicholas 2002. Constructing oral tradition: the origins of the concept in Enlightenment intellectual culture. In Adam Fox & Daniel Woolf (eds), *The Spoken Word: Oral Culture in Britain 1500–1850*. Manchester: Manchester University Press, 240–255.

McDowell, Paula 2010. 'The Art of Printing was Fatal': Print Commerce and the Idea of Oral Tradition in Long Eighteenth-Century Ballad Discourse. In Patricia Fumerton, Anita Guerrini & Kris McAbee (eds), *Ballads and Broadsides in Britain, 1500–1800*. Farnham: Ashgate, 35–56.

McLane, Maureen 2008. *Balladeering, Minstrelsy, and the Making of British Romantic Poetry*. Cambridge: Cambridge University Press.

Newbolt, Henry 1915. British Ballads. *English Review*, December 1915: 452–70.

Ong, Walter 2002 [1982]. *Orality and Literacy: The Technologizing of the Word*. London: Routledge.

Parry, Milman 1971. *The Making of Homeric Verse: The Collected Papers of Milman Parry*. Edited by Adam Parry. Oxford: Clarendon Press.

Percy, Thomas 1765. *Reliques of Ancient English Poetry*. 3 volumes. London: J. Dodsley.

Rieuwerts, Sigrid 1994. 'The Genuine Ballads of the People': F.J. Child and the Ballad Cause. *Journal of Folklore Research* 31 (1): 1–34.

Samuel, Raphael 1990. Grand Narratives. *History Workshop Journal* 29 (1): 120–133.

Smith, George Barnett (ed.) 1881. *Illustrated British Ballads*. 2 volumes. London: Cassell & Co.

St. Clair, William 2004. *The Reading Nation in the Romantic Period*. Cambridge: Cambridge University Press.

KYRRE KVERNDOKK

Disciplining the Polyphony of the Herbarium: The Order of Folklore in the Norwegian Folklore Archives

To put 3 bowls on the table

One should put 3 bowls on the table on Christmas Eve, one with water, one with beer and one with milk. He (she) should sit on a stool at some distance from the table, and at 12 o'clock the person one would marry would come and drink from a bowl. If he (she) drank from the water bowl, there would be penury, if one took the milk bowl, there would be wealth and if he took the beer bowl and drank from, there would be a drinker.

We immediately recognize this short description as folklore, as a traditional way of looking into the future and revealing the identity of a future mate. It was collected in Balestrand along the Sognefjord, in the northwestern part of Norway by the collector Sjur Bøyum in 1929 or 1930 and sent to the Norwegian Folklore Archives.[1] This is a typical folklore item from the early 20th century. After what could be termed as the communicative turn in folklore studies in the 1960s and 1970s (see for instance Ben-Amos 1972), archival records like this have been criticized for their lack of meaning and performative context (for a discussion of such critique see Anttonen 2013). Pertti Anttonen has argued that even though such kinds of folklore texts lack performative context, they do not lack context. The context is rather of another kind – it is archival. By being inscribed into an archive context as representations of traditional narratives or belief practices, folklore items have been entextualized in ways that facilitate recontextualizations in an endless number of new settings, through research, publication and translation (Anttonen 2013, 167). But how are traditional expressions recontextualized from a performative context to an archival context? What were the textual procedures for transforming oral utterances into archival documents? This article will discuss these questions by examining the production of folklore archival records in Norway in the early 20th century.

The institutionalization of folklore collections through the establishment of archives was a parallel tendency in the Nordic countries, and was based

---

1   Norsk Folkeminnesamling.

on similar ideas about folklore collection and archiving. The Norwegian Folklore Archives was founded in 1914, just a year after a similar archive was established in Lund in Sweden and seven years after the Danish Folklore Archive was founded in Copenhagen. Even though the folklore archives have been examined in a number of articles and dissertations in other Nordic countries over the last two decades (for instance Lilja 1996; Skott 2008; Nilsson 1996; Kurki 2002; Nyvang 2013; Ekrem 2014), there have been few studies on folklore archiving in Norway (a few exceptions are Hylland 2011; Kverndokk 2011; Kristoffersen 2013; Kristoffersen 2017).

This article shows how the foundation of The Norwegian Folklore Archives affected the practice of collecting folklore by establishing an infrastructure for collecting and organizing folklore items. The analysis traces the textual procedures for producing folkloristic archive documents, rather than focusing upon the content of the collected folklore. Using a Bakhtinian approach, it will first examine the technologies for collecting and archiving folklore, developed by the Norwegian Folklore Archives. Then follows a discussion on how these technologies regulated the collectors' practices of textualizing folklore. To be more specific, based on a dialogic approach, the article will examine how traces of both the dialogues between the archive and the collectors and the dialogues between the collectors and the storytellers are present in the archived folklore texts. Hence, the institutional regulations of the practice of collecting folklore are examined through a close reading of the presence or absence of the voices of the archive, the collectors or the storytellers in the archived texts (cf. Bakhtin 1986).

From private collections to a national archive

When the Norwegian Folklore Archives was founded in 1914, it was based on the private collections of Professor Moltke Moe (1859–1913), who had died the year before. These collections were astonishing. As the son of the bishop and folklore collector Jørgen Moe and as a close friend of his father's companion Peter Christen Asbjørnsen, he had inherited a considerable collection of folklore records. In 1886, at the age of 26, Moltke Moe was appointed as the first Norwegian professor of folk traditions, and held a unique position in both the academic and public sphere. Folklore collectors from around the country also sent him their collected material for his evaluation. He tended to keep this material, and his collections increased continually.

Moe was also an experienced fieldworker himself, and had collected a rich corpus of ballads and folktales. In 1878, at the age of 19, he went on his first trip to the parish of Bø, in the county of Telemark to collect folktales. In the following years he did extensive and thorough fieldwork in this county. Each of his fieldtrips lasted for several months, and he returned to the same community several times. From 1889 to 1891 he made three trips to the parish of Mo in the western part of Telemark to collect ballads, and he spent in total more than eight months in this small community. He lived with his informants and his fieldnotes reflect that he got to know them well.

The fieldnotes from Mo not only contain numerous ballads, but like other central collectors of the mid-19th century he also carefully documented the identity of his informants (B. Hodne 1979; Ø. Hodne 1979; Johnsson 2011). His notes contain biographical information about the singers and some of the singers' own comments on their songs. The field material from Mo further includes a collection of dialect words and sayings and about 50 pictures that documented traditional rural architecture, the everyday life at the mountain farm and portrayed some of people he got to know in the community. Hence, his practice of collecting folklore must be regarded as carefully performed ethnography. However, the new folkloristic archive institution he initiated a few decades later sat the course for a narrower and focused practice of collecting folklore.

In 1907 Moltke Moe and Professor Alexander Bugge (1870–1929) donated their collections of folklore to the Norwegian state. Alexander Bugge was a professor of history, but more importantly he was the son of recently-deceased Professor Sophus Bugge, and had inherited his father's folklore collection. Sophus Bugge was the editor of the first Norwegian scientific edition of medieval ballads, published in 1858. He continued collecting ballads until 1875, and he left at least seventeen handwritten volumes, containing about 1 200 records of ballads. Moe and Bugge donated their folklore collections on the condition that the Norwegian Folklore Archives would be established and that the necessary amount of money to preserve, register and catalogue the collections would be assigned. One further condition was that other folklore collectors would also donate their collections, and that folklore collectors in the future, at least those granted by the Norwegian state, would hand in a copy of the collected material to the archive.[2]

The program of the Norwegian Folklore Archives

The Norwegian Folklore Archives came to reality seven years later, and Moltke Moe's collections were transformed from a set of chaotic stacks of books and notes into a well-organized, modern archive. Knut Liestøl (1881–1952) was appointed as the director and, from 1917, professor of this new academic institution. He remained in the position until his death in 1952. In 1921 the internationally-recognized scholar Reidar Th. Christiansen (1886–1971) became the institution's first archivist, and he worked at the archive until he retired in 1956.

Soon after Knut Liestøl was appointed as the director of the archive he published the article "On the collecting of Norwegian Folk Traditions"[3] (Liestøl 1914), which could be considered as a manifesto for the new folklore institution. In this short and polemic article, he suggested a program closely based on what was already sketched in Moe and Bugge's donation letter. First

2   NFS Letters after Moltke Moe, letter from Alexander Bugge, dated 18 December 1907.
3   "Um innsamling av norske folketradtionar".

Moltke Moe in his working room, surrounded by his books and his private folklore collection. (Photo: The Norwegian Folklore Archives).

Knut Liestøl in the Norwegian Folklore Archives. The contrast to Moe's chaotic office is striking. (Photo: The Norwegian Folklore Archives).

of all, he emphasized that private folklore collections should be donated to the new institution. Private collections were at that time usually stored at home, and Liestøl remarked that the homes of the collectors were most often wooden houses and liable to catch fire. He rhetorically contrasted these houses with the modern archive institution. The archive was housed at the University Library, a brick building that was finished just the year before. While it was only a matter of time before the wooden houses of the collectors would burn down, the new and modern University Library was a secure archival environment, he argued (*Ibid.*, 114–115). Though his argument was right in a concrete and practical sense, it also signalized a new folkloristic order. His way of arguing for control over the folkloric material implied an institutional subordination of both folklore collections and folklore collectors.

In addition to preserving, registering and storing already-collected material, the new institution would continue to collect still-living folklore. Liestøl sketched a model for how this could be done. By registering and cataloguing the already-existing collections, lacunas in the collections would be uncovered. He argued that the task for further collecting was to systematically fill in these lacunas through nationally-coordinated projects, collecting folklore in underrepresented parts of the country, or collecting underrepresented types of legends (Liestøl 1914, 116–117).

Since the 1840s, a number of collectors had been given grants by the University of Christiania.[4] They operated as independent fieldworkers, working on their own, with few public obligations. Liestøl remarked that: "It seems that the holders of the scholarships do whatever they find appropriate. There has, in this respect, truly been a golden age for lone-wolves that lack understanding of what the major national tasks require" (*Ibid.*, 118).[5] This had to come to an end, he argued. He suggested using the grants for collecting folklore as a means to carry out the systematic and nationally-coordinated project of collecting. Moreover, to collect folklore was not something just anybody could do. It had to be based on scientific methods. Most of the collectors were farmers or school teachers, and did not necessarily have sufficient training to do satisfactory, scientific fieldwork. Liestøl therefore suggested organizing a group of collectors in a Norwegian Folklore Association,[6] which was supposed to be controlled by the archive and Liestøl himself. However, it took several years before such an association became a reality.

Liestøl's model for coordinating the collection of folklore was a radical attempt to discipline a field where people were used to operating fairly independently. Folklore collectors around the country were provoked and Liestøl's initiative resulted in an intense public quarrel that lasted for several

---

4 The city Christiania was renamed Kristiania in 1877, and again renamed as Oslo in 1925.

5 "Det ser mest ut som stipendiatane kann gjera som dei finn høveleg. Det hev reint vore ein gullalder i so maate for einstøingar, som vantar sans for det dei store nationale uppgaavor krev."

6 Norsk Folkeminnelag.

years. The leading folklore collectors of the early 20th century were quite self-conscious men, regarding themselves as key figures in the local cultural life of the rural communities where they operated. Two of them were Tov Flatin (1878–1945) and Rikard Berge (1881–1969). Flatin was the author and editor of books and journals on folklore and local history. He was a school teacher and the mayor of Flesberg municipality in Buskerud County for several years. Just like Flatin, Berge was the author and editor of books and journals on folk culture. He was appointed as the director of the newly-established regional museum for Telemark County in 1916, and held the position until he retired in 1951. Men like Flatin and Berge did not accept their autonomy being taken away from them, and refused to be controlled by Liestøl. They agitated against plans to move private folklore collections located around the country to a centralized institution, and they resisted the attempts to enforce academic control over the practice of collecting folklore.

In 1919 they founded the National Association for Folklore Collectors,[7] as a countermeasure to Liestøl's plan to discipline and control the collectors. The association was supposed to give out grants for collecting and to make it possible for collectors to publish the folklore they had collected (Kristoffersen 2013, 46–90). Flatin was elected as the leader, while Berge was the main spokesman. The language Berge used to characterize Liestøl's plans was not very flattering. He accused the plans as being old fashioned intellectual imperialism, undemocratic absolutism, and even called Liestøl's attempts to control the collectors the Kristiania Tyranny (Berge 1919, 10; Espeland 1974; Havåg 1997, 34). He suggested an alternative to Liestøl's model, with a network of regional and local folklore archives, located at regional and local museums. A national folkloristic institution, should, according to him, serve exclusively as a research center. Berge and Flatin resisted the scientification of the field of folklore. Based on rural nationalistic ideas, the objective for collecting folklore was in their opinion not first and foremost scholarly work, but rather to bring the folklore back to the folk – or to be more exact, to bring local folklore back to the local communities.

Berge and Flatin could not oppose Liestøl's plans in the long run. The association they founded only lasted for a couple of years. They had to accept that the grants for collecting folklore in the years to follow were to be administrated by Liestøl, and that the holders of these grants were obliged to hand in their collected material to the national archive. Finally, in 1920 the Norwegian Folklore Association was founded, whose main task was to publish manuscripts for folklore collectors around the country. Despite close relations to the Norwegian Folklore Archives, it operated as a fairly autonomous organization. Berge, on the other hand, continued his independent work, and he kept his folklore collections for himself for the rest of his life.

---

7   Landslaget for folkeminnesamlarar.

A technology for transforming vernacular culture to folklore items

Like folklore archives elsewhere, the newly-established Norwegian Folklore Archives operated within what could be termed as the rescuing paradigm in folklore studies. As suggested by Liestøl, the archive soon started up a systematic nationwide operation, collecting what was regarded as the last living remains of folklore in Norway. The architect behind this was, however, not Liestøl, but Reidar Th. Christiansen. In 1917 he worked out a detailed guide for collecting folklore. It was widely distributed to collectors around the country to make sure that their fieldwork practices had a reasonable, scientific approach (Christiansen 1917). The book was re-published in an extended edition in 1925 (Christiansen 1925).

The instruction book, *Norwegian folklore. A guide for collectors and others interested,*[8] draws a sharp line between folklore and other cultural expressions, such as modern popular culture and urban culture. It further distinguishes between folklore and cultural expressions belonging to the scientific domains of musicology, ethnology and history. Hence, the instruction book defined the Norwegian term *folkeminne* [folklore] as a fixed and precise cultural category. While the Norwegian term *folkepoesi* [folk poetry] was defined already in 1840 by Jørgen Moe (Moe 1988 [1840]), leaning on the genre system of the Grimm brothers, and the term *folkevise* [folk song] was defined by Magnus Brostrup Landstad in 1853 (Landstad 1968 [1853]), drawing on Herder's term *Volkslieder*, the conceptual content of the broader Norwegian term *folkeminne* and its equal *folketradition* [folk tradition] was still vaguely defined throughout the 19th century.[9] There was no need to fill the term with a precise conceptual content, as long as the practice of collecting folklore was not yet institutionalized. Though, when the Norwegian Folklore Archives was eventually established, it became crucial to clarify what the archive was supposed to contain.

Christiansen's instruction book was formulated as a questionnaire. It contained systematically-organized categories of customs, beliefs and narrative motifs, and was intended as a working tool for the collectors. Yet, these categories could also be regarded as a folkloric taxonomy. The book did not focus so much upon folktales and ballads, not because it was excluded from Christiansen's definition of folklore, but rather because he regarded the tales and ballads to be more or less extinct. Instead the questionnaire was to a large extent formulated after research interests of the time. Christiansen argued that one main task in folklore studies would be to examine the primitive spiritual life, or what he termed "the large common basis from which in the end all human culture is grown" (Christiansen 1925, 7).[10] While Liestøl claimed in 1924 that the main task for folklore research was to work on comparative studies of the development from primitive

---

8   *Norske folkeminne. En veildning for samlere og interesserte.*

9   While the term *folkminne* was already used in Swedish in the 1830s, it was not commonly used by Norwegian folklorists before the last decades of the 19th century.

10   "[...] det store almene grundlag, hvorfra til syvende og sidst al menneskelig kultur er grodd fram."

culture to civilization, they both agreed that the best way to examine such a development was through the study of folk beliefs and customs (Rogan 2013, 651). In line with these interests, the instruction book mainly focused upon these two main topics. Theoretically, the book was first and foremost based on the historical-geographical method, of which Christiansen was the main Norwegian exponent (see for instance Christiansen 1916). Hence, the systematic order of the questionnaire was developed as a tool for standardizing the folklore records to such an extent that it was possible to use them for comparative research. The questionnaire contained seven main categories:

A. The major events in life.
B. Daily life. Care and work.
C. Seasons of the year and holidays. Weekends.
D. Supernatural (magic) tricks. Aid and advice on illness and danger.
E. Legends and narratives.
F. Belief and narratives about nature phenomena.
G. Prose folklore.[11]

Each one of these categories was again divided into a set of subcategories. Underneath category E, "Legends and narratives", subcategory 2, "Supernatural beings", point c, "in the mountains and in the ground" were, for instance, "The hidden people" located.[12] On this last subordinated level, a number of detailed topics were listed, which was supposed to work as a checklist for the collectors, to make sure that they did not forget any crucial parts of the tradition they were collecting. Hence, the questionnaire worked efficiently as what the cultural historian Eirik Kristoffersen has characterized as a folkloristic vacuum cleaner (Kristoffersen 2013, 93). It was a tool for identifying and collecting folklore and, as importantly, a technology for dividing folklore from modern popular culture and urban culture and a technology for transforming rather different kinds of transitory, oral utterances into fixed archival records of the same kind – categorized as folklore.

Christiansen was not the only one to publish these kinds of guidelines. Tov Flatin also published a questionnaire for folklore collecting (Flatin 1918, second edition 1920). It is notable different from Christiansen's guide. Flatin's questionnaire contained eleven categories:

I.   Folk songs.
II.   Stev. [short, improvised verses].
III. Folk tunes.
IV.   Tales.

---

11 A. De store begivenheter i livet, B. Daglig liv. Stel og arbeide, C. Aarets tider og merkedager. Helg, D. Overnaturlige (magiske) kunster. Hjælp og raad i sygdom og fare, E. Sagn og fortælling, F. Tro og fortælling om naturens fænomener, G. Friere folkedigtning.

12 E. Sagn og fortælling, 2. Overnaturlige væsener. c. I berg og jord. Huldrefolket.

V.   Legends.
VI.   Beliefs and customs.
VII. Games.
VIII. Riddles.
IX.   Proverbs.
X.   Place names.
XI.   Folk art.[13]

While Christiansen's questionnaire was structured thematically, covering a variety of vernacular cultural practices, Flatin's was structured after a genre system, focusing on the aesthetics of folk culture. While Christiansen excluded folk music and folk art, both art forms were included on Flatin's list. It is worth noticing that he also included place names as a category. For Flatin, folklore was closely connected to local history, and he remarked that he had included both place names and folk art in the questionnaire to satisfy the interests of the local historians (Flatin 1920, 7). Flatin further emphasized that the questionnaire was merely intended as suggestions to what to ask about, not as a classificatory list of folklore (Flatin 1918, 13). The questionnaire presented an alternative to Christiansen's rather strict taxonomy. Yet it was soon to be forgotten.

Both Flatin and Christiansen were inspired by similar instruction books published abroad, especially the number of books and articles on the importance of collections of folklore published by the Swedish folklorist Carl Wilhelm von Sydow (von Sydow 1915; 1916; 1918; 1919). He was the director of the Folk Life Archives in Lund, and had already in 1915 published the instruction book *Folklore and its collection* (von Sydow 1915).[14] The instructions or rather recommendations were quite openly formulated, in comparison to Christensen's questionnaire. von Sydow did not strictly limit the term folklore to a set of categories in the way Christiansen did. Like Christiansen, he listed a number of topics, but these topics were not organized systematically as nomenclatural categories, as was the case in Christiansen's instruction book. In line with Flatin, his list of topics was merely a suggestion for what to collect, not fixed categories. Hence, he did not define a taxonomic order of folklore in the way Christiansen did.

In the introduction to the book, von Sydow discussed methodology and the practice of collecting. He gave some guidelines for interviewing techniques with an emphasis on strategies for getting people to talk, and he discussed what kind of documentation techniques that were most appropriate in the field. He further instructed the collectors to write down the names of the narrators or, to use von Sydow's own term, the tradition bearers, the places they live, and other sorts of information which could be useful, for instance whether he[15] had learned his stories from his parents or

---

13 I. Folkevisur, II. Stev, III. Folketonar, IV. Eventyr (Sogur), V. Segnir, VI. Truir og skikkar, VII. Leikir, VIII. Gaatur (Spuringar), IV. Ordtøkje og ordstev, X. Stadnamn, XI. Folkekunst.

14 *Folkminnena och deras insamling.*

15 The tradition bearer was referred to as a man.

whether he may have picked them up on a journey, and finally if he could date when he had first heard them (von Sydow 1915, 10–15).

Christiansen, on the other hand, did not give much attention to practical and methodological questions. He did not put any emphasis on the tradition bearers. He was interested in folklore as cultural items, and not the storytellers. In fact, he explicitly declared that he was not interested in individual stories:

> It is certainly the case that everything that happens will be reflected in people's minds and could become a story, but there would be little to gain by collecting all these narratives. One would only meet an endless series of individuals and just listen to their voices; it demands more to be termed as folk tradition. It has to be a material in which every single component of both form and content have lost the characteristics of its individual origin, so that it overall gets a shape and uniformity reflecting that there is no longer any single person speaking, but all those that have made it their own, polished it in their thought life and so given it on. Here is the folk speaking, "it tells" or "people are telling" is the right authority. One will obviously always meet this material in the individual, and applied to individual cases, but the character of the general is still striking, and the effort each bearer of the tradition eventually is doing, will not be of any interest, at least not in the first case. What we first and foremost are seeking is what the people at large have thought and felt in bygone times (Christiansen 1925, 14).[16]

This passage could be read as a theoretical statement about the characteristics of folklore. However, it could just as well be read as an instruction to the collectors, to make sure that they did not focus upon individual stories, but rather on de-individualized folklore. Thus, his remark that it is "the folk speaking" was not merely a theoretical statement. It might also be read as a description of an ideal folklore text.

The 1925 edition of Christiansen's instruction book was published by the Norwegian Folklore Association, and distributed to its 400 members, including more or less every single folklore collector in Norway. It was used actively by the collectors in the decades to follow. However, the questionnaire did not only work as a tool for fieldwork. It was also equivalent to the filing index Christiansen developed for the Norwegian Folklore Archives. The conceptual order in the archive's filing system corresponded in other words

---

16 "Det er nok saa at alt som sker, gir en refleks i folks sind og kan bli til beretning; men om en tænkte sig alle de fortællinger indsamlet, saa var det litet vundet ved det. En vilde deri bare støte paa en uendelig række individer og bare høre deres stemme; for at det skal kaldes folketradition kræves det noget mer. Det maa være et stof, hvori alle de enkelte bestanddele baade i utforming og indhold har tapt præget av sin individuelle oprindelse, saa at det hele faar en holdning og ensartethet svarende til at det ikke længer er nogen enkelt som fører ordet, men alle de som har gjort dette til sit, slepet det til i sit tankeliv og saa git det videre. Her er det folket som taler, "det fortælles" eller "folk fortæller" blir den rette autoritet. Naturligvis møter en altid dette stof hos de enkelte og anvendt paa individuelle tilfælde, men karakteren av det almene er like fremtrædende, og den indsats de enkelte bærere av traditionen vel undertiden gjør, blir ikke av interesse paa første haand iallefald. Det vi først og fremst søker, er hva det store folk har tænkt og følt i svundne tider".

with the recommended structure of the folkloristic fieldwork. Hence, if a collector used the instruction book carefully, his or her fieldwork material would already in the process of collecting and transcribing be structured as well-organized archival records.

The instruction book was a means of discursive control, regulating collecting practice among the various collectors around the country and synchronizing the variety of collecting practices among the collectors. It was furthermore a means to make sure that folklore was differentiated from other kinds of cultural expressions, and it offered the collectors a vocabulary for both interviewing the tradition bearers and for writing folklore records. Hence, it instructed the collectors in how to make some sort of order out of chaotic and unsystematic oral utterances. Liestøl and Christiansen at the archive appreciated the collections they received from the collectors being well organized. In fact, this seems to have been a criterion for being awarded a grant from the archive.[17] Yet, the collectors were not reduced to powerless marionettes. The instruction book could as well be regarded as a technology for delegating executive, discursive power from the archive to the collectors. The collectors were those who had to recognize and, so to speak, isolate folklore from other cultural expressions, and were those who gave the oral utterances a written shape. The book enabled the collectors to transform local practices and oral utterances into well-formulated written descriptions and narratives based on reasonable scholarly principles.

The collectors were positioned in between the archive and the tradition bearers. They represented the mid stratum of a three-staged hierarchical chain of knowledge production. The academic scholars located at the archive resided on top, while the tradition bearers, those delivering the raw material for the folkloristic knowledge production were at the bottom. I regard the production of folklore documents as a chained sequence of dialogues where these three instances participated – one set of source dialogues between the tradition bearers and the collectors, and another set of target dialogues between the collectors and the scholars (cf. Bauman 2004, 130–133). The latter set of dialogues framed and disciplined the first one. The folklore texts that today are stored in the archive were produced in the intersection between these two sets of dialogues and contain traces of both of them.

The institutional cleaning of the folklore texts

Let me now go back to where I started this article, with the quote from the collections of Sjur Bøyum (1884–1970). Bøyum was a typical collector of the 1920s and 1930s. He was a high school teacher, and he received grants from the Norwegian Folklore Archives from 1929 to 1934 to collect folklore during the summer holidays (*Norsk allkunnebok* 1949, 740). He handed in five volumes to the archive, containing the folkloric material he collected during his fieldwork along the Sognefjord from 1928 to 1933. The second of these volumes, dated 1929 and 1930, is 55 pages long. It contains mostly

17 NFS collection of letters, Letter of allocation, dated 3 April 1929.

legends, in addition to records on folk medicine and traditional sign-reading practices. The volume opens with an eight-page long chapter called "How one can get to know whom one would marry",[18] containing 43 different subtitled short texts. This is the full version of the first text of the chapter:

> To put 3 bowls on the table
> One should put 3 bowls on the table on Christmas Eve, one with water, one with beer and one with milk. He (she) should sit on a stool at some distance from the table, and at 12 o'clock the person one would marry would come and drink from a bowl. If he (she) drank from the water bowl, there would be penury, if one took the milk bowl, there would be wealth and if he took the beer bowl and drank from, there would be a drinker.
>
> A girl tried this once. At 12 o'clock one came and took the beer bowl, drank and left. She knew him well. Soon after came another one and drank from the water bowl and left, and then came a third man and drank from the milk bowl. The girl got married three times. The first became a drinker, the second a tramp and the third became a wealthy man (Balestr.[and])
>
> In Fjærland they tell it like this: They put up three glasses on Christmas Eve, one with water, one with wine, and one with beer. They should look into the glass on Christmas morning, and in one of the glasses they would then see the face of the one they would get. If the face appeared in the glass of beer, it would be a drinker, if it appeared in the glass of wine, it would be a wealthy man, and if it appeared in the glass of water, it would be penury and destitution.[19]

How are the instructions and institutional technologies for collecting and archiving folklore present in this text? And how do traces of the dialogues between the tradition bearers and the collector and between the collector and the archive appear in this text?

Already from the establishment of folklore as a cultural field in the early 19th century there had been a principle that the collector was not supposed to

---

18 "Korleis ein kan faa vita kven ein skulde verta gift med." NFS Sjur Bøym 2:1.
19 "Aa setja 3 skaaler paa bordet.
  Julafta skulde ein setja 3 skaaler paa bordet, ei med vatn, ei med øl og ei med mjølk. Han (ho) skulde sitja paa ein krakk eit stykke ifraa bordet, og kl. 12 skulde den ein vart gift med, koma og drikka or en skaal. Drakk han (ho) or vasskaali, skulde det verta armod, tok ein mjølkeskaali so vart det velstand, og tok han ølskaali og drakk or, so vart det ein drikkar.
  Ei gjenta prøvde dette eigong. Kl. 12 kom ein og tok ølskaali, drakk og gjekk. Ho kjende han godt. Nett etter kom ein annan og drakk or vasskaali og gjekk, og so kom det ein tredje mann og drakk or mjølkeskaali. Gjenta vart gift 3 gonger. Den fyrste vart ein drikkar, den andre ein fant og den tredje vart ein velstandsmann (Balestr.[and])
  I Fjærland fortel dei det soleis: Dei sette fram 3 glas paa julafta, eit med vatn, eit med vin, og eit med øl. Dei skulde sjaa ned i glasi juledagsmorgonen, og daa skulde dei faa sjaa andletet aat den dei skulde faa, i eit av glasi. Vart andletet i ølglaset, vart det ein drikkar, vart det i vinglaset, vart det ein velstandsmann, og vart det i vassglaset, vart det berre armod og naud."

do any substantial re-writing of the oral folklore or add anything by editing. The collector was not supposed to work as an author, but as a mediator of the local tradition. Hence, the collector was expected to silence his own voice in the text. However, when the collector translated transitory, oral utterances to fixed folklore items, it was not only a matter of intersemiotic translation, as Pertti Anttonen has pointed out (Anttonen 2013), but it was also a matter of recontextualization (Bauman 2004, 130) from a situated communicative and performative context, to an archival, scientific context. It required active and careful re-writing and editing to present the text as authentic folklore in this context.

The archive collections by Bøyum contain well-organized and well-edited manuscripts based on his fieldnotes. Four of the volumes, including the cited one, are even typed. The structure of the volumes does not necessarily follow the structure of the interviews with the informants. They are rather structured after the logic of Christensen's instruction book. The chapter "How one can get to know whom one would marry" could be recognized as a collection of texts within the genre of omen reading. The quoted passage is easily placed into Christiansen's nomenclature under category C, "Seasons of the year and holidays. Weekend," subcategory 2, "The feasts of the year", point a, "Christmas," under the topic "Omens and signs."[20] In this respect, Bøyum's manuscripts were certainly organized after the filing index of the archive. Hence, the dialogical traces of the archive as the addressee of the text are clearly visible in how the volume was structured.

The cited text reiterates the same omen three times, as three variants of the same folklore item – the first time as an instruction of how to perform the omen, then as a legend about how it worked and finally as a comparable description from another parish in the district. This way of compiling narratives and description of similar practices is quite typical for folkloristic archival records from that time. It was a way to uniform cultural practices to such an extent that they would become comparable units. While several of the folkloristic fieldworkers of the 19th century in Norway emphasized the performativity of the folklore utterance by writing down precise information about their informants, most collectors of the early 20th century, like Bøyum, paid little attention to the informants. The fieldwork as such, the interview and the dialogues with the tradition bearers, is systematically made invisible in his text. No tradition bearer is named, and the voices of the informants or the storytellers are almost entirely muted in the transformation from oral utterances to written texts. Hence, there are few traces of orality left in the text. The only possible linguistic trace of orality is the additive use of the conjunction *and* binding together the third and fourth sentences of the third paragraph: "They should look into the glass on Christmas morning, *and* in one of the glasses they would then see the face of the one they would get." According to Walter Ong, additive style indicated by the use of *and* is one of the main characteristics of orality in contrast to the reasoned subordination that characterizes writing (Ong 1988 [1982], 37). In a written utterance it is more likely that the two sentences would be separated, rather than linked

20 Aarets tide og merkedager. Helg. 2. Aarets høitider, a. Jul. Varsel og merker.

together by the use of an additive *and*. There are no other obvious traces of orality of the source utterance than this one left in the written text.

According to Pertti Anttonen, folklore archival texts "are intentionally stripped of their referentiality vis-à-vis the original event of interaction and its performer-audience relationship in order to function as a metonymic representation of collective tradition" (Anttonen 2013, 163). It is possible to study how this is done in detail in the short text from Bøyum's collections. Both the narrator and the protagonists of the text are generalized and anonymized. The text is narrated in third person; the first time about *one*, the second about *a girl*, and the third refers to *they*. Thus, it is impossible to read out of the text whether it is based on one or a number of source utterances. Bøyum is systematically striving to erase not only any traces of himself as the author, but also of the tradition bearers. The muting of the storyteller(s) is a rhetorical strategy to authorize the text as authentic folklore. Bøyum is actively inscribing the collective voice of the *local tradition* into the text. This becomes especially clear in the use of the collective instance *they* in the third paragraph. As emphasized by Christiansen in his instruction book, it is "the folk speaking" (Christiansen 1925, 14) in authentic folklore. In Bøyum's text, the storytellers are, like the collector himself, reduced to mediators, performing the voice of the people. The text is presented as de-individualized and generalized local tradition. Hence, it is actively traditionalized. To quote Richard Bauman, the source utterance is entextualized, it is endowed "with sufficient formal and functional boundaries and internal cohesion to allow it to be lifted out of its context of production and recontextualized in the target dialogue" (Bauman 2004, 147). The result is a text where the archive and the collective voice of the tradition are first and foremost the traceable dialogical parts.

The act of inscribing the oral utterance into the archive is not only an act of separating folklore from other kinds of oral discourse or cultural practices. Finding himself in the middle position of the hierarchical order of the folkloristic knowledge production, Bøyum is performing the first step of a folkloristic analysis by synthesizing the raw material of the local tradition, cleaning it for any indicators of individuality, and preparing it for reading and scientific work. The legend from Balestrand and the description from Fjærland are presented as comparable documentations of the same cultural phenomena. They are thus made suitable for historical-geographical analysis.

Another example from the same period is selected from the archival records collected by Rigmor Frimannslund (1911–2006). She was a different kind of collector than Bøyum. She was a folklore student during the 1930s, and as a fresh student in 1934 she was sent out by Knut Liestøl to do folkloristic fieldwork. Liestøl gave her Christiansen's instruction book, and we know from an interview late in her life that she used the book actively (Klepp 1990, 134–135; Telste 2012, 190–191). Frimannslund had a special interest for customs, which is reflected in her collections. In 1941 she presented a dissertation on traditional proposals, and became the first to get a licentiate[21] at the University of Oslo in the new academic discipline of ethnology.

---

21 Magistergrad.

Her collection of folklore, archived at the Norwegian Folklore Archives, is impressively well organized. In this collection we find this record from 1934:[22]

From <u>Samnanger</u> municipality, Hordaland. Written down after <u>Knut Tvedt</u> approx. 60–65 years?, 20 August 1934.

<u>Night proposals</u>
Night running was very common in the past. If the proposal was meant seriously, the boy did prefer to walk alone. Otherwise they went two by two. It was mostly at the summer pasture where they were doing night runs.[23]

In Christiansen's taxonomy this kind of proposal is classified underneath category A. "The major events in life", subcategory 1 "Proposals and marriage", point c, "Proposals and engagement."[24] The text following directly after this one is entitled "Working Life". It was collected from the same tradition bearer:

<u>Working life</u>
To put turfed roof on a house was <u>exchange work</u>. Then they gathered the neighbors to do it.

<u>Dugnad</u> was less used. I have only taken part in one.[25]

This kind of phenomenon is classified by Christiansen underneath category B. "Daily Life care and work", 1. "House and home."[26] Turning the page in Frimandlund's collection, the third folklore item collected by her after Knut Tvedt is about Christmas,[27] and is thus to be classified underneath Christiansen's category C. "Seasons of the year and holidays. Weekend," subcategory 2. "The feasts of the year", a. "Christmas".[28] Hence, in her editing of the fieldnotes, she has consciously and carefully organized her volumes of records after Christiansen's nomenclatural system, starting at category A, followed by B and C. In this sense, her collections could be considered as exemplary for archival purposes. It is worth noting that, in contrast to

---

22 NFS Rigmor Frimannslund 1:25.
23 "Frå Samnanger herad, Hordaland. Uppskrive etter Knut Tvedt ca 60–65 år? 20. august 1934.
   <u>Nattefriing.</u>
   Natteløperi var sers vanleg fyrr i tidi. Var friingi ålvorleg meint, gjekk guten helst åleine. Ellers gjekk dei gjerne tvo i lag. Det var helst på sætrene dei dreiv med natteløperi."
24 A. De store begivenheter i livet. 1 Frieri og Bryllup. c. Frieri og forlovelse.
25 "<u>Arbeidslivet.</u>
   Å leggja torvtak på eit hus var <u>bytesarbeid</u>. Då bad dei grannane saman til det.
   Dugnad var mindre brukt. Eg har berre vore med på ein."
26 B. Daglig liv. Stel og Arbeide. 1. Hus og hjem.
27 NFS Rigmor Frimannslund 1: 26–31.
28 C. Aarets tide og merkedager. Helg. 2. Aarets høitider, a. Jul.

Bøyum, she documented the name and age of the informant. However, this is not done with much emphasis. The information about his age is, for instance, a rough estimate, just as if she did not care to ask him.

Yet, Frimannslund still seems to have followed the same conventions as Bøyum when she edited the text. Just like in Bøyum's case, the voice of the tradition bearer, Knut Tvedt, is for the most part written out of the two quoted examples. Both the record on night proposals and the one about the working life are formulated in general terms, about *them*, and it is described in past tense, just dated to *in the past*. Both of the texts are held in a descriptive mode, cleaned of any direct speech. However, the last sentence breaks out of this generalized style. The way the informant mentions his own experience is referred to in direct speech: "Dugnad was less used. *I* have only taken part in one." Hence, the last sentence seems to be a direct quote from the source utterance.

The voice of the archive still seems to dominate the records by structuring them and by delivering the main terminology. Both the records are named after established archival or academic terms. The term *night running*[29] was a term used in Christiansen's questionnaire. While the term *dugnad* was not mentioned in Christiansen's book, but was generally used by ethnologists and folklorists to describe the social system of exchange work in rural communities (compare the contemporary standard reference, Visted 1923, 24). The utterance of the tradition bearer, Knut Tvedt, breaks out of the academic terminological framing. He was well aware of the system of exchange work, but obviously distinguished between exchange work in general and *dugnad*, which he seemed to have a far narrower understanding of. Hence, the archival records by Frimannslund contain quite noticeable traces of both the sets of dialogues – her dialogues with the tradition bearer as well as the dialogues with the archive.

The scientification of folklore

The institutionalization of folklore in the early 20th century implied a scientification of not only folklore as a cultural category, but also of the practice of collecting folklore and the shaping of the folklore records. Thus, an order of folklore was established, which, in addition to a near Linnaean system of genres, included the nomenclatural order of the archive and the nationwide synchronization of the practices of collecting folklore. The archival categories enabled the collectors to prepare the fieldwork material and present it as herbarium specimens of what could almost be mistaken for being natural categories. Hence, the archive system is fundamental for the naturalization of the cultural category of folklore and its subcategories. The institutional delimitation of the conceptual content of the term folklore was done due to quite specific theoretical interests and had epistemological consequences that are traceable in the archived folklore records.

---

29 Natteløperi.

There were some noticeable changes in the practice of collecting folklore from the late 19th century to the early 20th century. First of all, there was a shift of interest from performative genres such as folktales and ballads, towards a main focus on folk belief narratives, customs and various kinds of vernacular practices. A parallel tendency was the de-personalization of folklore records. While Moltke Moe and other central collectors of the 19th century so carefully collected information about their informants, the collectors of the early 20th century just as carefully strived to erase the traces of the informants in the folklore records. Though, this did not count for all the collectors. The example from the collections of Rigmor Frimannslund shows that some of the collectors still wrote down the name and age of their informants. However, I will still argue that there seems to be a tendency to anonymize the tradition bearer, and that this had to do with the instructions given from the archive. It is interesting to notice that the collector that actively resisted being subordinated to the institutional structure of the archive, Rikard Berge, also was the one that was most interested in the individuals performing the tradition. Berge's way of documenting folklore had similarities with the practices of the collectors of 19th century. He not only carefully documented biographical information about the performers, but even published a book about folklore as performative art, containing portrayals of storytellers (Berge 1924).

The folklore archival records have to be regarded as items of traditional knowledge co-produced in an intersection between the archive, the collectors and the tradition bearers. In this sense, the texts are highly polyphonic. The examples from the archival collections of Bøyum and Frimannslund illustrates that even though folkloric collecting was a method for preserving oral tradition, the archival records seems to contain few traces of orality. The textual technologies for collecting, preparing and archiving folklore were technologies for disciplining the polyphony of the texts, by entextualization and by transforming the singular oral utterances into collective representations of folk culture. It is a paradox that the technologies developed for collecting and preventing oral tradition at the same time worked as technologies for cleaning the folklore items of traces of orality. However, the close readings of texts from the collections of Bøyum and Frimannslund not only demonstrate how this is done, but also demonstrate that even though such texts have been through thoroughly performed cleaning processes, glimpses of the orality of the source dialogues may still pop up from the paper and reach the reader.

References

Unpublished sources from the Norwegian Folklore Archives

NFS Rigmor Frimannslund 1.
NFS Sjur Bøyum 2.
NFS Collection of letters, letter of allocation, dated 3 April 1929.
NFS Letters after Moltke Moe, letter from Alexander Bugge 18 December 1907.

Literature

Anttonen, Pertti 2013. Lost in Intersemiotic Translation? The Problem of Context in Folk Narratives in the Archive. *Arv. Nordic Yearbook of Folklore* 69: 153–170.
Bakhtin, Mikhail 1986. *Speech Genres and Other Late Essays.* Translated by Vern W. McGee, edited by Caryl Emerson & Michael Holquist. Austin: University of Texas Press.
Bauman, Richard 2004. *A World of Others' Words: Cross-Cultural Perspectives on Intertextuality.* Malden, MA: Wiley-Blackwell.
Ben-Amos, Dan 1972. Toward a Definition of Folklore in Context. In Américo Paredes & Richard Bauman (eds), *Toward New Perspectives in Folklore.* Bloomington: Trickster Press, 3–19.
Berge, Rikard 1919. *Decentralisation. Folkeminne – historielag – bygdemuse.* Fraa Landslaget for Folkeminnesamlarar 1. Risør: Erik Gunleiksons forlag.
Berge, Rikard 1924. *Norsk sogukunst: Sogusegjarar og sogur.* Kristiania: Aschehoug.
Christiansen, Reidar Th. 1916. *The Tale of the Two Travellers, or the Blinded Man: A Comparative Study.* FF Communications 24. Helsinki: The Finnish Academy of Science.
Christiansen, Reidar Th. 1917. *Veiledning ved indsamling av folkeminder.* Frå Norsk Folkeminnesamling 1. Kristiania: Det Mallingske Bogtrykkeri.
Christiansen, Reidar Th. 1925. *Norsk folkeminne. En veiledning for samlere og interesserte.* NFL 12. Oslo: Norsk Folkeminnelag.
Ekrem, Carola 2014. "Belysandet af vår allmoges andliga lif." Traditions insamlingen inom Svenska litteratursällskapet. In Carola Ekrem, Pamela Gustavsson, Petra Hakala & Mikael Korhonen. *Arkiv, minne, glömska. Arkiven vid Svenska litteratursällskapet i Finland 1885–2010.* Helsingfors: Svenska Litteratursällskapet i Finland, 22–197.
Espeland, Velle 1974. Desentraliseringsstriden. Ein strid om kva folkeminnesamling og gransking skal tena til. *Tradisjon* 4: 71–76.
Flatin, Tov 1918. *Spyrjelistor fyr folkeminnesamlarar.* Bergen: Gula Tidend prenteverk.
Flatin, Tov 1920. *Innsamling av Folkeminne.* Kristiania: Olaf Norlis Forlag.
Havåg, Eldar 1997. "For det er Kunst vi vil have": Om nasjonalitet og kunst i norsk oppskrivartradisjon og folkemusikkforsking. KULT 85. Oslo: Noregs forskingsråd.
Hodne, Bjarne 1979. *Eventyret og tradisjonsbærerne. Eventyrfortellere i en Telemarksbygd.* Oslo: Universitetsforlaget.
Hodne, Ørnulf 1979. *Jørgen Moe og folkeeventyrene. En studie av nasjonalromantisk folkloristikk.* Oslo: Universitetsbiblioteket.
Hylland, Ole Marius 2011. En gjenganger krysser sitt spor. Innhold, analytisk praksis og analytisk potensial i tekster om deildegasten. In Line Esborg, Kyrre Kverndokk & Leiv Sem (eds), *Or gamalt – nye perspektiver på folkeminner.* NFL 165. Oslo: Norsk Folkeminnelag, Instituttet for sammenlignende kulturforskning, 96–118.
Johnsson, Bengt 2011. *"Vil du meg lyde." Balladsångare i Telemark på 1800-talet.* Edited by Olav Solberg. Oslo: Novus forlag.

Klepp, Asbjørn 1990. Studenten som kom før faget. Rigmor Frimannslund – den første magister i norsk etnologi. *Norveg* 33: 131–144.

Kristoffersen, Eirik 2013. *Institusjonaliseringen av folkeminnene. Norsk Folkeminne-samling og Desentraliseringsstriden.* Master's thesis. University of Oslo, Cultural History.

Kristoffersen, Eirik 2017. *Kampen om Folkeminnesamlingen. Da folkeminnene ble et forskningsfelt og folket krevde dem tilbake.* NFL 172. Oslo: Scandinavian Academic Press.

Kurki, Tuulikki 2002. *Heikki Meriläinen ja keskusteluja kansanperinteestä.* (Summary: Heikki Meriläinen and discussions on folklore). Helsinki: Finnish Literature Society.

Kverndokk, Kyrre 2011. "Han ligner litt på nissen igrunn." Folkloristiske forestillinger om folketro. In Line Esborg, Kyrre Kverndokk & Leiv Sem (eds), *Or gamalt – nye perspektiver på folkeminner.* NFL 165. Oslo: Norsk Folkeminnelag, Instituttet for sammenlignende kulturforskning, 70–95.

Landstad, Magnus Brostrup 1968 [1853]. *Norske Folkeviser.* Oslo: Norsk Folkeminnelag, Universitetsforlaget.

Liestøl, Knut 1914. Um innsamling av norske folketraditionar. *Maal og minne* 1914: 113–122.

Lilja, Agneta 1996. *Föreställningen om den ideala uppteckningen. En studie av idé och praktik vid traditionssamlande arkiv. Ett exempel från Uppsala 1914–1945.* (The Notion of the Ideal Record: A study of Idea and Practice at Tradition-Collecting Archives: A Case from Uppsala 1914–1945). Uppsala: Dialekt- och folkminnesarkivet i Uppsala.

Moe, Jørgen 1988 [1840]. *Samling af Sange, Folkeviser og Stev i Norske Almuedialekter.* NFL 132. Oslo: Norsk Folkeminnelag.

Nilsson, Bo G. 1996. *Folkhemmets arbetarminnen: En undersökning av de historiska och diskursiva vilkoren för svenska arbetares levnadsskildringar.* Stockholm: Nordiska Museets.

Norsk allkunnebok 1949. Sjur Hansson Bøyum. In vol. II. Oslo: Fonna Forlag, 740.

Nyvang, Caroline 2013. Syn for sagn. Tre fotografiske dokumentationsprojekter, 1895–1927. *Tidsskrift for kulturforskning* 12 (1): 5–22.

Ong, Walter 1988 [1982]. *Orality and Literacy: The Technologizing of the Word.* New York: Routledge.

Rogan, Bjarne 2013. Instituttet for sammenlignende kulturforskning. In Anne Eriksen & Bjarne Rogan (eds), *Etnologi og folkloristikk. En fagkritisk biografi om norsk kulturhistorie.* Oslo: Novus forlag, 645–668.

Skott, Fredrik 2008. *Folkets minnen. Traditionsinsamling i idé och praktik 1919–1964.* Göteborg: Institutet för språk och folkminnen, Göteborgs Universitet.

Telste, Kari 2013. Rigmor Frimannslund (1911–2006). In Anne Eriksen & Bjarne Rogan (eds), *Etnologi og folkloristikk. En fagkritisk biografi om norsk kulturhistorie.* Oslo: Novus forlag, 185–198.

Visted, Kristoffer 1923. *Vor gamle bondekultur.* Ny forøket utgave. Kristiania: Cappelen.

von Sydow, Carl Wilhelm 1915. *Folkminnena och deras insamling.* Folkminnen och Folktankars skriftserie 2. Lund: Folkminnen och Folktankar.

von Sydow, Carl Wilhelm 1916. *Våra folkminnen och betydelsen av deras insamling.* Stenstorp: Särtryck ur Skaraborgs Läns Folkhögskolas i Stenstorp Redogörelse.

von Sydow, Carl Wilhelm 1918. *Samla folkminnen! Ett förslag och en vädjan.* Malmö: Ur folkminnen & folktankar.

von Sydow, Carl Wilhelm 1919. *Våra folkminnen. En populär framställning.* Lund: Domförlaget.

KIRSTI SALMI-NIKLANDER
http://orcid.org/0000-0003-0552-1801

Ideals, Practices and Debates Related to Oral Tradition in 19th-Century Finnish Student Culture

University students in 19th-century Finland played a crucial role in collecting folklore and establishing folklore studies as an academic discipline. However, few researchers have focused on discussions and practices related to folklore materials in student communities. My aim in this article is to explore the ideals, practices and debates related to the oral tradition in 19th-century provincial student organizations [*osakunta*, or "nation" in Swedish], focusing on the Western Finnish and Savo-Karelian provincial organizations [*Länsisuomalainen/Savokarjalainen osakunta*]. The material for this analysis was obtained from the large and well-preserved archives at the National Library.

The article is based on my long-term research project on hand-written newspapers and other examples of the oral-literary tradition in 19th- and early-20th-century Finland. I have explored oral-literary traditions in different conversational communities of young adults covering a time range from the 1850s to the 1920s. The communities include provincial student societies [*osakunta*], temperance and agrarian youth societies [*raittiusseura, nuorisoseura*] and working-class youth organizations.[1]

The student culture provides material for analysing the interaction between printed, manuscript and oral media. Because of the unstable political situation in Europe after the revolutionary year of 1848, student activities were strictly controlled by the Russian authorities. Publishing in print was difficult, therefore students discussed and disseminated their ideas via manuscript media and oral performance. The revolutionary movements in Europe in 1848 put Czar Nicholas I on the alert, which resulted in the strict censorship and prohibition of student organizations. The most extreme measure was the language statute of 1850, according to which the only materials that could be published in the Finnish language were religious books and practical advice to farmers. This was a serious challenge to the

---

1 See Salmi-Niklander 2006; 2013; 2014b; 2017. Oral-literary local tradition here means the expressive genres that involved both oral and written communication. Another key term in my research is conversational community, which means a group of people who in close interaction create, adapt and interpret texts presented in oral and literary form. (Salmi-Niklander 2013, 78–79.)

Swedish-speaking or bilingual intelligentsia in their attempts to disseminate nationalistic ideas to the common people. The statute was repealed in 1860. Provincial student organizations were prohibited in 1852. They were legalized in 1868, although many of them had continued their activities unofficially. (Kirby 2006, 101–102; Klinge 1967a, 135–136.)

Students in the 1850s revitalized hand-written newspapers as a means of serious political discussion. They were usually published as a single copy, but reached quite large audiences: being read out aloud at meetings was a form of distribution. As historian Matti Klinge pointed out, a hand-written student paper that was read aloud to 100–400 people could, in fact, reach an audience comparable to the readership of *Litteraturbladet*, the only literary journal to be published in Finland during the 1850s. Moreover, the readers and listeners could discuss issues immediately, whereas readers of print copies were scattered around the country. (Klinge 1967b, 11.) Hand-written newspapers remained a strong student tradition until the beginning of the 20th century.

As well as collecting folklore materials from the rural population, students documented their own oral traditions, songs and jokes in hand-written newspapers. However, these two traditions were separate: students did not donate collections of their own tradition to the Finnish Literature Society, but they kept their own records. These records included pieces of paper of various sizes, which were used as scripts for performances during students' social evenings.

In what follows I will explore the ideals, practices and debates related to the oral tradition in 19th-century student organizations that played a crucial role in the development of folklore archives and scholarship. I will focus on two provincial student societies. The first is the Western Finnish *osakunta*, which promoted the folklore-collecting tours of Berndt August Paldani in 1851–1852. This collection has played a significant role in Finnish folklore scholarship. The second society is the Savo-Karelian *osakunta*, in which the folklore-collecting activities were the strongest. The "nation" was a very lively intellectual community in the 1880s. New liberal ideas about the cause of women, socialism and realism provoked lively debates in the community, and most members supported the extreme Fennomanian K.P.T. movement[2]. It was during these years and in this community that the foundations of scholarship related to Finnish Folklore Studies and scholarship were laid. Kaarle Krohn, the first professor in Folklore Studies, was an active member of the society and it was on his initiative that the Savo-Karelian *osakunta* promoted projects involving the collecting, archiving and publishing of folklore materials. However, the oral tradition also provoked debate, and was used in various textual genres, often with ironic or parodic overtones.

I will consider the materials of these Finnish student organizations from three perspectives. First, from the perspective of folklore studies the student materials provide information on the practices and debates related to the

---

2   K.P.T. was an acronym with several interpretations: Kansan Pyhä Tahto [People's Holy Will], Koko Programmi Toimeen [The Whole Programme into Action] or Kaikki Punaiset Toverit [All the Red Comrades]. (Ruutu 1939, 206–223).

creation of folklore scholarship and archival collections. Second, from the historical perspective, Finnish student culture and other conversational communities of young adults provide interesting examples of the interaction among oral, manuscript and print media, which Robert Darnton (2000) and Margaret Ezell (1999), among others, studied in material from the 17th and 18th centuries.

Third, from the oral-history perspective, student culture provides materials on the writing of the group's history, and on the use of oral-history materials in this process. It became common practice in student organizations during the 19th century for somebody (often a history student) to write an annual historical record of the society based on written documents, observation and oral records. Oral presentations such as speeches were sometimes included in these histories word for word. (Salmi-Niklander 2006; 2013.) Examples such as these show that oral history certainly did not start with the invention of the tape recorder.

Kaukomieli *and Berndt Paldani's folklore-collecting journeys*

The folklore-collecting activities of the Western Finnish *osakunta* are depicted in the manuscript charting its history from 1822–1868, written by Rufus Saikku. It was probably written in the 1870s or 1880s, and Saikku cites many original sources. Antero Warelius (1821–1904) had a very strong influence on the nationalistic and folklore-collecting activities in the *osakunta*. He was from quite a modest background, born into a large peasant family in Tyrvää, but because of his talent and hard work he could continue his studies at university. He published a popular book, *Enon opetuksia* ["Uncles's teachings"], in 1845 in which he discusses natural science in the form of a dialogue. The book was circulated among students of the *osakunta* during the Christmas holidays and it sold very well. According to Rufus Saikku, Antero Warelius was both surprised and pleased about the amount of money his friends brought to him after the holidays.

Antero Warelius was in close contact with some young men in the Savo-Karelian *osakunta*, which was very active in collecting folklore. Together with August Ahlqvist, D.E.D. Europaeus and Paavo Tikkanen he founded a society for the advancement of the Finnish language among students. They also founded a long-lived and very influential newspaper *Suometar* in 1847. (Sulkunen 2004, 86.)

Antero Warelius, who had already graduated from university, was working as a priest in his home parish in 1851, but many younger students supported his initiative on folklore collecting. D.E.D. Europaeus gave a speech supporting these activities in the same meeting in November 1851 at which the first issue of *Kaukomieli* appeared, and suggested that the *osakunta* should raise money to "save from eternal destruction those pieces of folklore that might still be found in Western Finland". The *osakunta* quickly raised 76 rubles, which enabled Berndt August Paldani (1823–1860), a theology student, to make two folklore-collecting journeys to Ylöjärvi, Virrat, Ruovesi, Ikaalinen, Parkano and Kuru, the first one during the

113

Christmas holidays in 1851–1852 and the second in April 1852. He collected a considerable amount of fairy tales, riddles, proverbs, folk songs and poetry written in the Kalevala metre, which he reports in detail in his account. This collection made a significant contribution to Finnish folklore studies in proving that poetry in the Kalevala metre was also preserved in Western Finland. His collection of fairy tales has been influential in furthering research on this folkloristic genre.

Berndt Paldani described his field trip in a five-part travel story in *Kaukomieli*, a hand-written newspaper of which 28 issues were published between 11 November 1851 and the end of 1852, when student nations were prohibited. These travelogues appeared in print in 1904 in A.R. Niemi's anthology containing travel stories of folklore collectors.

The first part of Paldani's travel story covers his journey to his "field". He was travelling with a few other male students, first by horse and cart and then by sleigh, from Helsinki towards Tampere and from one inn to another. The narrator merges into the group of travelling companions and does not single out his own emotions and experiences. A major turning point came in Tampere, when the narrator continued on his journey alone towards his field and his great folklore-collecting mission. From here on he had to proceed and make decisions on his own, which was not very easy in the middle of winter in the countryside. At a farmhouse he hires a farm-hand to take him across a lake to a neighbouring village. This trip was an initiation of a kind, into Paldani's field: the farm-hand takes him on a breath-taking sleigh ride over the lake on ice that was still quite thin, and amuses him during the journey with "mostly very ugly and obscene" folk tales and legends. (Salmi-Niklander 2013, 1150–1153.)

In 2008, I gave a course for students in Folklore Studies (University of Helsinki) on oral traditions in 19th-century student culture. The students wrote essays in which they compared Berndt August Paldani's fieldwork stories with his folklore collections. They could link some fairy tales, songs and proverbs in Paldani's collection to lively storytelling situations, which he depicts in his travel tales. The students also noted Paldani's controversial relationship with oral traditions and literacy processes. On the one hand, he seeks the oral tradition, but on the other hand he praises the modernization and civilization he observes in the countryside: common people ordering and reading newspapers (*Suometar*), and the high rate of reading skills among the rural population. On his travels, he met various self-educated writers who sent their manuscripts to the Finnish Literature Society: one of them was Michael Hellen, a self-educated poet Paldani refers to as "*lauluseppä*", literally a "song-smith", a term that was in common use for peasant poets. One of Paldani's influential contacts was Joose Westerbacka from Karvia, whom he describes as "a genius", a literate man who later sent him collections of proverbs and riddles to be donated to Finnish Literature Society.

Paldani made his folklore-collecting journey on his own, which was quite exceptional. His great idols, Elias Lönnrot and Antero Warelius, were from quite modest artisan and peasant backgrounds. He was an officer's son from Virrat, which made his role as a folklore collector more contentious.

However, his Finnish was fluent. Berndt August Paldani experienced the classic phases of anthropological field work although he was travelling in his own home region. Many people living in rural areas ridiculed him, or were suspicious of him. Joose Westerbacka became his key informant, telling him about the suspicions of country people: some old women had suspected him of being a spy who would pass on information to the officials about religious superstitions in the countryside. Westerbacka defended him, but also made him conscious of these suspicions. Eventually Paldani learned to deal with the situation and things were much easier during his second trip: people were friendly and eager to speak to him, and even the girls looked pretty with their red cheeks. Paldani reflects on this in the fourth part of his travel stories: "Why is my collecting more successful now than in winter? It's because I'm more used to doing my work, and the common people no longer see it as something strange. What else? In the Winter I said almost everywhere I'll come again, keep your stories in your memory, when they complained they had forgotten them".[3] This comment has an ambiguous reference to writing: Paldani's advice "laittakaa juttunne muistoon" could be translated as either "keep your stories in your memory" or "write your stories down".

Peasant poets and writers could get their voices heard directly in *Kaukomieli*, which published two poems of the peasant poet Antti Puhakka, "The Birds' Counsel" ["Lintujen neuvonta"] and "Song of Sorrow" ["Surulaulu"], on 25 November 1851 (Kuismin 2012.) Antti Puhakka was one of the three peasant poets from Eastern Finland who were invited to Helsinki 1845 as honorary guests of Savo-Karelian *osakunta*. (Sulkunen 2004, 86.) However, *Kaukomieli* was a bilingual journal: the other half of the contents were essays, stories and poems written in Swedish. Many of these reflected the political controversies related to the Fennoman movement and the future of the Swedish language and Swedish-speaking population in Finland, but some were romantic or humorous depictions of student life.

The Savo-Karelian osakunta: *Liberal ideas and folklore collecting in the 1880s*

The second case study concerns the Savo-Karelian *osakunta*, in which the folklore-collecting activities were strongest. The hand-written newspaper *Savo-Karjalainen* was first published in 1864, and the oral tradition was a vital part of its contents during the first decades. Each issue included a "folklore column" featuring materials collected on field trips to Eastern Finland. Most

3   Berndt August Paldani, Letter from Ikaalinen, 15 April 1852: Published *Kaukomieli* 15, 27 April 1852.
"Mutta mintähden menestyypi kerääminen paremmin nyt, kun talvella? Sentähden, että minä olen tottunut asiani toimittamaan paremmin, ja rahvas ei tätä enää pidä ihmeenä. Mitä vielä – talvella sanelin mennessäni melkein joka paikassa: vielä tulen, laittakaa juttunne muistoon, kun valittivat muistosta pois menneen." All translations by Kirsti Salmi-Niklander.

of these were folk songs in the round [*"piirileikkilaulu"*]. The first issue dated 5 October 1864 included the following contextual information:

> Once in Savo when the country people were singing in the round, I heard songs that I would like to have a better fate than to be forgotten. Moreover, I think these are typical of Finnish people and I haven't come across any of them in any printed poetry collection. This song has its own melody, which is not bad.[4]

Bilingual student traditions were also documented in the paper, in Swedish and Finnish (songs, anecdotes, parodic news and advertisements), in a section entitled "Bugge Bugge". The anecdotes tended to depict comic situations in which Swedish-speaking officials attempted to explain official issues to Finnish-speaking peasants, leading to comic misunderstandings. Anecdotes supported the agenda of Fennomanian students, which promoted equal rights for the Finnish language. The third element referring to the oral tradition comprised translations of folklore-related materials. The first issue also included Finnish translations of "Fairy tales of Christ" (legends) from Bohemia.[5] These legends combine fairy-tale and legend motifs: the story "Proud shepherd girl" ["Ylpeä paimentyttö"], is about a shepherd girl who refuses to give water to an old man. The man turns her and her herd into white stones. "The Old man was Lord Jesus, who hates all proud souls".

The same translations of Bohemian fairy tales appeared in print a few years later in the first volume of the printed album *Koitar*, which was published by Savo-Karelian *osakunta* in six volumes in 1870–1899. These albums include materials adapted from the oral tradition, both in fictional stories and in accounts of local history and traditions. One of travel stories written by the pen-name A.Hm. (K.A. Hällström)[6] was published in the third *Koitar* album in 1880. It was based on the journey he made with A. Borenius in 1877 collecting folklore and folk music in the parishes of Liperi and Polvijärvi in Northern Karelia. This travel story reflects the changing attitudes to folklore and traditional folk music in the Finnish countryside: young people were only interested in "modern" rhymed folk songs. The two travellers eventually find a fine old *kantele* hanging on the wall in a farmhouse, but the master of the house shows his contempt for this instrument and threatens to throw it against the wall. They manage to buy it for the modest sum of 20 pennies. They find another old man who can sing many songs written by peasant poets, but all of them have the same melody.

My research on the Savo-Karelian *osakunta* focuses on the 1880s, during which time it was a very lively intellectual community. Provincial student

4 "Savossa kerran rahvaan rinkisillä ollessa, kuulin laulettavan wirsiä, joille soisin paremman kohtalon kuin unohtuksiin jäännön. Semminkin kun luulen näitä Suomen kansan ihan ominaisiksi, ja kuin yhtään näistä en ole tavannut missään painetussa runokokouksessa, niin tulkoon eräs näistä täten ilmi. Tällä laululla on oman nuottinsakin, joka ei ole huonompia."

5 The fact that legends have been translated from German folk tales is only indicated in the list of contents for *Savo-Karjalainen*.

6 Real names of writers with pen-names are indicated in inscriptions in *Koitar*-volumes at the library of Finnish Literature Society.

organizations were legal again, and students could publish printed albums and contribute to printed newspapers and journals. However, hand-written student newspapers were still an influential medium: editorial positions were highly competitive, and some individual essays raised heated debate. The ideals of realistic literature gave a new impetus to the oral tradition, which was followed as an integral element of the fictional stories published in printed albums and hand-written newspapers. More students were recruited from the rural lower classes during this decade, when the folklore-collecting projects of the Finnish Literature Society expanded considerably, and a network of collectors was formed that included many self-educated people from the countryside (Mikkola 2013). Initiated by Eliel Aspelin and, later, Kaarle Krohn, the folklore collecting focused on folk tales and fairy tales, as well as on folk songs, charms and proverbs. (Ruutu 1939, 329–342; Sulkunen 2004, 200–201.)

Savo-Karjalainen included submissions in both Finnish and Swedish during the 1860s, but the Finnish language dominated both official and informal student activities in the 1880s. "The Oxen Boy" ["Härkäpoika"; a pseudonym] makes an appearance in *Savo-Karjalainen* on 4 October 1882, recalling his first experiences as a newcomer and a young man from the countryside in Helsinki, which he calls "Babylon". Among the tall buildings he finds out that his own language is not understood. Walking into the university and going to a student meeting fail to meet his great expectations: the speeches reflect the grand ideals of patriotism and nobleness of character, but the informal socializing among students is a disappointment. He finds the superficial informality of his fellow students, and above all the singing of "Swedish trash songs" instead of Finnish folk songs, irritating. "He wonders what might be the reason for this: perhaps a Finn should not listen to those songs, or perhaps they are just trash, and can't be sung in Finnish".[7]

The establishment of academic Folklore Studies in Finland was closely linked with the Savo-Karelian *osakunta* in that Kaarle Krohn was one of the active members. In the early 1880s he promoted projects involving the collecting, archiving and publishing of folklore materials, above all fairy tales and folk tales. The archives of the Savo-Karelian *osakunta* provide evidence of the debate about projects such as collecting and publishing folklore materials. In 1881, students P.J. Hannikainen (who became a well-known composer) and K. Bäckström initiated the publishing of folk songs collected on fieldwork trips organized by the Savo-Karelian *osakunta*. However, they suggested that new lyrics should be written because "the words in the songs collected from the common people nowadays are low-grade in both form and content". Two collections of folksongs with traditional melodies but mostly new lyrics were published 1881 and 1886, under the title *Uusi Kannel Karjalasta* I–II [New Kantele from Karelia I–II]. Many songs in these collections became very popular. (Ruutu 1939, 249–251.)

---

7 "Siinä hän sitten aprikoi syytä tuohon, ja kohta pälkähtää päähänsä, että nuo laulut lienevät semmoisia, joita ei suomalainen saa kuulla, tai ovat ne sitten roskaa, jot'ei suomeksi viitsitä eikä osatakaan laulaa."

Even though the lyrics of contemporary folk songs were considererd low-grade, late-19th-century students appreciated peasant poets of the earlier generation: an anthology of poems by eighteen peasant poets, edited by Kustavi Grotenfelt, was published by the Finnish Literature Society in 1889. In the preface Grotenfelt cites Elias Lönnrot, who defended peasant poets in his literary periodical *Mehiläinen* (February 1840). For one thing, Lönnrot considered the Finnish language of the peasant poets more pure and beautiful than the Finnish used by the originally Swedish-speaking intelligentsia. Second, Grotenfelt reminds readers that peasant poets depict the minds and lives of the common people much better than educated men, who are estranged from rural life, do. He also mentions the peasant poets' literary achievements, linking them with the new generation of Finnish writers from modest rural backgrounds. They wrote realistic prose rather than poems, but nevertheless Grotenfelt praises their achievements. He provides information about the poets, and gives long citations from their poems. (*Kahdeksantoista runoniekkaa* 1889.)

Kaarle Krohn encouraged (even put pressure on) his fellow students to collect folk tales in their home regions during their holidays. Some of them were enthusiastic about this, whereas others were more sceptical. Among the latter was A(ugust) B(ernhard) Mäkelä, who later became a socialist journalist and together with his fellow student Matti Kurikka founded the Utopian socialist community of Sointula in British Columbia. A.B. Mäkelä commented in a somewhat ironic manner on Krohn's projects in his 1883 history of the *osakunta*: "I cannot say if other members of the *osakunta* returned from their Christmas holidays as empty-handed as yours truly did, but at least the purpose was good".[8] Grants were given to many students to collect information on oral and material traditions in their home region during the summer holidays: the focus was on folklore, ethnological information and objects. This was how many poor students survived the summer holidays, but apparently, many of them never provided the expected materials.

A project involving the collecting and publishing of folk tales was established in November 1883, on Kaarle Krohn's suggestion, to be led by three students: Kaarle Krohn, Kustavi Grotenfelt and Pekka Hartikainen. Apparently, it never produced concrete results. Krohn and Grotenfelt became established scholars in Folklore Studies and History, but the third member, Pekka Hartikainen was to be the "legendary loser" of his generation. However, his memory lived on among his peers, who reflected on it soon after his early death 1889 and again many decades later when Martti Ruutu collected material for the history of the Savo-Karelian *osakunta*, published in 1939. (Ruutu 1939, 316–318.)

Pekka Hartikainen (1861–1889) was born in Rantasalmi, Eastern Finland in 1861, where his father was a gravedigger, and later a farmer and a house-owner. Pekka matriculated from the boys' secondary school in Kuopio in 1880 and soon started his studies at the University of Helsinki, supported by

---

8 "En voi sanoa tulivatko muutkin osakuntalaiset joululuvalta yhtä tyhjinä kuin alle-kirjoittanut, vaan tarkoitus ainakin oli hyvä."

some wealthier relatives. He never graduated, although he pursued studies in various humanities subjects. He is depicted in the stories of his peers as a talented, promising and popular student, and he was praised for some of the short stories he published in student albums. However, he could not withstand the temptations of student life, alcohol and debt. He left Helsinki for the countryside in 1887, worked as a journalist and contributed to several newspapers, led a restless life and died at the age of 28 in Viipuri in 1889, of either pneumonia or lung disease. (*Ibid.*; Salmi-Niklander 2010; 2014a.)

Pekka Hartikainen did not leave any personal archives or autobiographical notes. I therefore gathered the basic facts about his short life from a few obituaries, the student register of Helsinki University and the archives and printed publications of the Savo-Karelian student organization. Arvid Järnefelt, a well-known writer and Hartikainen's friend during his study years, devoted a whole chapter to him in his autobiographical and family-history novel *Vanhempieni romaani* ("A Novel about my Parents" 1948 [1928–1930], 361–368), and Martti Ruutu discussed his fate in his history of the Savo-Karelian student organization (1939, 316–318).

The key event in Pekka Hartikainen's life story was his first "singing session" at the Old Student House in Helsinki, during his first study year 1880–1881. Arvid Järnefelt gives a dramatic account of this spontaneous session in his autobiographical novel: "The rooms resounded with his singing. The second, the third, the fourth... the seventh verse. The young companions sitting around the tables looked up towards the singer. The words and the melody were familiar to them all. What surprised them was how this folk song from the mighty forest reverberated around these mighty rooms under the decorated columns."[9]

According to Arvid Järnefelt, this was the first of numerous singing sessions that finally sealed Pekka's fate: "He was fed and made drunk, and he fed his audience with his spicy and popular songs and stories". His humour was "very close to irony", which was directed at the intelligentsia and, especially, people who had made fast money and were imitating the upper classes. This also reflected the content of many of the popular songs he performed.

Unfortunately, very little is documented from Pekka Hartikainen's singing sessions. Arvid Järnefelt cites just one verse of the song he sang in the first session:

Many big factory owners
were born in Finland
but few log drivers
live a long life.

9   "Salit kajahtelivat hyvästi. Toinen, kolmas, neljäs... seitsemäs värssy. Nuoret toverit kaikista pöydistä kurkoittivat päätään laulajaa kohden. Sekä sanat että nuotti oli kaikille tuttu. Mutta että tuo salomaiden rekilaulu nyt kajahteli näissä upeissa saleissa ja korupylvästöissä, se oli toki odottamatonta jokaiselle. [--] Laulun kapinoiva tendenssi tuntui näissä saleissa melkein samalta kuin jos joku frakkiin ja valkoisiin hansikkaisiin pukeutunut herrasmies olisi ilmestynyt tänne sontainen talikko kädessä." (Järnefelt 1948 [1928–1930], 361–362).

On noita Suomessa syntynyt
noita suuria patruuneita
mutta harvat on vanhaksi elänyt
noita tukkijunkkareita!

Pekka Hartikainen's last public performances in his student life were in April 1886 during the so-called club evenings, which *Savo-Karjalainen* depicted in much detail. The programme of these evenings consisted of short, humorous pieces called "surprises". One of them was a drag-show-style sketch about a family in which the gender roles are reversed: the father takes care of the home wearing an apron and a bustle, and the mother and daughter are masculine characters. The daughter is a university student who boozes from the bottle. (*Savo-Karjalainen*, 10 April 1886). Even though women were not admitted to the university until the 1890s, gender roles were intensely discussed among the male students.

Pekka Hartikainen's was not a unique case: many students from both wealthy and poor families never graduated, consumed too much alcohol and spent their money on various amusements in the notorious quarters of Helsinki. The special expression in Helsinki student slang for this phenomenon was (and still is) "*olla deekiksellä*" ["in the gutter"]: it originates from Stockholm slang and the English word "decadence". The sons of wealthy families who were "*deekiksellä*" could get some nominal job in state administration or in a family enterprise, or they lived on inherited money. The peasant students had no easy way out of the gutter, most of them having to borrow money on which to live and with little or no social support from their families. As Arvid Järnefelt (1948 [1928–1930], 367) points out in his novel, peasant students were not used to consuming alcohol in the same manner as the sons of wealthy families.

The oral tradition, dialect stories and realistic prose

Materials related to the oral tradition played a different role in *Savo-Karjalainen* in the 1880s than in the earlier issues of the 1860s. Replacing the separate "folklore columns" are motifs and plots embedded in humorous textual genres. These texts take an ironic step back from the oral tradition rather than celebrate its cultural value. "Pekka the Trickster's Pranks" ["Peijari-Pekan kujeet"] was a two-part story in *Savo-Karjalainen* (8 February and 8 March 1882), with the subtitle "Adapted from a folk tale" ["Mukaelma kansansadusta"]. The author was probably Pekka Hartikainen, who was an active editor of the paper in those years and often used the pen-name "Pekka". The story belongs to the genre of "Numskull tales", in which stupid people are fooled by a skillful trickster. This is not a dialect story, even though the narrative style follows the oral tradition.

Another interesting genre in *Savo-Karjalainen* is the simple, popular poem imitating the style of popular broadsheets with a focus on melodramatic love stories and violent crimes. An example is a poem entitled "A new and enlightening tale of Pekka Pursiainen's love affairs in Japan", to which "translated by Uoti" is added (*Savo-Karjalainen*, 10 November 1883). It is about the love affairs and adventures of a Finnish sailor, Pekka Pursiainen. The exotic setting, the awkward rhymes and the occasional Swedish word support the interpretation that the text is parodic:

Olj merimiesi ennen
Iloinen vekkuli;
Hän Japanihin mennen
Rakastui, seikkaili.

Once there was a seaman
A merry fellow;
He went to Japan,
Made love and had adventures

Kun kerran satamalla
Hän soutel' illalla,
Niin hellun suudelmalla
Sai Japan' neidolta

Once when he was rowing
around the harbour in the evening
He got a kiss
from a Japanese maiden.

Mut tytöll' ol'kin, näähän,
isänä mandarin,
Kiireestä kantapäähän,
Hän oli hieno, "fin".

But you see, the girl's father
was a Mandarin
Elegant, "fine" [expressed both in Finnish and in Swedish]
From head to toe.

The literary use of dialect required special skills, and people who could write in dialect were highly appreciated. In his guide for collecting folk tales (1885), Kaarle Krohn recommends writers not to attempt to use dialect unless they are familiar with Finnish linguistics. Most stories written in dialect in *Savo-Karjalainen* represented comic genres. The newspaper also sometimes published light-hearted speeches in dialect given on festive occasions and "club evenings" organized by Savo-Karelian *osakunta*.[10] In fact, Pekka Hartikainen won a prize for his short story, "The Czar's Friend", which the literary album published in honour of Elias Lönnrot's 80th birthday in 1882.[11] The story is about a simple peasant, Olli from Hakolahti. He makes acquaintance with the Czar, who behaves in an unpretentious manner. The

10 E.G. "Huiska", 27 October –1 November 1884.
11 *Suomen Ylioppilaskunnan albumi Elias Lönnrotin kunniaksi. Hänen täyttäessään 80 vuotta 9/IV 1882. Helsinki 1882.*

story is written in the third person and in Savo dialect, conveying Olli's naïve images of "The Good Czar" who sits next to him at the table serving liquor, bread and salt, and shows him his fields, houses and "fine war horses".

"The Czar's Friend" bears some resemblance to the family history of Matti Kurikka (1862–1915), who was one of Pekka Hartikainen's close friends and among the leading figures in the Savo-Karelian *osakunta* during the first years of the 1880s (Ruutu 1939, 323–324). He became a well-known and controversial character in Finnish history, and had a long career as a journalist, playwright, socialist agitator and founder of Utopian communities in Australia and British Columbia.[12] He was the son of a wealthy Ingrian peasant from Tuutari near St. Petersburg. His father was, in fact, a friend of Czar Alexander II, who visited his farm now and then. Matti Kurikka and his siblings were sent to school in Helsinki. In 1883, he obtained a scholarship for collecting Ingrian folklore from his home parish of Tuutari. These experiences provided material for his first and most popular dramatic work, *Viimeinen ponnistus* [The Last Struggle, 1883].

Matti Kurikka was bullied because of his "Russian" identity when he was at secondary school in Helsinki (Kalemaa 1978, 28–33). This Russian identity followed him in his future political shipwrecks. He wrote a short story on Ingrian folk life, "How Ingrians propose marriage" ["Kuinka Inkerissä kosissa käydään"], which was published in *Savo-Karjalainen* 29 March 1884. This was the first part of a serial, but apparently, the second part was never published. The story comprises a dialogue between an Ingrian peasant and his wife: they are worried about their son, who spends his time loitering and getting into fights. After blaming each other, they find a solution: the boy should get married to calm him down. A suitable bride is found, a strong girl and a hard worker. The dialogue includes some words in the Ingrian dialect. *Savo-Karjalainen* did publish some stories written entirely in the Karelian or Ingrian dialect, but they merely give a comic and ethnocentric picture of Greek Orthodox Karelians. "A Karelian in a Lutheran Church" (11 October 1884) is a short, anecdotal tale in strong East Karelian dialect, in which the narrator, a Greek Orthodox Karelian, recalls his strange experiences in a Lutheran church: instead of money, he puts some pastry in the offertory bag. When he joins the queue for Holy Communion the priest drags him away forcibly and he is put in the stocks.

Matti Kurikka, A.B. Mäkelä and Pekka Hartikainen were dissidents among their peer group. Kurikka left university and became the editor-in-chief of the newspaper *Wiipurin Sanomat* in 1886. A.B. Mäkelä was his co-worker, and Pekka Hartikainen spent his last years in Viipuri. His obituary in *Wiipurin Sanomat*, 29 September 1889 was written either by A.B. Mäkelä or by Matti Kurikka, who gave a speech at his funeral.

12 Matti Kurikka's life and times are being studied in the research project, "Fragmented visions. Performance, authority and interaction in early 20th-century Finnish oral-literary traditions" (www.fragvis.net), led by Kirsti Salmi-Niklander and funded by the Academy of Finland. See Heimo et al. 2016; Kalemaa 1978.

Forgotten alternatives and hidden power struggles

There are many observable differences between the two case studies, the Western Finnish *osakunta* in the 1850s and the Savo-Karelian *osakunta* in the 1880s. The Fennoman movement had become quite militant by the 1880s, and folklore-collecting activities had been established. The complex relationship between the oral and the literary tradition is evident in both cases. The students were looking for specific genres of the oral tradition on their folklore-collecting journeys. They observed and documented processes of literary and bilingual practice among the common people, which they discussed in the form of anecdotes in their hand-written student papers. Travelogues of folklore collecting journeys were not archived to Finnish Literature Society, but published in hand-written newspapers or printed albums. The oral tradition was intensely present in many genres and practices of student life, and these traditions are documented in archival sources and manuscripts.

The comparison of the manuscripts and printed sources produced by students brings to light the forgotten alternatives and hidden power struggles in the creation of Finnish folklore scholarship. The value of the oral tradition was debated in student societies: some students requested its refinement so that it could be used for artistic or educational purposes, whereas others defended its intrinsic value as an object of scientific study. Students from upper-class or intellectual families differed from those with a poor, rural background in their ideas on the role and value of the oral tradition: the latter had direct access to contemporary traditions in their unrefined form, which had romantic or exotic connotations among upper-class students. Some genres were selected to be documented and studied, but other, contemporary genres were only presented orally or published and discussed in hand-written student papers.

The folklore collectors of the Western Finnish *osakunta* in the 1850s have been recognized as pioneers in folklore scholarship, even though they did not forge a career in this field. Berndt August Paldani died young without knowing how highly his folklore collections would be valued by later generations. Members of the Savo-Karelian *osakunta* in the 1880s had very different career paths. Kaarle Krohn and Kustavi Grotenfelt built excellent academic careers in Folklore Studies and History, and many of their peers became forerunners in their own fields. Matti Kurikka's life could be depicted as a series of political and personal shipwrecks, and politically he ended up on the opposite side from his former friends. The images and verses of the Kalevala followed him for the rest of his life, both in cartoons, in stories written by his enemies and in his own visions: he named one of his Utopian communities *Sammon takojat* [Forgers of the Sampo], and during his last years in the US he was an active member of the Finnish secret order Knights of Kaleva. He is buried in Greenwood Cemetery, Brooklyn, in the same grave as two other Knights of Kaleva, with the symbol of the order engraved on the top.[13]

Pekka Hartikainen lived in the memories of his friends as "a lost promise": when Martti Ruutu interviewed former members of the Savo-Karelian *osakunta* in the 1930s he was depicted as the most talented and promising writer, even though his published texts constitute only a small corpus, and his friends had vivid memories of his "singing sessions". It is unfortunate (although quite understandable) that the folk-tale collection Kaarle Krohn, Kustavi Grotenfelt and Pekka Hartikainen were supposed to edit never materialised. They probably had very different ideas about it. However, lost and forgotten alternatives have had their effect on the scholarly practices and theoretical frameworks that have been accepted over time. The analysis of oral, manuscript and printed sources brings to light the dialogic process in which Finnish folklore scholarship and archival practices were created.

References

Archival sources

Archives of Savo-Karelian provincial student society [*Savokarjalainen osakunta*], National Library
    Savo-Karjalainen, hand-written newspaper
    Manuscript annual history records

Archives of Western Finnish provincial student society [*Länsisuomalainen osakunta*], National Library
    Kaukomieli, hand-written newspaper 1851–1852
    Saikku, Rufus. Manuscript history of the Western Finnish student society

Unpublished sources

Student essays: "Representations of oral tradition and the 19th-century student culture", spring term 2008, University of Helsinki. In the author's possession.

Literature

Darnton, Robert 2000. An Early Information Society: News and the Media in Eighteenth-Century Paris. *The American Historical Review* 105 (1): 1–35.
Ezell, Margaret 1999. *Social Authorship and the Advent of Print*. Baltimore: Johns Hopkins University Press.

13 *Kalevan ritarit* [Knights of Kaleva], was a secret society of Finnish immigrants, which was founded in 1898 in Belt, Montana. It became popular among Finnish immigrants and still functions in Finnish immigrant communities in the U.S. The society was ideologically conservative, but also tolerant to different opinions. See Koivukangas 2008; Heimo et al. 2016.

Grotenfelt, Kustavi (ed.) 1889. *Kahdeksantoista runoniekkaa*. Helsinki: Finnish Literature Society. Available from
http://neba.finlit.fi/kirjasto/digi/index.php?%20pagename=teokset-nimio&set=954

Heimo, Anne, Mikko Pollari, Anna Rajavuori, Kirsti Salmi-Niklander, Mikko-Olavi Seppälä & Sami Suodenjoki 2016. Matti Kurikka – A prophet in his own country and abroad. *Siirtolaisuus/Migration* 43 (3): 6–10.

Järnefelt, Arvid 1948 [1928–1930]. *Vanhempieni romaani I–III*. Second edition. Porvoo: WSOY.

Kalemaa, Kalevi 1978. *Matti Kurikka. Legenda jo eläessään*. Porvoo: WSOY.

Kirby, David 2006. *A Concise History of Finland*. Cambridge: Cambridge University Press.

Klinge, Matti 1967a. *Ylioppilaskunnan historia. Ensimmäinen osa 1828–1852*. Porvoo: WSOY.

Klinge, Matti 1967b. *Ylioppilaskunnan historia. Toinen osa 1853–1871*. Porvoo: WSOY.

Koitar. Savo-Karjalaisen osakunnan albumi III. Helsinki: Savo-karjalainen osakunta, 1880.

Koivukangas, Olavi 2008. Siirtolaiset veivät Kalevalan mukanaan maailmalle. *Siirtolaisuus/Migration* 35 (1): 1–6.

Kuismin, Anna 2012. Building the Nation, Lighting the Torch: Excursions into the Writings of the Common People in Nineteenth-Century Finland. *Journal of Finnish Studies* 16 (1): 5–24.

Mikkola, Kati 2013. Self-Taught Collectors of Folklore and their Challenge to Archival Authority. In Anna Kuismin & M.J. Driscoll (eds), *White Field, Black Seeds: Nordic Literacy Practices in the Long Nineteenth Century*. Helsinki: Finnish Literature Society, 146–157.

Niemi, A.R. 1904. *Runonkerääjiemme matkakertomuksia 1830-luvulta 1880-luvulle*. Suomalaisen Kirjallisuuden Seuran Toimituksia 109. Helsinki: Finnish Literature Society.

Ruutu, Martti 1939. *Savo-karjalaisen osakunnan historia II. 1857–1887*. Porvoo: WSOY.

Salmi-Niklander, Kirsti 2006. Tapahtuma, kokemus ja kerronta. In Outi Fingerroos, Riina Haanpää, Anne Heimo & Ulla-Maija Peltonen (eds), *Muistitietotutkimus. Metodologisia kysymyksiä*. Tietolipas 214. Helsinki: Finnish Literature Society, 199–220.

Salmi-Niklander, Kirsti 2010. Menetetty sankaruus. Mahdollisuuksien retoriikkaa. In Ilona Kemppainen & Ulla-Maija Peltonen (eds), *Kirjoituksia sankaruudesta*. Helsinki: Finnish Literature Society, 288–324.

Salmi-Niklander, Kirsti 2013. Monologic, Dialogic, Collective: The Modes of Writing in Hand-Written Newspapers in 19th- and Early 20th-Century Finland. In Anna Kuismin & M.J. Driscoll (eds), *White Field, Black Seeds: Nordic Literacy Practices in the Long Nineteenth Century*. Helsinki: Finnish Literature Society, 76–88.

Salmi-Niklander, Kirsti 2014a. Kansankirjailija ja talonpoikaisylioppilas. Vertaileva elämäkerta myyttejä purkamassa. In Heini Hakosalo, Seija Jalagin, Marianne Junila & Heidi Kurvinen (eds), *Historiallinen elämä. Biografia ja historiantutkimus*. Helsinki: Finnish Literature Society, 223–239.

Salmi-Niklander, Kirsti 2014b. Adventurers, Flâneurs, and Agitators: Travel Stories as Means for Marking and Transgressing Boundaries in 19th and Early 20th Century Finland. *Culture Unbound: Journal of Current Cultural Research* 6 (2): 1145–1164. Available from http://www.cultureunbound.ep.liu.se/v6/a63/

Salmi-Niklander, Kirsti 2017. Small stories, trivial events – and strong emotions: Local event narratives in hand-written newspapers as negotiation of individual and collective experiences. In Monika Tasa, Ergo-Hart Västrik & Anu Kannike (eds), *Body, Personhood and Privacy: Perspectives on Cultural Other and Human Experience*. Approaches to Culture Theory 7. Tartu: University of Tartu Press, 163–178.

Sulkunen, Irma 2004. *Suomalaisen Kirjallisuuden Seura 1831–1892*. Helsinki: Finnish Literature Society.

Suomen Ylioppilaskunnan albumi Elias Lönnrotin kunniaksi. Hänen täyttäessään 80 vuotta 9/IV 1882. Helsinki: Suomen ylioppilaskunta, 1882.

Uusi kannel Karjalasta, soitto sointuva Savosta. 1. Uusia suomalaisia kansanlauluja Savokarjalaisen osakunnan kokoelmasta mieskvartetille. Adapted by R. Faltin. Helsinki: Savo-Karjalais-osakunta, 1881.

Uusi kannel Karjalasta, soitto sointuva Savosta. 2. Uusia suomalaisia kansanlauluja Savo-Karjalaisen osakunnan keräyttämiä yksinlaululle ja seka-ääniselle köörille. Adapted by Ilmari Krohn. Porvoo: WSOY, 1886.

Wiipurin Sanomat 29 September 1889, Pekka Hartikainen's Obituary. Available from https://digi.kansalliskirjasto.fi/sanomalehti/binding/480224?page=2&term=Hartikainen

Wiipurin Sanomat 3 October 1889, News on Pekka Hartikainen's funeral. Available from https://digi.kansalliskirjasto.fi/sanomalehti/binding/480877?page=2&term=Hartikaista&term=Hartikaisen

Diarmuid Ó Giolláin

Books, Manuscripts and Orality: Notes on Reading, Writing and Narrating in Irish

In a 1937 lecture on the Irish Folklore Commission, of which he was director, Séamus Ó Duilearga (J.H. Delargy, 1899–1980) noted that the material lodged in the Commission's archives had been faithfully recorded from illiterate informants. His staff, he said, respected the integrity of this material and did not change or edit it in any way: "...we consider ourselves not as creators or adapters, but as literary executors of earlier generations". Stressing the remarkable continuity in the Gaelic[1] tradition from a medieval aristocratic culture, he explained that after the destruction of the native elite in the 16th and 17th centuries the common people saved "in spite of all persecution some of the culture of the upper classes and admitted it into their age-old treasury of oral tradition". Thus "a large part of our medieval literature exists in oral form..." (Ó Duilearga 1943, 12).

In a later lecture, Ó Duilearga argued that "Irish literature, both written and oral, must be studied as a continuous whole", that each had considerable influence on the other "while, in more recent times, the paper manuscripts of the seventeenth to nineteenth centuries have exercised a greater influence than has hitherto been suspected on Gaelic oral literature" (Delargy 1969 [1945], 30). He noted that the compilation of manuscript miscellanies continued until the beginning of the 20th century in a few places.

In this last stage of the tradition the orthography had reached the lowest ebb, the manuscript being written in a barbarous spelling based on the local form of English. The poor scholars[2] had gone; the small farmers and cottiers were now

---

1   Gaelic refers to a branch of the Celtic languages spoken in Ireland, Scotland and the Isle of Man – Irish (Gaelic), Scottish Gaelic and Manx – and to the cultures associated with those languages.

2   The Poor Scholar [scoláire bocht] is described in Fr Dinneen's dictionary (1927, 980) as "a class of itinerant students dependent on the ready hospitality of those near his educational centre" up to the middle of the 19th century. This was usually a "hedge school". From the late 17th until the mid-19th centuries, owing to the anti-Catholic Penal Laws and their aftermath, such fee-paying schools, run in a clandestine fashion in makeshift premises (hence "hedge schools"), provided the main means of education especially to rural Catholics. They were often taught by Gaelic poets and scribes.

the scribes, and into these miscellanies they wrote, or had written by people no better educated than themselves, the Ossianic ballads and tales for which they hungered. These poor tattered copy-books mark the end of a continuous literary tradition; they are the last link in the long chain of Gaelic literature which stretches back unbroken for over twelve hundred years... (Delargy 1969 [1945], 27–28.)

Ó Duilearga's notion of an oral culture was strongly influenced by literary models, and by his own philological and literary training.

These old tradition-bearers, like the old manuscripts, are libraries in themselves. Questioning them, we can turn over page after page in their capacious memories, and listen to what we would have told, whether it be a heroic tale, a place-name legend such as we have in the *Dindshenchas*[3], a religious tale which might have come from a saint's life, a *fabliau*, a *cante-fable*, a collection of aphorisms, genealogies of local families, and so on. (*Ibid.*, 8.)

While the negative assessment of this last stage in manuscript culture is part of the cultural pessimism that characterized much of Ó Duilearga's writing on the Gaelic tradition (and can probably be traced back to Ernest Renan's 1854 essay "La Poésie des races celtiques"), the interplay between Gaelic learned and oral tradition is well known, as well as the continuity between them. There is plenty of evidence of continuity of topics, themes and personages from medieval literature to the modern folk tradition in Irish; several studies treating such topics have indeed appeared (see, for example, Müller-Lisowski 1948, and Ó Crualaoich 2006). Folklore studies, drawing on antiquarianism, Celtic philology and the literary engagement of Ireland's Anglo-Irish elite with the peasantry, became an important part of the activities of the cultural revival begun in the late 19th century, and was institutionalized in the Irish Folklore Institute (1930–1935) and in the Irish Folklore Commission (1935–1970), supported by the Irish state established under the 1921 Anglo-Irish Treaty (Briody 2007). Folklore collection and research from the cultural revival on mostly focused on Irish-speaking districts, in order to document a disappearing oral and linguistic – or as folklorists implied, national – tradition as well. The collections, largely in Irish, are immense and are of major importance.[4]

Adverse historical circumstances make the relationship between the Gaelic oral and literary traditions particularly interesting; it is largely this political context that will inform the following discussion. The legacy of the anti-Catholic Penal Laws, instituted from the 1690s, largely deprived native Ireland of a public sphere until well into the 19th century. The ethno-religious divide was not impermeable (conversion to the established church was a well-known 17th and 18th century Catholic strategy to maintain family estates, for example), but the monopoly of power exercised by the Protestant Anglo-Irish Ascendancy from the 17th century helped to create a sense of

3 A body of tradition about prominent places preserved in medieval and later manuscripts.
4 In 2017, they were added to the UNESCO Memory of the World register.

Catholic identity that to a good extent transcended social boundaries and limited the separation of high and popular culture that various scholars see as characterizing Western European culture in the modern period (Bakhtin 1984, 33; Burke 1994, 270–271; Muchembled 1991, 342–343). The subaltern status of Irish, the language of the great majority of Catholics at the beginning of this period, narrowed the gap between the Gaelic literary and oral tradition, and kept it at a remove from print culture, while the gradual growth in literacy was in English only. Almost none of the Gaelic literature of the period appeared in print, but circulated widely in manuscript. Of all the modern manuscripts that survive, the most popular one, originally composed in the 17th century, was political, giving a native reading of Irish history, and it was copied down to the beginning of the 20th century. The 18th and 19th century literary poets all composed political songs, many of which remain in the oral song repertoire to this day.

This essay will give an overview of the relationship between oral, manuscript and print culture in the Irish language. It will look at the fortunes of the Irish language itself. It will consider how the development of a positive idea of oral tradition facilitated the reception of Macpherson's *Ossian* and how that work's authenticity was rejected on those grounds by Irish writers who wished to stress its literariness. It will give an account of the dissemination of printed religious texts, the circulation of historical manuscripts and the dual oral-literary transmission of the works of 18th and 19th century poets, but also show how Gaelic learned culture came to inform an Anglo-Irish re-imagining of an Irish nation at the end of the 19th century.

The concept of oral tradition and the problem of Macpherson's Ossian

The Irish language is among the oldest written vernaculars of Europe. The partial 12th century Anglo-Norman conquest introduced English as the language of the towns and especially of the region around Dublin that became known subsequently as the (English) Pale. From this period, the King of England claimed the title of Lord of Ireland, but effective English control did not go beyond the Pale. Until the 17th century, Irish flourished as a language of high culture alongside Latin and English. The Reformation did not take root among the native inhabitants, the Gaelic Irish and the "Old English" (the later term for the descendants of the 12th century settlers), but Catholic Ireland became a geopolitical threat to Protestant England, which had powerful Catholic enemies on the continent, and the incomplete conquest of the 12th century was completed over the 16th and 17th centuries. The Catholic Gaelic and Old English aristocracy was largely replaced by a group of Protestant English investors and soldiers that facilitated the conquest and took possession of most of Ireland's land; this group formed the nucleus of what later came to be known as the Anglo-Irish Ascendency. In Ulster, planned and informal colonization brought in large numbers of English (mostly Anglican) and Scottish (largely Presbyterian) settlers. The new established, or official, church, the Anglican Church of Ireland, appropriated all the existing parish churches, but since there were not enough settlers or converts (Anglicans never numbered more than 10% of the population), most of these fell into ruin.

"There is hardly another country in Western Europe where a high culture was carried on in the Middle Ages in which so few of the treasures of learning still survive ..." (Ó Corráin 2004, 7). The Elizabethan and Cromwellian conquests were very destructive of the cultural heritage. Only about 250 manuscripts survive from the period before 1600 and about 200 from the 17th century (Gillespie 2007, 43). Without Catholic elite patronage, the position of Gaelic learned culture became fragile. The Irish Catholic colleges on the European mainland, the first of which, in Salamanca, was founded in 1592, took on a significant role in this respect. They trained Irish priests for the home mission, served the large Irish refugee communities established especially during the 17th century, and promoted the Counter-Reformation. The colleges of Leuven, Paris and Rome, especially, became important centres of learning. In Leuven, a major historical work, the *Annals of the Four Masters* [*Annála Ríoghachta Éireann*, the "Annals of the Kingdom of Ireland"], was compiled in the 1630s by the Franciscans with the help of scholars from the old hereditary learned families (and remained in manuscript until a scholarly edition was published in the 19th century). With the end of the learned ("bardic") schools of poetry[5], dependent on patronage, literary poetry took on more demotic forms.

Printing in Irish in Ireland began with 16th century Protestant texts as part of a state effort to promote the Reformation. Early Catholic printing in Irish was associated with the continental Irish colleges. The first English-Irish dictionary was published in Paris in 1732 by a Catholic priest, Conchubhar Ó Beaglaoich, who appears to have been connected with the Irish College, with the help of the scholar and poet Aodh Buidhe Mac Cruitín, a member of a hereditary learned family from Clare and then a soldier in one of the Irish regiments in the French army (Mac Amhlaigh 2008, 24–33; Morley 1995). In the dictionary, we find the word *béaloideas*, "tradition". In a survey of the semantics of this word, Dáithí Ó hÓgáin (2002) finds *béaloideas* initially referring to the oral tradition of the church [*béal-*, "oral", *oideas*, "instruction"], then shifting semantically to include oral tradition in general, thus reflecting the wider development of the notion of oral tradition.[6] The first two known instances of *béaloideas* are indeed in two religious works, by Geoffrey Keating (Seathrún Céitinn), dated to c. 1630 and 1631 respectively (Ó hÓgáin 2002, 85). In his celebrated history, *Foras Feasa ar Éirinn* (1634–1635), Keating characterized the three sources of history other than the Bible as "oral tradition [*béaloideas*] of the ancients, old documents, and antique remains, called in Latin *monumenta*" (Keating 1908, 324).

Initially, the notion of oral tradition was limited to the domain of theology. According to a Catholic understanding developed in the 15th century and which later became a dogma of the Counter-Reformation, truth resided both in Scripture and in unwritten tradition. While Protestants

---

5   The bardic schools originated in the early 13th century and survived until the mid-17th century in Ireland and early 18th century in Scotland.

6   Since the early 20th century *béaloideas* is the standard Irish word for "folklore".

dismissed the value of oral tradition, continental jurists had outlined the principles of an unwritten "natural law" underlying statutory law, and the authority of the unwritten traditions of English customs and law had been invoked since the mid-17th century as the "Ancient Constitution" (Hudson 1996, 162, 164). Gradually the notion of oral tradition expanded from the theological into the ethnological domain. The Jesuit missionary Lafitau's *Moeurs des sauvages amériquains, comparées aux moeurs des premiers temps* (1724) contended that despite the absence of writing, a people could have a sophisticated culture and social system (see Hamm 1975; Cocchiara 1981, 95–103). 18th century comparisons of native American peoples to the Greeks and Romans is also evidence of a subtler understanding of the European classical age itself. Scholars began to see the power of Homer's language as coming from the primitive state of his own society. Both Vico and Rousseau had questioned Homer's literacy, but "[a]fter about 1760, the number of British (especially Scottish) texts advancing arguments for sophisticated oral societies rose dramatically" (McDowell 2010, 238–240). Primitivism in literature was a late 18th century literary phenomenon that was largely British. Writers saw their "savage" contemporaries in terms of an earlier stage of civilization and attributed a Homeric spirit to their poetry, as Scottish Lowland intellectuals did with the Highlanders. Fiona Stafford points out that the epic form – used by James Macpherson in his *Ossian* poems (1760–) – was situated in an antique past: "To impose epic form on a contemporary society may thus be seen as an attempt to control that society by imprisoning it in the safe distance of antiquity" (Stafford 1996, 85–86). Macpherson's case for the orality of *Ossian* derived then both from specific Scottish and British developments and from a more general European intellectual tendency. His case for *Ossian*'s orality – that he had merely recorded an ancient oral tradition – and his inconsistency on the question, point to a key issue in the study of the Ossianic or Fenian[7] tradition: the relationship between folklore and learned culture and between oral and literary versions.

The Ossianic tradition is particularly well represented in literature from the 12th century as well as in modern folk tradition in Ireland and Scotland (as well as in the Canadian Scottish Gaelic-speaking community of Cape Breton, Nova Scotia). Gerard Murphy (1953) attempted to establish the relationship between the literary and the oral tales in his notes on *Duanaire Finn* [the poem book of Fionn], a 17th century compendium of Ossianic tales made for Somhairle Mac Dómhnaill, a captain in the Spanish Army in Flanders, which had survived in the Irish College in Leuven. This theme has since been followed up by other scholars. Narrative poems – "lays" or "ballads" – were an important part of the tradition; "they were composed in the literary syllabic metres of the later Middle Ages... and some of them were probably not written down until they were recorded from oral tradition in the past two centuries" (Bruford 1987, 27). Bruford points out that "[m]anuscript copies of some prose tales circulated throughout the

---

7   The terms are synonymous, "Ossianic" deriving from Macpherson's rendering of the name of the eponymous hero, "Fenian" from the band of warriors (Fianna) to which he belonged.

Gaelic-speaking area from Co. Cork to the Hebrides in the seventeenth century", and were read out in farmers' houses in Munster as late as the 19th century (*Ibid.*). He outlines three categories of narrative in the history of the Ossianic cycle:

> first, written narrative, composed more or less on to paper, though not therefore designed necessarily for solitary silent reading; second, literary narrative, composed by professional *seanchaithe*[8], historians and storytellers, or poets, but passed on generally though not exclusively in oral forms; and third, folk narrative, told by storytellers or sung by singers with no formal training, which might derive mainly or only in small part from written or literary sources. (*Ibid.*).

The first[9] Irish-English dictionary also was published in Paris, in 1768, the work of Bishop John O'Brien (Seán Ó Briain, 1701–1769) who had studied in France and spent time in the Irish colleges in Toulouse, Bordeaux and Leuven (Mac Amhlaigh 2008, 42–50). O'Brien was among the first Irish scholars to attack *Ossian*, in an article that appeared in *Le Journal des Sçavans* between 1764 and 1765, where he challenged in detail the authenticity of Macpherson's versions of the poems and asserted their Irish origin, renewing his attack in the introduction to his dictionary (O'Halloran 1989, 81). As his criticism shows, Irish opposition to Macpherson's claims for the authenticity of his translations, for *Ossian*'s Scottishness, for the priority of the Scottish literary tradition over the Irish, and to Macpherson's dismissal of Irish historians such as Keating was almost immediate. One of the contributors to the debate was the scholar and activist for Catholic rights Charles O'Conor (1710–1791). His ancient aristocratic background (he was a descendent of the last High Kings of Ireland), his education in traditional Gaelic scholarship and his later published writings in English aiming to vindicate Ireland's ancient civilization meant that he had little sympathy for Macpherson's claims nor for his primitivist views:

> [F]or O'Conor the notion of an exclusively oral medium of communication undermined his portrayal of early Ireland as a sophisticated, aristocratic and, above all, literate society, and [*Ossian*] had thus to be attacked as part of the established British tendency to depict the Irish as barbaric (O'Halloran 2004, 102).

But O'Conor's projection of an Irish learned and literary culture back to a time before the coming of Christianity was wishful thinking.

---

8   Often glossed as "antiquarian" or "historian", the *seanchaí* (plural *seanchaithe*) preserved ancient knowledge in Gaelic learned culture. The term in the spoken language has come to mean someone specializing in oral historical, genealogical, toponymic, etc. traditions.

9   Strictly speaking, an earlier lexicon had appeared in the pages of the first volume of *Archaeologia Britannica: an account of the Language, Histories and Customs of Great Britain, from Collections and observations in Travels through Wales, Cornwall, Bas-Bretagne, Ireland and Scotland*, published in Oxford in 1707; it was the work of the Welshman and pioneering Celtic scholar Edward Lhuyd.

The marginalization of Irish manuscripts

Looking at the period from 1760 to 1845, Joep Leerssen argues that "*native Ireland had no public space*" (Leerssen 2002, 31, his italics). The public sphere for most of that period was English-speaking, loyal to the crown, and Protestant, and print publication in Irish was extremely limited. Between 1700 and 1750, only four titles were published in Irish as opposed to 9,000 in English and in the next fifty years nineteen Irish but 16,000 English titles appeared (Ó Tuathaigh 2017, 56). Of the Irish titles that appeared in the second half of the 18ᵗʰ century, seven were editions of the century's most popular work in the language, Bishop Gallagher's *Sixteen Sermons in an Easy and Familiar Stile*, which first appeared in 1736; in Scotland, by contrast, fifty-nine works appeared in the same period in Scottish Gaelic. In the 18ᵗʰ century, numerous collections of poetry and song appeared in Scottish Gaelic, including Jacobite[10] works, while not a single work by an Irish-language poet appeared in print. Only about 150 books and pamphlets in Irish appeared in all of the 19ᵗʰ century, as opposed to a thousand in Scottish Gaelic (Ó Ciosáin 2013, 348–350, 353).

Some 4,000 manuscripts have come down from the 18ᵗʰ and 19ᵗʰ centuries (Morley 2011, 116; Ní Úrdail 2000) and during that period they circulated widely among an Irish-speaking population that was socially becoming more and more marginalized (while a mostly English-speaking Catholic middle class began to develop from the late 18ᵗʰ century). The majority of the manuscripts are from the southern province of Munster and, to a lesser extent, from South East Ulster. Evidence for the copying and use of manuscripts is extensive for this period. An unsympathetic source from the early 19ᵗʰ century mentions the usual practice of Catholics gathering to play cards and tell stories, with the "historian" narrating "a whole pack of nonsense" either known by heart or read out of an old manuscript (de Brún 1983, 288–289). Writing in the 1820s, Thomas Crofton Croker (1798–1854), an important antiquarian and folklorist *avant la lettre*, observed that "[m]odern manuscripts, in the Irish character, may be met with in almost every village, and they are usually the produce of the leisure hours of the schoolmaster; there is little variation in their contents, which consist of verses wherein Fingal, Oscar, Ossian[11] and St. Patrick are important characters". He states that "large numbers will assemble on a winter's evening around the turf fire of a farmer's cabin" to hear one of these "monotonous olios" read out, considered by the peasantry to be "a treat of the highest order" (Croker 1981 [1824], 331–332). According to the antiquarian Standish Hayes O'Grady (1832–1915) they were

> for the most part written by professional scribes and schoolmasters, and being lent or bought by those who could read but had not leisure to write, used to be

---

10 Supporting the claim of the Catholic King James II and VII and the House of Stuart to the thrones of England, Scotland and Ireland.
11 Fingal is Macpherson's version of Fionn (earlier Finn), chief of the Fianna, Ossian [in Scottish Gaelic Oisean, in Irish Oisín] is his son and Oscar is Ossian's son.

read aloud in farmers' houses on occasions such as wool-carding in the evenings; but especially at wakes. Thus the people became familiar with all these tales. (Cited in Ó Duilearga 1943, 27.)

Croker gives an account of "Buckaughs" [Irish *bacaigh*], "a description of mendicant", who often sought a night's accommodation in a peasant's house:

> It is not uncommon to find these men with considerable literary acquirements; they are generally the possessors of several books and Irish manuscripts, which they have collected, and bear about from place to place with incredible fondness, nor can money always purchase part of their travelling library; their knowledge of writing renders them acceptable guests to many farmers, whose correspondence is often entirely carried on by such agency. (Croker 1981 [1824], 236.)

Irish manuscripts were, as Niall Ó Ciosáin outlines, "commissioned by patrons ranging from farmers to clerics, and written by itinerant scribes, who were often poor, and usually combined transcription with teaching" (Ó Ciosáin 1997, 157). Ó Conchúir (1982) has identified well over 200 scribes who were active in Co. Cork alone (and to whom manuscripts can be attributed) in the period 1700 to 1850. Scribes were often tutors in affluent households but as this type of patronage waned they became more involved in setting up schools (Cullen 1990, 17–21). If most poets were also scribes, then those of comfortable farming or gentry background did not engage in teaching. The teacher-scribes were of very modest origin, unrelated to the comfortable farmers and gentry around them. "They were essentially men of few ties, migrating frequently between districts, trying to establish at least a temporary foothold." (*Ibid.*, 24–25.)

Literacy in Irish between 1750 and 1850 was characterized by two different types: one among the socially diverse Irish-speaking population in Munster, where a rich scribal culture existed and where some Catholic printed works circulated, and the other a result of Protestant proselytizing activities, leading largely to reading-only literacy (Ó Ciosáin 1997, 157). Catholic and secular texts used Roman typography, "probably because... [they] were being produced commercially, within a printing trade that functioned almost entirely in English" (*Ibid.*, 159), and – especially in the broadside ballads and Catholic catechisms – they broke with the historical orthography, using a phonetic spelling based on English (*Ibid.*, 160–161). Between 1800 and 1850 there was a considerable production of popular works in Irish, foremost among them *Timothy O'Sullivan's Irish Pious Miscellany*, which had numerous editions between its initial publication in 1802 and 1850. The early poetry of O'Sullivan (Tadhg "Gaelach" Ó Súilleabháin, 1715–1795) includes Jacobite works, but he later had a religious conversion and dedicated himself to religious verse. Many of the poems, in traditional song metre [*amhrán*], circulated in manuscript before they appeared in print. Later manuscript copies probably derive from the printed book, and some of them survived in oral tradition into the 20th century (Ó Ciosáin 1997, 123, 131).

Protestant proselytising efforts among Catholics in the early and mid-19th century used the Irish language. The Irish Society for Promoting the

Education of the Native Irish through the Medium of their Own Language (1818) provided free elementary education and distributed Irish-language devotional literature. The society, according to its own rules, aimed to use Irish-language literacy "as a means for obtaining an accurate knowledge of English", with the Scriptures in Irish for "moral amelioration" while "disclaiming, at the same time, all intention of making the Irish language a vehicle for the communication of general knowledge" (de Brún 1983, 281). The educational aim in places won the initial toleration of Catholic priests, but the teaching of the Scriptures without commentary was contrary to Catholic teaching. Most of the society's teachers were Catholics, a number of them poets and scribes, who found a source of paid employment, "and it would seem that very few persons who were literate in Irish can have been completely untouched by the work, those not involved in it busy opposing it" (*Ibid.*, 287). The society published and distributed tens of thousands of copies of religious texts in Irish using purpose-made Gaelic fonts based on scribal script. Proselytism was a major source of religious conflict but also had a negative side effect on the Irish language.[12] The resulting widespread Catholic clerical condemnation of printed works in Irish later in the 19th century (*Ibid.*, 285) led to many scribes giving up copying and circulating manuscripts: by this time, the Catholic church, cognisant of political realities and of language shift, used English almost exclusively and was indifferent, if not hostile, to Irish.[13] The widespread destruction of manuscripts in the second half of the 19th century can at least in part be attributed to church opposition; Ní Uallacháin shows that was the case for South-East Ulster and Co. Louth, where most, if not all, of the Irish Society's teachers were local Catholic scribes (Ní Uallacháin 2005, 21–22, 26). No manuscripts have survived in the hand of the poet from that region Art Mac Cumhaigh (c. 1738–1773), author of the *aisling* [see below] poem *Úirchill an Chreagáin* that has been called "the national anthem of South Ulster" owing to its popularity. Mac Cumhaigh's manuscripts apparently were used to pack goods in a shop and children destroyed those that survived about 1907. The account of the poet's life in Ó Fiaich's edition of his poems is based in part on oral tradition (1973, 8, 20–21). The rescue or destruction of manuscripts, of course, is a not uncommon phenomenon in literary history. Well-known is the story of the rescue from the flames of the 17th century manuscript that was to provide the basis for *Reliques of Ancient English Poetry* by Bishop Percy – who in 1782 was appointed Church of Ireland Bishop of Dromore, in South East Ulster (Groom 1999, 6). Reports of manuscript destruction became a useful weapon to Douglas Hyde at the turn of the 20th century when he campaigned for recognition of the Irish language in the educational system (see Sharpe 2017).

12　Derisory terms for Catholics who converted to Protestantism and their descendants included "soupers", who converted for food, and *cat breacs*, so named for the textbook used for their instruction, which had a picture of a speckled cat [*cat breac*]. These terms were still in use a century later.

13　Ó Ciosáin has demonstrated the key role of the institutional churches, or of elements within them, in creating reading publics and print cultures in the other Celtic languages, Scottish Gaelic, Welsh and Breton (Ó Ciosáin 2013, 362).

The first estimate for Gaelic-speakers in Scotland is for 1755, when they numbered less than three hundred thousand, almost 23% of the country's then population (Withers & McKinnon 1994, 109), while Irish-speakers around the same time were two thirds of Ireland's much larger population estimated at 3.2 million. Estimates for the number of Irish speakers before the Great Famine (1845–1848) vary: in 1821, perhaps 3.7 million or so out of a total population of 6.8 million, in 1841 4.1 out of 8.2 million – about half. From 1851, the census probably under-enumerated them, but showed the obvious decline: in 1851 23.3% of a total population of 6.55 million, in 1861 19.1% of 5.8 million, in 1871 15.1 % of 5.4 million (Hindley 1990, 15, 19). The earliest reliable source for literacy is the 1841 census, when 47% of those more than five years old could read (Ó Ciosáin 1997, 32). In the 18th and 19th centuries, literacy was acquired in English, even by Irish speakers, among whom literacy in their native language was extremely rare: an 1806 estimate was that 20,000 could read Irish (*Ibid.*, 157; Daly & Dickson 1990), perhaps not a lot more than 1% of the linguistic community at the time. A dialect continuum for a long time existed between Irish and Scottish Gaelic, and the same literary language, most commonly called Classical Irish today, was shared until the 18th century. Most of the surviving classical manuscripts are Irish; Black enumerates 138 that originated in Scotland or are associated with Scottish literati (Black 1989, 167). The translation of the New Testament in 1767 and its later revision established a new literary norm for Scottish Gaelic. The fact that the literary history of the shared language is mostly Irish until late is possibly one of the reasons why Macpherson stressed the orality of the sources for *Ossian*, though he was well aware of the existence of manuscripts; indeed he was responsible for bringing to light the most important Scottish Gaelic manuscript, the early 16th century *Book of the Dean of Lismore*.

Gaelic poets and the oral circulation of manuscripts

The Elizabethan and Cromwellian conquests were catastrophic for Ireland, politically, socially, culturally and demographically. In adversity, a new identity of Irish Catholics developed, transcending the centuries-old ethnic divide between Gael and *Gall* ["Old English"], and in opposition to the "New English" Protestant settlers, and this is when the term *Éireannach*, "Irish person", begins to be used in place of the earlier ethnic terms and when the word "nation" [in the form *náision*] is borrowed into Irish.[14] This new ideological construction is exemplified in *Foras Feasa ar Éirinn*. The work, whose title can be translated as "a foundation of knowledge about Ireland", was completed in 1634–1635. It gives an account of Ireland's history from the Creation to the 12th century, but also absorbs the Old English, the author's ancestors, into a new national narrative, contrasting them implicitly with the contemporary colonists. It was written by a Catholic priest from Co.

---

14 It is in a will made by a member of the Old English community entering the Franciscan order in the Irish College in Leuven in 1610 (Mac Craith 1995, 152).

Tipperary whom we have already mentioned, Geoffrey Keating (c. 1580–1644), who appears to have studied at Rheims and was later associated with the Irish College of Bordeaux (Cunningham 2000, 26–31). Other than *Foras Feasa*, Keating's fame rests on his theological writings, strongly influenced by the ideas of the Counter-Reformation, and on his poetry. His prose style has long been considered exemplary: he has been called "the father of modern Irish prose" (Ó Buachalla 1987, eight).

A contemporary Latin translation of *Foras Feasa* survives in manuscript copies while an English translation appeared in print in 1723. The text did not appear in print in Irish until the 1902–1914 scholarly edition of David Comyn for the Irish Texts Society. It circulated widely in manuscript: twenty-nine copies have survived from the 17th century alone and it continued to be copied throughout the 18th and 19th centuries. Morley (2011, 114–119) has itemized the surviving manuscripts by period copied, with seventy-five in the 18th century, nineteen in the first half of the 19th century and four in the second:

> *Foras Feasa* maintained its status as a historical standard from generation to generation. It was an authoritative source for seventeenth century conservative authors under the influence of bardic poetry, for eighteenth century bilingual poets who practised popular song metre, and for nineteenth century popular poets whose compositions lived in folklore until the beginning of the revival.[15] (*Ibid.*, 107).

Oral traditions about Keating being hunted by English soldiers were recorded by Croker (1844, 5) in Keating's home district, and in the 20th century from the famed Blasket Island storyteller, Peig Sayers (1873–1958) (Fitzgerald 2014). Whatever about the tradition heard by Croker, learned culture must surely have influenced the narrative of Sayers, who was literate in English, but not in her native Irish.

The great popularity of *Foras Feasa* can be seen in the influence it had on other works, such as the long poem *Tuireamh na hÉireann* ["Ireland's elegy", c. 1655–1659]. By Seán Ó Conaill (fl. c. 1650), it covers much the same ground as Keating's history, but also deals with contemporary events, culminating with the Cromwellian conquest (1649–1653), *an coga do chríochnaigh Éire*, "the war that finished Ireland", as the poem describes it (O'Rahilly 1952, 75). The number of surviving manuscript copies – between two and three hundred – and 19th century English translations, suggests an extraordinary popularity. In the Royal Irish Academy, the most important repository of Irish manuscripts, *Tuireamh* has the most copies – followed by the Ossianic poem of the debate between Oisín and St. Patrick (Morley 2011, 128). Of the 19th century copies, Morley (*Ibid.*, 129–137) breaks them down by period: one hundred and twenty-five from the first half of the century and fourteen from the second; two were even written in the United States in the early 20th century. Only two 17th century manuscript copies, and those from the century's end, have come down to us, and 101 from the 18th century.

---

15 The late 19th century language revival movement spearheaded by the Gaelic League.

According to an 18th century account, the poem was "repeated and kept in memory on account of the great knowledge of antiquity comprehended in it" (O'Rahilly 1952, 58), and there is evidence of other political poems, or at least of songs, deliberately not being written down. Crofton Croker was interested in popular song, and was troubled by the seditious sentiments that characterized most of them (he was unsympathetic to Irish Catholics and worked as a clerk for the Admiralty in London). He noted "few have been committed to paper: this may be ascribed to two causes; first being that short compositions, they are easily remembered, and secondly, their treasonable nature" (Croker 1981 [1824], 336; Morley 2011, 127). Morley argues that *Tuireamh*, "more than any other literary work, taught the Gaelic version of history to the native population and made it a dominant narrative" (*Ibid.*, 138).

Poems by 18th century Gaelic poets circulated widely in manuscript and orally. Many of them were political, especially the *aisling* or "vision" poem, which originated in the late 17th century. In the *aisling*, a woman using various poetic or mythological names that identify her with Ireland appears to the poet in a vision. She laments the suffering of the Irish people and foresees their liberation with the return of her rightful spouse. The *aisling* in effect linked the ancient sovereignty myth to the ideal of the rightful king in the century following the 1688 overthrow of the Catholic King James[16] – the native Irish literati recognizing James' dynasty, the Stuarts, as legitimate kings of Ireland owing to their supposed descent from Milesius, putative ancestor of the Gaels. Ó Buachalla, in his monumental study of the *aisling*, points out that the literary and the oral were complementary media in its dissemination (Ó Buachalla 1996, 604).

The most famous 18th century poet, generally considered the greatest of the modern language, was Aogán Ó Rathaille (c. 1670–1729), who is transitional between the centuries-old professional bardic tradition – in which he was schooled – and the more demotic verse that flourished after the demise of the old order, which reduced him to destitution. Two copies of *Foras Feasa* in his hand are preserved in the National Library of Ireland. The Gaelic scholar Fr Patrick Dinneen (1860–1934), a native of Ó Rathaille's home district in Co. Kerry, observed that in his youth "the splendid O'Rahilly tradition... had subsided to a faint murmur", but he tells that he "heard some snatches of his most musical songs sung by my mother, who also taught me some folk-tales of which he was the hero" (Dinneen 1929, 20).

Eoghan Rua Ó Súilleabháin (1748–1784) was a native of the same district and led a short dissolute life, as itinerant labourer, as tutor (to the Nagles of Ballyduff, Co. Cork, the family of the statesman Edmund Burke's mother [Cullen 1993, 17]), as schoolmaster of a hedge school and as sailor in the British Navy in the West Indies.[17] A few poems of his in English are

16 He ruled as James II in England and Ireland and as James VII in Scotland until his overthrow in 1688 in the coup led by the Dutchman William of Orange, James' son-in-law: the "Glorious Revolution". James was the last Catholic monarch of Britain.

17 It seems from the evidence of his poem in English, "Rodney's Glory", that he took part in the naval battle of Ile des Saintes in 1782, when Admiral Rodney's British fleet defeated the French.

known. His poetic work in Irish, however, was of great popularity – "some of the sweetest and most musical poetry ever composed in Irish" – and in his political poems, especially the *aislingí*, he disseminated Jacobite rhetoric that linked traditional cultural references, as already stated, to contemporary politics (Ó Buachalla 1996, 605). The literary critic Daniel Corkery (1878–1964) tells of his visits to the Irish-speaking parts of Munster as a young man:

> I found there were two subjects which never failed to arouse the dying fires, to bring light into the fading eyes, and a flood of speech to the toothless gums: the Great Famine of '47 was one, and Eoghan Ruadh, the wastrel poet, whose voice had been stilled for more than a hundred years, whose poems they had never seen printed, whose life they had never seen written, was the other. (Corkery 1967 [1924], 220.)

The first editor of his poems, Fr Dinneen, recounts that "[s]eldom did a social gathering separate without having heard several stories in which he figured; without some of his songs being listened to; without having enjoyed some of his drolleries" (Dinneen 1929, 25).

A favourite song that is still well-known is *Amhrán na Leabhar*, the "song of the books", the work of Tomás Rua Ó Súilleabháin (1785–1848), poet and itinerant schoolmaster. His songs – both on religious and on political themes, especially in support of Daniel O'Connell (1775–1848), winner of Catholic Emancipation[18] in 1829, were very popular in oral tradition. *Amhrán na Leabhar* tells of the loss of the poet's collection of books and manuscripts when the boat carrying them capsized. The lost volumes are lamented by name and included a copy of *Foras Feasa* (Fenton 1922, 46). Clearly such a song, with its numerous references to literary works, could hardly be transmitted by oral tradition alone. Yet the texts in the first edition of Ó Súilleabháin's work were all recorded from oral tradition, "not one was found in manuscript", according to the editor (*Ibid.*, 25). In a later edition of his poetry, additional poems appear, but they were found in the Irish folklore archives and had all been recorded from oral tradition (Ní Shúilleabháin 1985, 5).

From about the 1820s, Gaelic scribes noted the names of tunes to which the poems they copied were to be sung (Morley 2011, 124; Ó Buachalla 2002–2003, 112), evidence that the oral was envisaged as one of the media for the poem's transmission. Pádraig A. Breatnach has argued that in this case the accurate transmission of the poem depended on the singing ability of the transmitter (Breatnach 1987, 59). He shows how 18th century Munster poets maintained close contact with each other, sometimes using messengers to memorize poems and orally transmit them to other poets, sometimes over great distances (*Ibid.*, 61–62). Usually, in the absence of abundant documentary evidence, oral tradition from the late 19th and early

---

18 The Emancipation Act allowed Catholics, till then subject to a range of discriminatory laws, to be elected to and sit in parliament and opened most public offices to them.

20th century has added to our knowledge of the lives of the poets, of the popular role and power attributed to poets, and has added compositions that have not survived in manuscript; the work of Tomás Rua Ó Súilleabháin, as we have shown, is a case in point of a literary poet whose compositions have survived only through oral tradition. *Cante-fables* about poets were very popular, both about oral and literary poets; the introduction to the first edition of Tomás Rua's poems largely consists of these (Fenton 1922, 5–24). An abundant amount of relevant material is in the folklore archives, much of it tapped in Ó hÓgáin's study on the supernatural powers attributed to poetry. His data are particularly rich in oral traditions of Eoghan Rua Ó Súilleabháin, Raftery, Aogán Ó Rathaille, Tomás Rua Ó Súilleabháin and Diarmuid "na Bolgaí" Ó Sé (c. 1755–1846) (Ó hÓgáin 1982). In 1943, the Irish Folklore Commission's collector Seán Ó Cróinín recorded from the tailor and poet Pádraig Ó Crualaoich (1861–1949) an extraordinary body of oral traditional lore concerning more than fifty poets who lived in Cork and east Kerry between 1700 and 1850, which included poems, biographical information and *cante-fables*. Among the poets about whom *cante-fables* were recounted in this corpus were Ó Rathaille, Eoghan Rua Ó Súilleabháin and Cearbhall Ó Dálaigh (c. 1590–c. 1640) (Ó Cróinín 1982).

The son of a weaver, Raftery[19] (1779–1835) was blinded by smallpox as a child. An oral poet, the popularity of his songs in the West brought them to the attention of two major figures in Irish cultural life, Douglas Hyde (1860–1949) and Lady Augusta Gregory (1852–1932)[20], to whom his later literary fame is largely due. Hyde published two editions of Raftery's work, the bilingual collection *Abhráin atá leagtha ar an Reachtúire or Songs ascribed to Raftery* (1903) and a fuller scholarly edition, *Abhráin agus Dánta an Reachtabhraigh* ["The Songs and Poems of Raftery", 1933]. One of Raftery's compositions is *Seanchas na Sceiche* ["History of the bush"], a long oral poem – some 400 lines – clearly influenced both by *Foras Feasa* (it invokes Keating's authority) and *Tuireamh na hÉireann*. It recounts Ireland's history from the Flood up to the calamities of the 17th century as witnessed by the thorn bush under which the poet was forced to shelter from the rain. It has been recorded from oral tradition into the 20th century and was very popular in the West of Ireland.

Marcas (c. 1789–c. 1846) and Peatsaí Ó Callanáin (1791–1865) were Raftery's contemporaries and rival poets. They were literate in English and wrote their poetry in a phonetic script based on English orthography (of the kind to which Ó Duilearga refers). The poems were copied in a similar way,

19 Many versions of his surname appear in manuscripts. He was usually known simply as Raftery, the anglicization of the surname Ó Reachtabhra (itself sometimes rendered in gaelicized spelling as Raiftearaí), and it appears that this was the form he used himself (Ó Coigligh 1987, 3).
20 Both were members of the Anglo-Irish elite and important figures in the cultural nationalist movement. Gregory was a dramatist, folklorist, translator and one of the founders of the national theatre. Hyde's translations from the Irish were seminal works of the Irish literary revival. A notable scholar of Irish literature and folklore, he was the leader of the key organ of the language revival movement, the Gaelic League, founded in 1893, and, much later, first president of Ireland.

but also circulated orally and as such came to the attention of Hyde and Lady Gregory. The latter famously tells in *Poets and Dreamers* (Gregory 1903, 1–2) of an argument between two old women in the Poorhouse[21] in Gort, Co. Galway, as to the respective merits of Raftery and Peatsaí Ó Callanáin; Seán Ó Ceallaigh (1916–2003), the editor of their poems who was a native of the same district, tells of hearing similar debates among the local old people (Ó Ceallaigh 1967, 5). Ó Ceallaigh's edition includes poems recorded only from oral tradition as well as manuscript texts. Raftery was an oral poet, yet learned historical traditions were key influences on *Seanchas na Sceiche*. The historian Louis Cullen argues that *Seanchas na Sceiche* is so sophisticated that it cannot be considered as folk poetry nor could it have survived in the form that it did had it depended on oral transmission alone. He points out that "there was great demand for these poems and the wide dissemination of them especially depended on a complex interaction between the written form and the oral form, with the written form at least as important as the other". He sees poetry like *Seanchas na Sceiche* and other public poetry in late 18th century Connacht, where there was not a significant modern scribal tradition and where manuscripts were transmitted in phonetic scripts based on literacy in English, as being modern and innovative (Cullen 1996, 174–175). The phonetic scripts begin to appear in the 1790s. They were rare in Munster and in South-East Ulster, but much more common in Connacht. "[W]here they appear they emphasised that individuals were drawing their reading knowledge from English, and that they proceeded to literacy in Irish through models already picked up from English" (Cullen 1990, 32).

Máirtín Ó Cadhain (1906–1970), the greatest modern prose writer in Irish, saw 19th century Irish-language manuscripts in East Co. Galway, across the River Corrib from his native Connemara; his grandfather learned to read Irish in a hedge school in a rough phonetic script (Ó Cadhain 1969, 14). The young Ó Cadhain and his contemporaries used a similar script to write down songs they liked; he had one in his possession written in 1930 and remembered a traditional charm, *an Mharthain Phádraig* ["St. Patrick's preserving prayer"], being written much later in the same script to be sent to America and to be sewn into the lining of a coat as protection against harm. Contemporary popular poetry from his own district circulated in the same type of script (Ó Cadhain 1990, 151–152). Ó Cadhain grew up in a family of storytellers and as a young teacher collected folklore, though his political radicalism was later to turn him against the folklorists' project – he had particular vitriol for Ó Duilearga's cultural pessimism (Ó Giolláin 2000, 149–153).

---

21 Poorhouses, officially known as workhouses, were established under the 1838 Poor Law Act to cater for the destitute poor, with a punitive regime of manual labour. Families, but not individuals, were eligible for relief but were separated on being admitted.

Concluding remarks

As we have seen, the reading of manuscripts in communal contexts was a relatively well-known phenomenon in parts of the country. Morley shows that a Gaelic narrative of national history derived from learned culture was consolidated among the Catholic population, both literate and illiterate, and we can take it that the rambling house type of venue was an important forum in this respect.[22] Learned cultures until the modern period depended on elite patronage. But it is through them that modern nations have tended – where possible – to assert a historical depth and a national history. Some of the custodians of Gaelic learning, the remnants of the old learned families, found new roles after the turmoil of the 17th century and often repurposed their expertise in the service of the new order, helping to translate Protestant literature and, from the middle of the 18th, functioning as assistants to the nascent antiquarian societies, which initially had a wholly Protestant membership. Charlotte Brooke (c. 1740–1793), a member of the Anglo-Irish ascendancy, was inspired by hearing a labourer on her family's estate reading an Ossianic poem aloud from a manuscript. She was helped by native Gaelic scholars and encouraged by Bishop Percy, and in 1789 published *Reliques of Irish Poetry*. This work included literary texts and a discussion of popular song, and helped to foster an interest in native Irish culture among the Protestant elite. With Brooke, the influence of Macpherson's *Ossian* and of Bishop Percy's *Reliques* came together and helped to shape a seminal work in Irish cultural history. Referring to these native Gaelic scholars from the old learned families, Joep Leerssen writes:

> All these were men who, in lending support to Protestant propaganda, placed themselves outside the mainstream of the post-bardic Gaelic tradition, which was vigorously Catholic; in so doing, however, they created the middle ground needed for the transfer of information that eventually was to create a new, non-sectarian audience for the heritage guarded by that tradition. (Leerssen 1996, 287.)

This paved the way for the late 19th century cultural revival, which was largely led by Anglo-Irish writers, and which was to inform the cultural and political revolution that followed.

---

22 Much later, in the 1930s, the anthropologists Arensberg and Kimball wrote of the rambling house frequented by the elders of a peasant community in West Co. Clare that "[i]t is the clearing house of information and the court of opinion in which the decisions of the community are reached and the traditional knowledge of the peasantry applied and disseminated". They concluded that "[i]t is here public opinion is formulated" (Arensberg & Kimball 2001 [1940], 183, 185).

References

Arensberg, Conrad M. & Solon T. Kimball 2001 [1940]. *Family and Community in Ireland*. Third edition. Ennis: Clasp Press.

Bakhtin, Mikhail 1984. *Rabelais and His World*. Translated by Hélène Iswolsky. Bloomington: Indiana University Press.

Black, Ronald I.M. 1989. The Gaelic Manuscripts of Scotland. In William Gillies (ed.), *Gaelic and Scotland: Alba agus a' Ghàidhlig*. Edinburgh: Edinburgh University Press, 146–174.

Breatnach, Pádraig A. 1987. Oral and Written Transmission of Poetry in the Eighteenth Century. *Eighteenth-Century Ireland / Iris an Dá Chultúr* 2: 57–65.

Briody, Mícheál 2007. *The Irish Folklore Commission 1935–1970: History, Ideology, Methodology*. Studia Fennica Folkloristica 17. Helsinki: Finnish Literature Society.

Bruford, Alan 1987. Oral and Literary Fenian Tales. In Bo Almqvist, Séamas Ó Catháin & Pádraig Ó Héalaí (eds), *The Heroic Process: Form, Function and Fantasy in Folk Epic. The Proceedings of the International Folk Epic Conference, University College, Dublin, 2–6 September 1985*. Dublin: The Glendale Press, 25–56.

Burke, Peter 1994. *Popular Culture in Early Modern Europe*. Revised edition. Aldershot: Scolar Press.

Cocchiara, Giuseppe 1981. *The History of Folklore in Europe*. Translated by John N. McDaniel. Philadelphia: Institute for the Study of Human Issues.

Corkery, Daniel 1967 [1924]. *The Hidden Ireland: A Study of Gaelic Munster in the Eighteenth Century*. Dublin: Gill & Macmillan.

Croker, Thomas Crofton 1844. *The Keen of the South of Ireland*. London: The Percy Society.

Croker, Thomas Crofton 1981 [1824]. *Researches in the South of Ireland: Illustrative of the Scenery, Architectural Remains and the Manners and Superstitions of the Peasantry with an Appendix Containing a Private Narrative of the Rebellion of 1798*. Dublin: Irish Academic Press.

Cullen, Louis M. 1990. Patrons, Teachers and Literacy in Irish. In Mary Daly & David Dickson (eds), *The Origins of Popular Literacy in Ireland: Language Change and Educational Development 1700–1920*. Dublin: Department of Modern History, Trinity College Dublin & Department of Modern Irish History, University College Dublin, 15–44.

Cullen, Louis M. 1993. The Contemporary and Later Politics of "Caoineadh Airt Uí Laoire". *Eighteenth-Century Ireland / Iris an Dá Chultúr* 8: 7–38.

Cullen, Louis M. 1996. Filíocht, Cultúr agus Polaitíocht ["Poetry, Culture and Politics"]. In Máirín Ní Dhonnchadha (ed.), *Nua-Léamha. Gnéithe de Chultúr, Stair agus Polaitíocht na hÉireann c. 1600–c. 1900* ["New readings: aspects of Irish culture, history and politics, c. 1600–c. 1900"]. Dublin: An Clóchomhar Tta.

Cunningham, Bernadette 2000. *The World of Geoffrey Keating: History, Myth and Religion in Seventeenth-Century Ireland*. Dublin: Four Courts Press.

Daly, Mary E. & David Dixon 1990. *The Origins of Popular Literacy in Ireland: Language Change and Educational Development 1700–1920*. Dublin: Department of Modern History, Trinity College.

De Brún, Pádraig 1983. The Irish Society's Bible Teachers, 1818–27. *Éigse* 19: 281–332.

Delargy, J.H. 1969 [1945]. *The Gaelic Story-teller: with some notes of Gaelic folk-tales*. Reprinted from Proceedings of the British Academy, Volume XXXI (1945), 177–221. Chicago: University of Chicago Press.

Dinneen, Rev. Patrick S. 1927. *Foclóir Gaedhilge agus Béarla. An Irish-English Dictionary*. Dublin: Irish Texts Society.

Dinneen, Rev. Patrick S. 1929. *Filidhe Móra Chiarraighe. Four Notable Kerry Poets*. Dublin: M.H. Gill & Son, Ltd.

Fenton, James 1922. *Amhráin Thomáis Ruaidh .i. The Songs of Tomás Ruadh O'Sullivan the Iveragh Poet (1785–1848)*. Second edition. Dublin: M.H. Gill & Son, Ltd.

Fitzgerald, Kelly 2014. "Between the Army and the Altar": The Function of Folk Narrative and the Image of Geoffrey Keating. *Béaloideas* 82: 116–132.

Gillespie, Raymond 2007. The Ó Cléirigh Manuscripts in Context. In Edel Bhreathnach & Bernadette Cunningham (eds), *Writing Irish History: The Four Masters and Their World*. Dublin: Wordwell, 43–51.

Gregory, Lady 1903. *Poets and Dreamers: Studies and Translations from the Irish*. Third edition. Dublin: Hodges Figgis & Co. Ltd.

Groom, Nick 1999. *The Making of Percy's Reliques*. Oxford: Clarendon Press.

Hamm, Victor M. 1975. Greeks and Indians: A Study in Mythic Syncretism. *Thought: Fordham University Quarterly* 50 (4): 351–366.

Hindley, Reg 1990. *The Death of the Irish Language: A Qualified Obituary*. London: Routledge.

Hudson, Nicholas 1996. 'Oral Tradition': The Evolution of an Eighteenth-Century Concept. In Alvaro Ribeiro, SJ & James G. Basker (eds), *Tradition in Transition: Women Writers, Marginal Texts, and the Eighteenth-Century Canon*. Oxford: Clarendon Press, 161–176.

Keating, Geoffrey (Seathrún Céitinn) 1908. *The History of Ireland [Foras Feasa ar Éirinn]*. Part II. Edited and translated with notes by Rev. Patrick S. Dinneen. London: Irish Texts Society.

Leerssen, Joep 1996. *Mere Irish and Fíor-Ghael: Studies in the Idea of Irish Nationality, its Development and Literary Expression prior to the Nineteenth Century*. Second edition. Cork: Cork University Press.

Leerssen, Joep 2002. *Hidden Ireland, Public Sphere*. Galway: Arlen House.

Mac Amhlaigh, Liam 2008. *Foclóirí & Foclóirithe na Gaeilge* ["Irish dictionaries and lexicographers"]. Dublin: Cois Life.

Mac Craith, Mícheál 1995. The Gaelic Reaction to the Reformation. In Steven G. Ellis & Sarah Barber (eds), *Conquest and Union: Fashioning a British State 1485–1725*. London: Longman, 139–161.

McDowell, Paula 2010. Mediating Past and Present: Toward a Genealogy of "Print Culture" and "Oral Tradition". In Clifford Siskin & William Warner (eds), *This is Enlightenment*. Chicago: University of Chicago Press, 229–246.

Morley, Vincent 1995. *An Crann os Coill: Aodh Buidhe Mac Cruitín, c. 1680–1755* ["The tree above the wood: Aodh Buidhe Mac Cruitín, c. 1680–1755"]. Dublin: Coiscéim.

Morley, Vincent 2011. *Ó Chéitinn go Raiftearaí. Mar a cumadh stair na hÉireann* ["From Keating to Raftery: how the history of Ireland was created"]. Dublin: Coiscéim.

Muchembled, Robert 1991. *Culture populaire et culture des élites dans la France moderne (XVe–XVIIIe siècle)*. Second edition. Paris: Flammarion.

Müller-Lisowski, Käte 1948. Contributions to a Study in Irish Folklore. Traditions about Donn. *Béaloideas* 18: 142–199.

Murphy, Gerard 1953. *Duanaire Finn: The Book of the Lays of Finn*. Vol. III. Dublin: Irish Texts Society.

Ní Shúilleabháin, Máire 1985. *Amhráin Thomáis Rua* ["The songs of Tomás Rua"]. Maigh Nuad: An Sagart.

Ní Uallacháin, Pádraigín 2003. *A Hidden Ulster: People, Songs and Traditions of Oriel*. Dublin: Four Courts Press.

Ní Úrdail, Meidhbhín 2000. *The Scribe in Eighteenth- and Nineteenth-Century Ireland: Motivations and Milieu*. Münster: Nodus Publikationen.

Ó Buachalla, Breandán 1987. Foreword to 1987 reprint. In *Foras Feasa ar Éirinn le Seathrún Céitinn, D.D. The History of Ireland by Geoffrey Keating, D.D.* Part I. Edited by David Comyn. London: Irish Texts Society [1902], two–nine.

Ó Buachalla, Breandán 1996. *Aisling Ghéar. Na Stíobhartaigh agus an tAos Léinn 1603-1788* ["Bitter vision: the Stuarts and the learned class 1603-1788"]. Dublin: An Clóchomhar Tta.

Ó Buachalla, Breandán 2002-2003. Ceol na Filíochta. *Studia Hibernica* 32: 99-132.

Ó Cadhain, Máirtín 1969. *Páipéir Bhána agus Páipéir Bhreaca* ["White papers and speckled papers"]. Dublin: An Clóchomhar Tta.

Ó Cadhain, Máirtín 1990. *Ó Cadhain i bhFeasta* ["Ó Cadhain's writings in the journal *Feasta*"]. Edited by Seán Ó Laighin. Dublin: Clódhanna Teoranta.

Ó Ceallaigh, Seán 1967. *Filíocht na gCallanán* ["The poetry of the Ó Callanáin family"]. Dublin: An Clóchomhar Tta.

Ó Ciosáin, Niall 1997. *Print and Popular Culture in Ireland, 1750-1850*. Basingstoke: Macmillan.

Ó Ciosáin, Niall 2013. The Print Cultures of the Celtic Languages, 1700-1900. *Cultural and Social History* 10 (3): 347-367.

Ó Coigligh, Ciarán 1987. *Raiftearaí: Amhráin agus Dánta* ["Raftery: songs and poems"]. Dublin: An Clóchomhar Tta.

Ó Conchúir, Breandán 1982. *Scríobhaithe Chorcaí 1700-1850* ["Cork scribes 1700-1850"]. Dublin: An Clóchomhar Tta.

Ó Corráin, Donnchadh 2004. Cad d'Imigh ar Lámhscríbhinní na hÉireann? ["What happened to Ireland's manuscripts?"]. In Ruairí Ó hUiginn (ed.), *Oidhreacht na Lámhscríbhinní* ["The manuscript legacy"]. Léachtaí Cholm Cille XXXIV. Maigh Nuad: An Sagart, 7-21.

Ó Cróinín, Donncha (ed.) 1982. *Seanchas Phádraig Í Chrualaoi*. Dublin: Comhairle Bhéaloideas Éireann.

Ó Crualaoich, Gearóid 2006. *The Book of the Cailleach: Stories of the Wise-Woman Healer*. Cork: Cork University Press.

Ó Duilearga, Séamus 1943. Volkskundliche Arbeit in Irland von 1850 bis zur Gegenwart mit besonderer Berücksichtigung der "Irischen Volkskunde -Kommission". *Zeitschrift für Keltische Philologie und Volksvorschung* xxiii: 1-38.

Ó Fiaich, Tomás 1973. *Art Mac Cumhaigh: Dánta* ["Art Mac Cumhaigh: poems"]. Dublin: An Clóchomhar Tta.

Ó Giolláin, Diarmuid 2000. *Locating Irish Folklore: Tradition, Modernity, Identity*. Cork: Cork University Press.

Ó hÓgáin, Dáithí 1982. *An File* ["The poet"]. Dublin: Oifig an tSoláthair.

Ó hÓgáin, Dáithí 2002. "Béaloideas": Notes on the History of a Word. *Béaloideas* 70: 83-98.

Ó Tuathaigh, Gearóid 2017. Languages and Identities. In Eugenio F. Biagini & Mary E. Daly (eds), *The Cambridge Social History of Modern Ireland*. Cambridge: Cambridge University Press, 53-67.

O'Halloran, Clare 1989. Irish Re-Creations of the Gaelic Past: The Challenge of Macpherson's Ossian. *Past & Present* 124: 69-95.

O'Halloran, Clare 2004. *Golden Ages and Barbarous Nations: Antiquarian Debate and Cultural Politics in Ireland, c. 1750-1800*. Cork: Cork University Press.

O'Rahilly, Cecile 1952. *Five Seventeenth-Century Political Poems*. Dublin: Dublin Institute for Advanced Studies.

Sharpe, Richard 2017. Destruction of Irish Manuscripts and the National Board of Education. *Studia Hibernica* 43: 95-116.

Stafford, Fiona 1996. Primitivism and the "Primitive" Poet: A Cultural Context for Macpherson's Ossian. In Terence Brown (ed.), *Celticism*. Amsterdam: Rodopi, 79-96.

Withers, Charles W.J. & Kenneth McKinnon 1994. Gaelic Speaking in Scotland, Demographic History. In Derick S. Thomson (ed.), *The Companion to Gaelic Scotland*. Glasgow: Gairm Publication, 109-114.

Marija Dalbello

Threshold Text and the Metaphysics of Writing

In exploring the question of textuality, writing, and material-conceptual identities of texts, this article presents "micro-readings" of several texts. Such hermeneutic process offers insights into the layering of text and analysis, pace Paul Ricoeur, and the disclosures of materiality, textuality, and of transformative dimensions of writing as a kind of material criticism. An example of non-literary letter writing, a literary letter-poem by Emily Dickinson, and a remediated modernist poem by Guillaume Apollinaire – all edited for a digital archive – are contrasted with contemporary artistic practices in conceptual drawings by Molly Springfield in which a work's artistic strategy is focused on revealing its materiality. The actualization of text in these examples addresses everyday inscription (letter writing), expressive literary writing (visual poems), and an artistic "meta-textual" project (text art). Thus ordinary writing is situated against "meta-textual" projects that explore the limits of scriptural, graphic (as in drawing), printed, and electronic forms. The features of texts across these widely divergent forms vary but they reveal a conceptual identity of text as a "material metaphor" and text as metaphor (Hayles 2002, 43) in that all treat inscription as a medium rather than as "transparent interface."

In text as a "material metaphor," the metaphor's materiality encompasses the physical and poetic features of texts across their widely divergent forms. Their micro-readings disclose text technologies and tensions inherent in the central notion of text that is enshrined in the socializations of text integral to production, reception and transformations (Chaudhury 2010, 82). Microreading unlocks the discourses of textuality as a core problem of what constitutes an actualization of text, a foundational question of the "metaphysics" of writing and textual space. The poetics of typographic space and writing surface activated within the toponyms of "material imagination" (Bachelard 1994 [1958]) are accompanied by oneiric experiences of text beyond its signification leading towards its actualization. The "metaphysics" of writing concerns chirographic inscription and remediation, especially in threshold texts that straddle across different forms of language and electronic text. Ordinary epistolary writing is contrasted with a literary letter and a modernist poetic text. Recovery of the core and irreducible identity that constitutes their presence as unique and distinct entities surfaces when peeling away the layers that make up conceptual identities of texts (Chaudhury 2010, 5) and our own assumptions about what constitutes a particular discourse of textuality and in contrasting different types of texts.

In its conclusion, the essay offers a reflection on writing as inextricable to creation (rather than instrumental and contextual) through the fourfold distanciation of writing, after Paul Ricoeur: (1) in suspension from signification, (2) in distanciation from the addressee but open to microreading, (3) in drawing attention to its own structure and visibility as graphic form, recognizing its sonic and resistive sensory elements, and (4) the autonomy of the text as distanced through intervention of its unintended reader – an editor of a digital archive (Dalbello 2011b; Van der Heiden 2010).

The purpose of this reflection is to discuss texts and their actualization as belonging to the larger system of language in which texts are tied to speakers or writers (*I*) as well as listeners or readers (*you*) (Altman 1982, 117) and the phenomenology of the everyday inscriptions in their material metaphors shaped by the history and "socializations" of text. Texts are realized in action, by being "made real." Their making and unmaking in the context of inscription, remediation, and actionable performance of textual form discloses the discourses of textuality.

Writing and material criticism

The (micro-)reading of exemplary resistive texts is prefaced by several theoretical points that organize them in this section, starting from the assumptions by Hans-Georg Gadamer about the "hidden" nature of language that needs to be interpreted, that "the emergence of new and unexpected interpretations has the purpose of not just extending but also *changing* [italic in the original] how we think about a subject matter" (Davey 2006, 32–33). In that context, micro-readings validate the hermeneutic project and the value of analysis reveals the layering of text. The "disclosive space of the hermeneutic encounter" in the practice of reading resistive texts and recognizing the "polarity of familiarity and strangeness" in their reading are integral to disclosure (*Ibid.*, 15). The inseparability of the physical and meta-physical in what "constitutes an actualization of text" is at the core of a new agenda for the study of texts. This form of material criticism originates in Katherine Hayles' *Writing Machines* (2002) and her call for media-specific analysis (MSA) to focus on instances and material situations. Hayles analyzes an "altered" book by a British artist Tom Phillips, *A Humument: A Treated Victorian Novel*, the unique form of art exploring the idea of the book. A "treated book" is the reverse palimpsest writing/drawing that uses the surface of an existing text, which is then altered through an artistic process to produce new work. The meta-physical – "beyond"/or behind the physical realm that is introduced in writing as an act of creation – is in dialogue with the physical – of how texts must exist in the world and their embodiment. Insofar as revealing non-stable meanings within a text is deconstructive by means of "the dismantling of conceptual oppositions, the taking apart of hierarchical systems of thought which can then be *re-inscribed* within a different order of textual signification" (Norris 1988, 19), this project is Derridarian.[1] *Arche-writing* is a phrase formulated by Jacques Derrida, to indicate writing capable of expressing that speaking and writing are simply two different forms of the same thing: the play of difference within language (Derrida 1997, 80).

Clearly, at the core of actualization is the material origin of text, conceived not only as a text-body but also an inner logic of its embodiment. Actualization operates through remediation, and not through representation. Therefore, close reading reveals different thresholds of text and the in-between forms. Thus, a text is actualized through "multi-layered inscriptions that create the book [or a letter, or any other inscription surface such as document, journal, map, *added MD*] as a physical artifact to imagine the subject as a palimpsest, emerging not behind but through the inscriptions that bring the book into being"; actualization is in itself a metaphysical inquiry "in which representation is short-circuited by the realization that there is no reality independent of mediation" (Hayles 2002, 110).

The letter-text is a material metaphor formed through "specific possibilities and constraints that shape texts" (*Ibid.*, 30) and a prime example of writing. When contrasted with artistic strategies, which are deliberative and force certain readings of text's materiality, in its actualization the letter-text belongs to a larger system of language in which texts are tied to speakers or writers, and listeners or readers.

Writing at the limit of orality: Letters of migration (Micrography 1)

Letters are socialized texts insofar as they are part of an epistolary discourse (Altman 1982, 117). One such form of epistolary writing is represented by the "letters of migration," which are non-literary texts that engage poetics and subjectivity through their rhetorical and affective nature. Letters of migration are a special category of texts that can connect writing closely to orality in the expressions of autodidacts, i.e. self-taught writers without formal training as evidenced by their use of grammar and orthography; or, in dictation that implies editorial interventions in the transposition of sound at the point of creation. Micro-reading of these letters focuses on

---

1   According to this Derrida scholar, deconstruction can be summarized as a three-step process: the first step involves identifying the binary oppositions that structure a text and the hierarchical relation that defines one term as central and the other as marginal. The next step is to reverse this hierarchical relationship by placing the marginal term at the center. This has the effect of showing the original relationship to be constructed and produces an alternative reading of the text. However, as Derrida consistently pointed out, the goal of deconstruction is not merely to replace one hierarchy or reading with another but to demonstrate that both (and many others) are equally possible. Thus, the final step of deconstruction requires the formulation of a more fluid and less coercive conceptual organization of terms that transcends the binary logic and acknowledges the mutual interdependence of both terms.

the interplays between orality and writing, invoking external realities of text that bear on its nature as meta-text at a particular historical moment of epistolary writing (Shemek 2015). Because texts and letters by autodidacts and dictated writing are ordinary in that particular historical moment, they can reveal operations within the text unique to that moment. The letters are historical documents but they are also material metaphors in the sense that they encode inherent constraints and the materiality of writing that shaped them. As an artifact of literacy's materiality and a material metaphor of transnational epistolarity, the migration letters construct writing as a social and material practice (Vieira 2016, 60). Personal letters reflect a range of cultural practices and modes of literacy, as shown in the following example of migrant letters.

The process of editing letters for a digital archive of letters written at the turn of the 19th and the 20th centuries in the context of the Great Migration and preserved at the University of Minnesota's Immigration History Research Center, the *Digitizing Immigrant Letters (DIL)* project[2] prompted a particularly intimate and close material reading.

The evolving analytical and immersive character of editing entailed multiple manipulations: with the sequencing of transcription, translation, and "transliteration," followed by the transposition of hand written to typed and representation as digital text, and ultimately reflecting on the juxtapositions of archival and digital facsimiles and their unique forensic versus semantic elements. These analytical stages prompted the disclosure of a letter as *inter-text* (at the threshold of orality, writing, and digitality); as a document (historiographic object); and in how it revealed its media specificity as *techno-text*. I will present these stages of recovery as a heuristic if subjective journey of microreading that brought about the "second ontological moment" as the texts were prepared for a digital archive. The recovery starts with the letters' finding, their "archive story" (Burton 2005), which is presented next.

The task of recognizing archival-worthy material for the *DIL* project was meant to be a simple process of selection, translation, and contextualization of a few exemplary letters from Austria-Hungary, – or so the task seemed at first. The four letters finding their way into this project were written to Milko Vukašinović of St. Paul, Minnesota by his mother from the village Plavnice in northwestern Croatia. Initially, I was attracted by the sparseness and a certain "dramatic" epigrammatic quality offered by the

---

2   Letters of migration project at the University of Minnesota Immigration History Research Center focuses on the "America Letters" and "homeland letters" written from and to America. These letters document the experience of migration through immigrant epistolarity and analysis of sentiment. These letters are distinct from epistolarity subsumed by the state and exemplified in Kate Vieira's ethnographic study of official documentation and communication with the state (2016, 59). The *Digitizing Immigrant Letters (DIL)* project was started by Donna Gabaccia, Daniel Necas, and Sonia Cancian, and involves an international group of collaborators with a common aim to study letter writing, transnationalism, and "America" discourse. The project continues through periodic symposia and ongoing additions to the letter archive.

juxtapositions of dates and records in the archival folder and a dearth of artifacts telling this story of immigrant life. Four neatly folded letters in the elongated shape that, when opened, easily fit into a palm of one hand, a typical contemporary format for personal correspondence. In addition to the letters, the file contained a checkbook with various recorded dates of transactions, a check for 4.75 dollars issued to Milko ("Mike") in 1920, his death certificate dated 31 January 1935, and the coroner's report from the same time. Apparently, Mike died at 54 of "natural causes," of pneumonia and coronary arteriosclerosis and his last known address was in St. Paul, Minnesota. We can deduce from this record that Milko was born in 1881 and that most likely he spent much of his working life in America, during the period when millions were immigrating from the European heartlands. Other facts are deducible from this sparse evidence contained in the archival folder. The letters were written before the dissolution of the Habsburg monarchy,[3] which was at least 17 years before the earliest moment at which this archive comes together as an artifact. The time before its institutional life as an archival folder is without an exact provenance. Someone must have kept these records before they were deposited in the university's collections in the 1970s. Clearly, there are several ontological moments in play, some with complex implications that Jacques Derrida recognizes in any archive in his work *Archive Fever* (1996) – related to how texts become part of a system of memory.

From the mother's letters, we see a world unfold – a family drama and economic crisis that shaped Milko's story of emigration, typical of many others of that time. In the letters, his mother begs Milko to return home, she relates events from village life including some feuds and a legal or criminal case in which he was implicated. The historical recovery could be one way in which one can proceed with the contextualization of the letters: by exploring the migrational dimension of this story and the two places that frame it – the place of origin (departure) and the place of arrival and settlement; and, recovering the historical moment that produced the letters as epistolary discourse; by focusing on their language and dialectal expression; or, by recovering the *sentiment of the époque* (after Raymond Williams). Historicizing the letters would be one way of localizing this collection – situating it within the patterns of a larger archive of immigrant experience. While it is relevant to explore further the locale and the story using archival and census material that is still available in Croatia to understand more about the kinship context, in this particular case the historical recovery is not explanatory in the sense I want to pursue here.

Reading the inscription itself offers another entry point and readings of letter-texts as material metaphor. First, the visual response to the graphic identity of letters was one of wonder, the presence of the otherness of untrained handwriting and, an aesthetic response to their "strange beauty" and their counter-cultural dimension that prompted disclosure. The letters belong to a subaltern culture of writing in which written forms are deeply

3   From the content of the letters it was clear that they were written between 1900 and 1918.

rooted in the oral performance of language, and a materiality of inscription that such "residual" orality produced. The process of preparing the letters for a digital archive made these qualities visible in surprising ways.

The "processing" of letters for a digital archive called for multiple transpositions that engaged the visual experience. That is no surprise for anyone who contemplated or engaged in the practices of digitization: that digitization defamiliarizes the experience of text and that one can be gratified by the intimacy of a close-up that reframes seeing as one can inspect every tremor in the gesture of handwriting. Digitization is just one rhetorical element in the process of translation, with several other preceding it. The stages of construction of a digital archive involved the letters' transcription and translation. A subjective account of multiple thresholds of construction, each in turn leading to surprising insights about my own assumptions about literacy, writing, and the epistolary form, is presented next.

(1) Encountering each letter was reading it as if Mike would – silently processing and hearing an inner voice, as if they are spoken to me, declaratively. This process is familiar and somewhat intuitive, as one's eye skips and glides across the surface of the page. Expressed colloquially, one "gets a drift," even if not compelled to understand every word or thought: one can have a general sense and emotion of the letter. These are imagistic events. Transmission of a letter occurs in a private space that provides multiple contextual dimensions and links between a reader and a writer. We are left in the state of ambiguity that is integral to such an intimate reading. Clearly the letter-text as a material metaphor is legible although the socialization of the text (i.e., its recognition as communicative writing) is not complete or final.

(2) Transcription. As I transcribed each letter, its reading forced another analytical engagement: transposing handwriting to typewritten surface required visual interpretation. The graphic disambiguation in the articulation of script (e.g. distinguishing "p"s and "t"s), to be expected in a document written in an awkward hand, offered no resistance. And yet, the transcription was dislodging. The letters had been written in a continuous gesture. Unbroken text, un-punctuated, is not the familiar *scriptura continua*. Here, only the punctuation was absent though the spacing between words retained the appearance of a standard morphemic structure. The units of text were maintained but in an entirely idiosyncratic orthography. Breaks between words and phonetic-semantic units could be re-interpreted to mirror spoken language. In this form of writing, visual parsing by means of a comma or a full stop had no place. The end of sentence was without a question mark or an exclamation point. Except for the end of a line, or end of a page, the text was delivered in a single breath. An unbroken form of writing accommodated the gesture and the form of language in which spoken Word is dominant and writing is oralized and embedded within a graphic form.

The actualization of text in this form of writing pointed to a voice and inscription having a common origin; there was no translation from one to the other apart from phonemically – the transposition of voice to writing stopped at the morphemic and syntactic articulations.

Mike Vukasinovich papers (IHRC2807). Letter to Mike Vukasinovich from his Mother – No Date. Immigration History Research Center Archives, University of Minnesota.

The transcription posed only minor difficulties in the decoding of handwriting, which was otherwise articulate and logical. The struggle around legibility resided in the material form and in the text itself that resisted, interstitially, the transposition from orality to literacy: the text did not "fit" standardized morphological units of language (the expected "words"). What counted as a word was defined phonetically. And, even without encoding the rhythm of pauses and silences in the stream of sound that corresponded to spoken language from which this letter originated, the flow of handwriting allowed for ambiguity to be maintained in the written form. Increasingly, the letter that seemed more or less legible became illegible in the moment of attempted remediation via typewritten transcription. Thus, the transcription revealed that the letter was an impossible textual object resistant to logical ordering (Hayles 2002, 116).

My struggle with the disciplinary order of the word processing program was visceral. The Word program (Croatian mode) refused to parse words in order to normalize the text to conform to its appearance on the page, as if emphasizing "violence" that orthography exercises upon spoken language. In order to make sense and make the text and its transcription intelligible, I found myself vocalizing these nebulous streams of writing in order to figure out what is being said, where the thought stops (if it does), and where it picks up again, then shifts. I often found that there were overlaps in thoughts and repetition of the same thought metonymically, and words melded with other words. Repetition aimed to subvert the text and bolster the voice, disorganizing the visual space in the process. Clearly these letters were resistant but also pointing to multiple simultaneous systems in play. My co-editor on this group of letters, with whom I corresponded about the problematic dimensions of the letters and the transcription, thought that the letters had been dictated. While writing by dictation was a common practice in letter writing, historically speaking, in this case each letter must have been spoken to someone who was similarly an autodidact and who merely transcribed, as if tape-recorded, what he or she heard, without intervening. Why would the person taking dictation – and therefore assumed being functionally "literate" and schooled – give precedence to the logic of the spoken word rather than observing rules of early 20th century orthography? In the historical studies of spacing and punctuation (Parkes 1993; Saenger 1997) such document forms connect writing and reading to oral performance. In this example, the raw forms of orality enshrined in the text were unsuspected points of socialization of the text that was integral to its production and reception. In the actualization of writing analyzed in the process of editing, the letter-text clearly asserted its connection to spoken language.

(3) Translation brought yet another interesting perspective in understanding writing at the limit of orality. The issue of un-translatability was not one of isolated concepts transmitted in language but the un-translatability of the structure of thought. The attempts at the actualization of text in translation only emphasized the illegibility in the original. Comparable to an attempt of interpreting a dream that resists narrative ordering, the attempts at translation resulted in being lost in the stream of

someone else's consciousness – as if inhabiting the text of a modernist novel but without its aesthetic, literary, or semantic associativity. The text could only be described as "nebulous, hazy, and fuzzy." Idiosyncratic! The text was an inversion in which a floating (i.e., multi modal or "empty") signified is attached to a fixed graphic signifier. That has been a most dislocating experience for a reader socialized in the forms of standard literacy and orthography. The effect was not by authorial intent or "by design"; instead it prompted an experience of the text one would expect in the anti-aesthetics of the Dada movement. Nevertheless, the effect of a nebulous text that could not be semantically completed is sublime and poetic. A surreal effect and its strange beauty may be an editorial hallucination or a mirage created by the expectations of literacy brought to the letter by its unintended reader (myself). The text as material metaphor (as a written letter-text) in this found text was formed through specific possibilities and constraints introduced by text technologies that tied these texts to orality within a tension that made orality surface within the text but not being fully produced.

Even though the meaning of some words may have remained unclear, particularly interesting were those cases in which there were overlapping sentences that in speech propel thought metonymically. In written form such expressions are breaking the rules of literacy, the rational expression enforced through syntax. The rules of sentence formation require a subject, predicate, object connected by prepositions and augmented with adjectives, adverbs and relative clauses. Not here! In this subaltern form of literacy in the letters of migration, referents are lost and antecedents are left ambiguous. The letter in this form is socialized within the language of orality that shapes the relationship of *I-you*, which corresponds to a historical situation (i.e., an epistolary culture within which autodidacts, dictation are common, and epistolary conventions are distinct).

When faced with difficulties in finding resolutions for particular ambiguous situations, it becomes interesting how each of the two editors approached the problem. Wladimir Fischer, who is a native speaker of German yet a trained Slawicist, could see the comparative forms via Old Church Slavic. As an educated native speaker of Croatian language and familiar with its dialects, I opted for intuitive associations, fitting form to various possibilities of dialectal traces, literally "listening" to the text in order to understand it. For example, the grapheme that could be transcribed as any of the following: "*Košto, Pošto, Hošto*" would each lead to a different interpretation and sequencing of (preceding and the following) text. And, each of these could be semantically interesting: "*Košto*" [adverbial "like"] introducing an analogy with an antecedent thought; "*Pošto*" ["because"] establishing causality; and finally, "*Hošto*" ["as if"] indicating a dialectal archaism. We could not tell which form is "correct" or even whether the pursuit of correctness can be the goal here. We decided to retain ambiguities in the edited version, establishing a sort of critical edition of this text of ordinary writing. The possibilities of digital editing allow for editorial glosses that at least symbolically would make the process of transposition transparent. Leaving ambiguities intact (i.e., not resolving them editorially) was not a failure of writing, or reading. Enforcing fixity, on the other hand, would be.

(4) Presentation in a Digital Archive. Digital archives can record the alternatives and point to juxtaposition of multiple layers of textuality contained in a performative text (Broude 2011). The interpretive moments by which the cultures of writing can be de-standardized in a digital archive and the archive could be emancipatory for critical editions of non-literary texts is comparable to retaining interpretive layers that textual bibliography accomplishes in the realm of print culture (McKenzie 1999). Editing letters for a digital archive opened the realm of writing to critical reading of various thresholds of text, moving the letter-text across the oral, literate, and the historical-contextual dimensions of immigrant letter writing, as shown here. The editing also pointed to the interstitial nature of enunciation, revealing a joined visual-oral-written form that is experienced in a synesthetic fashion. The fourfold distanciation of writing that enabled this interpretive reading revealed the nature of text at the limit of orality in surprising ways. Because the letters of migration belong to ordinary writing, they present these relations involuntarily and without authorial intent. Only in the process of being transposed to electronic text within a context of their re-socialization in a digital archive, they became open to unintended analytical reading that revealed their formative discourse of textuality.

The next section focuses on "technotext" as another threshold text. Techno text conceptualizes text as compositional-structural form in which the physical dimension of a text artifact is foregrounded. The digital archive is itself a writing machine, a "technotext" (Hayles 2002, 29). The first example to be interpreted is a literary letter-poem in which the composition is a deliberative poetic device and not an example of ordinary writing. The second example is a visual poem with its multiple mediations.

Techno-text – digitized Dickinson, digital Apollinaire (Micrography 2)

Emily Dickinson's letter-poems epitomize a genre, exemplifying sensory writing that melds epistolary conventions with poetry, which she blended for a wide-ranging purpose and effect.[4] Their presentation in one of the

---

4   From *DEA*: "… In his 1958 introduction to *The Letters of Emily Dickinson*, Thomas H. Johnson remarked the oft-quoted editorial "doubt where the letter leaves off and the poem begins" (L, xv). Sixteen years later, her eminent biographer Richard B. Sewall identified producing "letter-poems" as a familial as well as an artistic practice: '[Dickinson's father] Edward's sister Elizabeth was not only the chronicler but the bard of her generation. She once sent her young nephew Austin a rhymed letter of fifty stanzas on his toothache' (*Life* 32). Sometimes Dickinson enclosed poems on a separate sheet with a letter; sometimes poems (especially to Susan Dickinson) constitute the entire text of a letter; sometimes a few lines of a poem recorded in the fascicles or in another letter or on a sheet not bound to any manuscript book, either literally with string or figuratively by being sent to a particular addressee, are woven into the prose of a letter." Available from http://archive.emilydickinson.org/letter/letintro.htm.

155

Emily Dickinson. Autograph letter and poem sent to Susan Dickinson, c. 1884. Houghton MS Am 1118.5 (B90) Houghton Library, Harvard University.

pioneering digital humanities projects, the *Dickinson Electronic Archives (DEA),*[5] mediates their materiality and presence as digital inscriptions.

Martha Nell Smith argues in one of her essays reflecting on the *DEA* archive and its editorial construction that the electronic format can preserve Dickinson's authorial intention, her poetry being "determined by the codes of hearing (metrical conventions) rather than the codes of seeing" (Smith 2002; quoted in Dalbello 2011a, 495; Dalbello 2013a). The epistemologies of hearing and seeing conflated in this digital archive point to the oral

---

5 There are several Emily Dickinson projects on the Internet, all available through the *DEA* home page that relates "the recent unveilings of digital archives – the Emily Dickinson Collection produced and hosted by Amherst College and the Emily Dickinson Archive produced and hosted by the Houghton Library and Harvard University Press – have stirred up a new iteration of an old conversation with Dickinson Studies" (http://www.emilydickinson.org/bound-a-trouble). There are commonalities in the library efforts – of making accessible their Dickinson manuscript collections on the open web with hopes of creating a new participative model for Dickinson scholarship. The *Dickinson Electronic Archives (DEA)* project started in 1994 and is still available from the main menu of *DEA 2* and at http://archive.emilydickinson.org. *DEA 2* was launched in 2014. The model for presentation changes with different interfaces.

roots of all writing, making a link with the letters of migration. In these letters, orality is encoded in the compositional-structural dimensions that resurfaced in the process of editing to render them in electronic form, their *texton* (as a unit distinguished from *scripton* in Espen Aarseth's *scripton-texton* distinction [1997, 62–63; 2003, 767]).

Dickinson's poetry presents editorial challenges because she circulated hand-written copies and included objects with her poetry, defying finiteness of text and the reductionist conventions of printed poetry. The scriptural dimensions of her letter-poems (the imagist text or *scripton*) can be found as well, as in the close up of a digital autograph of a letter-poem in *DEA*, "Morning Might Come."[6] In its various versions, the poem becomes a *text-image* (Mitchell 1994) and even the individual words within the poem can be experienced imagistically, a feature supported by the ability to zoom in and out of the digital facsimile.

As *intertext* (transcription), the sonic dimensions of the document and individual letter-poem are normalized (lines and stanzas vary in different printed versions, compact and rhythmically ordered). The accompanying *peritext* links outwardly; to information about editions, location of the original in the *DEA*. At the time of writing, the contextual elements in the image metadata included credits and extensive publication history, space for "my notes" inviting interaction, searching and filtering functions. The searching/browsing for manuscript images (by first line, date, recipient, or edition) are connecting individual poems to the entire Dickinson archive. The participatory engagement is also fore fronted in the latest version. These are the general properties of digital textuality and presentation within an electronic collection. While the archive is a topographic frame within which letter-poems are embedded, it also mediates the interface. The presentation of text in the digital archive recirculates representations of documents located elsewhere. The digital form of a letter-poem is actualized in the interactions that are embedded in the materiality of inscription technologies and augmentation of experience such as the ability to flow along different paths through the text, close up view, and forensic examination.

The deliberation with which sensory writing of letter-text engages sight through its graphic rhythms on the Dickinson's page or her idiosyncratic autographs intensely remind us of their materiality, authorial origin, and irreducibility. As noted, her poetry defies finite-ness and completeness. The digital archive does not complete it through the erasure of its irreducible quality but by contiguous multiple drafts of extant manuscripts presented in the digital archive, in itself presenting a challenge to the fixity of text. The affordances of electronic text in the context of a digital archive are better suited to Dickinson's poetic practice than the printed editions. In the

---

6   Dickinson, Emily, letter to Susan Huntington Dickinson, "Morning Might Come," MS Am 1118.5 (B90). Houghton Library, Harvard University, Cambridge, Mass. Houghton Library – p. 1, L912, Fr1658, HCL (H B90); 2008 addition to the *DEA*. The letter-poem was written in pencil c. 1884. It was first published in 1924 "as penciled message," and in 1958 as "Letter 912." Published in *Open me Carefully* in 1998, Ellen Louise Hart & Martha Nell Smith (eds).

augmentation of writing that tends to the specificity of the letterform and a topographic environment within which each letter-poem is embedded, we are pointed once again to chirographic forms (in the insistence on the "image") to be the outcome of searching and filtering. In the archive, it is the editorial authority and Emily Dickinson's handwriting that authenticates the irreducible dimension of text and her poetic practice as well as its role as a literary document.

The next example of technotext are several digitized versions of Guillaume Apollinaire's concrete poem "Il pleut" that were published in *E-ratio Poetry Journal*, including an electronic rendition of the poem created by Gregory Vincent St. Thomasino and Mary Ann Sullivan (2008) at: http://www.eratiopostmodernpoetry.com/editor_Il_Pleut.html

On a single scrolling page there is a digital version (first), followed by the autograph from 1916 and a typeset version first published in the avant-garde journal *SIC: sons, idées, couleurs, formes* (12 December 1916). In these transformations of the poem, from an autograph and print to electronic text, its "materiality emerges from interactions between physical properties and a work's artistic strategies" (Hayles 2002, 32–33) as each of the forms presents a contrast to the other. (The autograph and the printed/typeset versions are digital versions, too, in this context.)

In the digital edition, the display of sound is "graphic" and representational, an ironic reflection on the processes of signification. The inscription on the page is set to sound. In less than a minute of sonic rain that accompanies the reading of letters, dropping on the electronic page in the speed and rhythm of rain-drops pouring downward and clicking against glass of a "windowpane" page, in the re-appearance of "play again" button once the text is complete while the sound continues for 10 more seconds, we are reminded that we are reading a text machine that can be turned off and on, reminiscent of a *vergula*, the mechanical instrument that plays a repeating melody by the turn of a handle. The text can be played over and over from start to finish. Thus, a text is actualized in its appearance, which simulates a mechanical tool, the typewriter. (Is it possible not to link this with the appearance of text marching to the sound of typewriter from the early days of PowerPoint? Here, the text is flowing down the page with the sonic rhythm of rain.)

"Il pleut" is not punctuated. Accordingly, its linear translations preserve the rhythm of the poem and its mood created by the slanting lines that create "the sensation of rain running downward across a windowpane," as in one widely available rendition through the Poetry Foundation on the public Internet. This version is curated by Edward Hirsch in an interpretive essay, "Winged Type" and notes that the graphic form and verbal music of the poem are "coming together as each long vertical line becomes a rhythmic unit of meaning," while "the sound of the unpunctuated lines in French creates an incantatory murmuring that evokes the sadness and melancholy of a rainy day in Paris" (Hirsch 2006).

In this electronic text, the sound is not oralization or a "naturalistic" imitation of the sound of the writing tool (rain, typewriter?). Neither is it the cracking of the electric wiring of neon signs that light up letters (Samoyault 2011). The sound of rain is a concretist and associational device in the electronic pictorial poem. Leading the comparison of this poem created in 2008 to the 1916 typeset version "original" is the visible structure on which the electronic text is modeled. The descending lettering inserted in the geometrical grid of a printed page is already complete but not atemporal because we need to scroll to reveal it. A certain mechanical rhythm can be recognized in the broken lines when letters shift around the grid. The lettering in the printed version imitates the typography of a typewriter. The title IL PLEUT frames the poem, as does the lettering GUILLAUME APOLLINAIRE. The title points to its place on the page of a printed book (i.e., the modernist magazine *SIC*) from within an electronic Apollinaire museum. In the digital scan of the printed page, we also see a mirror image on verso that is bleeding through. The "see-through writing" is spectral, as it breaks the autonomy of the page (recto) or the autonomy of electronic rendition, its representation.

A digital scan of the autograph text of "Il pleut" in *E-ratio* edition is positioned between the digital rendition and the printed edition, perhaps to break the similarity of the two that is obvious in both of them referencing a spurious manuscript text that would be written using a typewriter. The comparison of the three texts on this scrolling page lends itself to material criticism by a casual reader. An autograph (also from 1916) reminds us of the origin of this poem in a text that is hand written rather than structured with type, a version that is modeled in the electronic rendition.

The autograph is visually complex: two types of ink, creases, texture of hand-made paper, smears and corrections. There are two or three levels of text here. The "corrections" in darker ink in the second, third and fourth parallel dropping lines respectively (in the words "*gouttellettes*," "*à*" and "*que le regret*"). These appear as corrections, possibly added at a later time in darker ink as is the poem's title "Il pleut" (double-underlined) and a compressed doodle ("Apollinaire"?). The autograph also features "dic 16" in the upper right section of the page, which is tilted upward and against the descent of graphemes of the text of the poem itself. Handwriting leaves un-answered questions, un-fixes the text.

As shown in the analysis of Apollinaire's poem, "meta-textual" projects employ artistic strategies to explore the limits of scriptural, graphic, printed and electronic form. These projects are similar to the avant-garde typographic experiments such as Stéphane Mallarmé's, "Un coup de dès jamais n'abolira le hasard" (Shaw 2011) or Guillaume Apollinaire's *Calligrammes* that offer multiple non-linear readings and surreal effects of typography and the arrangements of words on a page. Revealing texts enshrined in material metaphors, they are the phenomenological-poetic investigations of intentionality, material form and the everyday experience of text.

Meta-text: Simulacra of writing (Micrography 3)

Drawings by a contemporary Washington, D.C. artist Molly Springfield are a meta-text that imitates writing. They record multiple simultaneous re-mediations and examine the relationship of reality, inscription and replication. The actualization of text in a drawing that appears to be an enlarged photocopy (or printout) of a printed page maintains traces of simultaneous spectral presences of these material contexts of replication. These contexts are encoded but visible because of our preconceived notion of what is a text. Springfield's meta-text confronts transmission itself as an "ensemble of media, practice, and thought" and not a "purely mechanical affair" (Chandler, Davidson & Johns 2004, 6). Her work is similar to the genre of "treated books" exemplified by *A Humument: A Treated Victorian Novel* (Phillips 2012 [1970]) by using the relationship to "originals" and "origin" as well as materiality in her critical analysis of transmission.

Molly Springfield's *Chapter IX* (2008) appears to be a photo-copy of the first page of a chapter titled "On Drawing from Flat Copies." The original of this apparent photocopy (enlarged to an "un-natural" page dimension that indicates a departure from the original) is the first page of the ninth chapter of *Handbook of Drawing*, a Victorian pedagogical treatise on elementary drawing published in London in 1879 by the drawing master William Walker.[7] In his text, Walker commented on the advantages and pitfalls of careful copying. He also championed the *art* of drawing as an act of creation according to formal rules – as opposed to the *craft* of drawing in which students imitate the work of others. This observation gestures to the signifying practices of writing as creation and drawing as its special case.

In her drawing, Springfield removes the printed book page from its source by creating a copy of it. This does not appear to be a neat and clean photocopy; the artist seems to have made it carelessly, as if she had left open the lid on a photocopier, resulting in some distortion and thick black borders. The narrow white margin around these black borders leads us to wonder whether this framed object may even be an inkjet printout of a digital scan of a photocopy – the ubiquitous Portable Document Format (PDF) that pervades our reading experiences today.

Gradually we become aware that what we are seeing and reading is actually a remarkably masterful manual copy – a drawing – of a printed/photocopied/digitized page. Springfield painstakingly traced each letter and word on the page by hand, so that this drawing is not simply a page copied from a book, but a page of a copy invoked in drawing, a framed scribal copy. We are now truly participating in a mirage of writing and we are faced by an *imagetext* overcome by the graphic. This drawing (copy of a copy of a copy) is a near-photographic record of the visibility of a typographical

---

7   There are British and American editions of this work: the English editions were published by London's Seeley, Jackson and Halliday (in 1880) and the American by New York's C. Scribner's Sons (in 1890, 1905, and 1907). This drawing was shown in *Art=Text=Art: Works by Contemporary Artists (4 September 2012 – 6 January 2013)* (Dalbello 2013b).

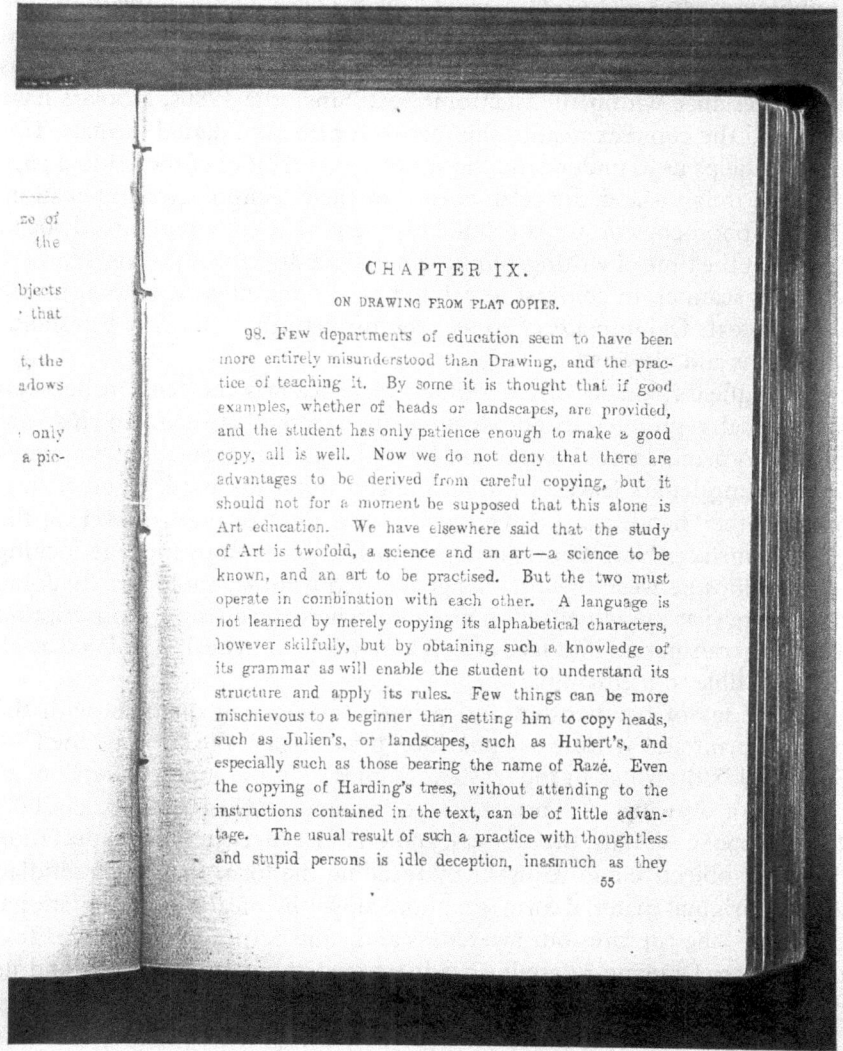

Molly Springfield. Chapter IX, 2008. *Graphite on paper 55.9 x 43.2 cm. Sarah-Ann and Werner H. ("Wynn") Kramarsky Collection. Photograph and permission granted by the artist.*

page (including the book cover). Yet Springfield also emphasizes the book as an expressive material object, in a slightly inappropriate copy. She has captured all the residual marks of the binding, gutter, and margin, as they would be recorded in a photocopy.

Springfield's choice to situate her drawing within the context of a methodological treatise on drawing is a reflection on both the current age of photomechanical reproduction and the material nature of the book. We live at a time when digital copy can upstage printed matter but digital text is not a new form. It is steeped in the resistant nature of the print interfaces that materialize within the electronic text. Since the 1980s, scholars have pondered the complex relationship between print and digital formats. This drawing helps us to understand the various materialities of the printed page available today – and the relative ease of their technological replication. One can photocopy or Xerox printed texts, a practice that may already be in decline at the time of writing, or one can make a digital copy using a camera lens or a scanner. In contrast to printed page – ink pressed onto a surface – digital texts feel immaterial to us, seen through their material thresholds (platforms and viewers).

Springfield's fantasy of the printed page realizes the tension between mechanical reproduction and hand-written copy, between drawing and writing. A printed page is organized by its design constraints; the symmetry of repeating letters leaves a formal imprint upon the page. Handwriting, on the other hand, can fill the page with a river of marks covering the writing surface. Here Springfield prompts us to explore the interlocking relationships between drawing, language, and print technologies. By doing this, she reverts the actualization to a point where the medium of inscription is not the transparent interface even if it may appear to be. It is imbued by all of its possible re-mediations.

Drawings of handwritten and printed texts are in dialogue with the fixity of print and writing as apparition if we engage the "trompe l'oeil" of Springfield's drawings in the "ecstatic mimesis" of the multiple versions of text that a drawing of a printed page insinuates (Gosetti-Ferencei 2007, 185). The joke is on us, the viewers, and on our experience and expectation of text as objective and realistic. By recalling the form that is a quotidian and un-original material form – a photocopy – by means of an imitational drawing – she ruptures our awareness and simulacrum of coherence. Text is a mirage. Drawing re-establishes the connection between a text and its material expression.

Springfield's further meditation on the incompleteness of visible text is her work titled, *A Translation*, the series of 28 drawings of the first chapter of Marcel Proust's *In Search of Lost Time*. The visual work of "translation" is patched together from "photocopies of sequential pages from the first chapter of the novel, pieced together from every existing translation … This patchwork results in the repetition and omission of text from page to page, resolving into an incomplete and not-fully-readable rendition of the original" (commentary from artist's web site). Are texts and their readings present in sequential re-mediations? The elision of words and passages transforms the experience by making texts objects and their reading conditional on our own insertions of missing signs.

Springfield's interest in the conceptual dimensions of writing includes objects such as annotations as readers' interventions. *The Marginalia Archive* is an expanding interactive installation that explores relationships between texts and readers, with a photocopier/scanner available in the exhibit, with the invitations to viewers to submit photocopied or scanned book pages that readers had marked or inscribed (Dabkowski 2012). Springfield is a self-styled "artist-qua-text explorer" whose work, using detailed realist painting techniques, revisits the technologies of reproduction (calotypes), memory, identity and collecting and cataloguing in correspondence art (postcards and letters), offering meditations on digital text (see her exhibitions *The Proto-History of the Internet*, 2012) or objects (*The World is Full of Objects*, 2008). Engaging in a meditation on the nature of textuality and originality is also a meditation on falsehood and mimesis.[8] The illusion of text surface points to the transformations of intentionality expressed in visual works of art.

Text art, library art, and book art are becoming a theme for the 21st century conceptual artists whose works on paper resurrect text technologies and make *techno-textual* environments by making them visible in the interstices of text that resists. They leave us with a question of what is a book, what is a text, pointing us to reflect on the phenomenology of everyday writing and its material metaphors.

Digital renditions of non-literary and literary texts and reflection on text in the context of visual art have shown that studying writing, rather than being instrumental and contextual to text, is inextricable from studying the creation of text. The micrographies (descriptions originating from micro-reading) pointed to the fact that text is actualized through multilayered inscriptions that create it as a material body, emerging not behind but through the inscriptions that bring it into being (Hayles 2002, 110). The last example especially pointed to actualization becoming a metaphysical inquiry in itself, integral to an artistic program, and that there is no reality independent of mediation.

In the next section, the actualization of text is revisited one more time to assess the consequences of analysis and questions that it may open up about writing as a larger problem of language.

Fourfold distanciation of writing

The previous sections have shown how material criticism can be used in media-specific analysis (MSA) (Hayles 2002, 29). The program for material criticism focused on the actualization of text and writing in specific embodiments of text. Following from the reflections on the micrographies that disclose text discourses (of ordinary writing close to orality and different types of meta-text) is Paul Ricoeur's fourfold distanciation of writing. The fourfold distanciation presents itself (1) in suspension from signification, (2) in distanciation (from the addressee/reader/viewer) but open to microreading, (3) in drawing attention to its own structure and visibility as graphic form, and (4) the autonomy of the text distanced through interventions (by unintended reader – such as editor of a digital archive) (Dalbello 2011b; Van der Heiden 2010).

---

8   *False Documents and Other Illusions* is the name of a group exhibition at The Portland Museum of Art in 2010 that featured work by Molly Springfield.

The analysis has shown that while expressive, the texts are (1) in suspension from signification. This is integral to the artistic approach in the drawings by Molly Springfield, which are fully engaged with the processes of replication. When the form engages representation (as in digital Apollinaire, by completing the vision), it does so through the text itself. The auditory expression that is non-textual is relegated to digital rendition of natural sound (a looping gif file) and the rain by the pouring of letters down a page/windowpane. The sensory experience is illustrative but it allows us to contemplate the fully realized text on the page, now conflating the epistemologies of seeing and hearing through these two inscriptions (one, textual that prompts imagistic response; the other, naturalistic that introduces sound). The text becomes suspended in the interplay of differences and signification. This text depends on a relationship with the "exterior absence" of its opposite, a static text.

The letters of migration point to text resistant to logical ordering of literacy and its inability to control oral forms. They reveal a type of socio-materiality that resides in what Dorothy Smith calls "active text" in her sociology of the people (Campbell 2003) and a type of arche-writing (after Derrida's contemplation of written speech). The hand written text is an inscription that resists reproduction and orthography. Emily Dickinson's letter-poems cease to be letters in their digital renditions, the digital presenting itself as a superior inscription technology that produces multiple simultaneous effects, graphic overflow (*textimage* to *imagetext*) and text that is fully realized within a digital archive and "technotext" as another form of threshold text.

While these examples point to texts that are not fully descriptive of the phenomenon (world connected to the word) they are still evocative (even if not complete). The emotional content of mother's letters imploring an absent son to return are appropriated in an editorial reading and their translation appropriated into a project that can open multiple forms of understanding and bring into presence the sentiment of a historical situation. Reading letters in suspension from the everyday world (Van der Heiden 2010, 83–85) in which they figure in one singular event, and to opening a possibility for them to configure a poetic world, is an editorial intervention and frames the purpose of this interpretation. Thus the letters assume their status as discourse (2) in the distanciation from the addressee (reader, viewer) when opened to editorial microreading.

The texts are engaged in conveying a deeper human truth because of their uniqueness and origin. For example, the letters of migration are associated with non-elite writers and are generated outside of the canons of graphic form and orthographic organization (spacing, and punctuation). Their distanciation originates in the writing itself with the consequence of the reader being faced with obstacles when attempting to determine the exact meaning. This text disallows to be contained and its origin in an oral culture of speaking is visible in the orthographic transgressions of its writing. Thus, (3) in drawing attention to its own structure and visibility as graphic form the letters abduct the reader, they have the potential for disorienting literate readers who expect a particular order. The other examples variously point to their own visibility and graphic formations and involve a viewer. The machinery of inscription surfaces beyond the signification and semantics in the digital texts, exemplified in Dickinson letter-poem and the different versions of Apollinaire's "Il pleut." The invisible codes that produce text (Hayles 2004, 8) are its compositional-structural elements or *textons* within the *scripton-texton* pair (Aarseth 1997, 62–63). In contrast, *scripton* is the imagist text, i.e., the image of page/screenic representations that we experience as text in the case of concrete poems and Dickinson letter-poems, their visible graphic surface. Meta-textual experiments with the imagist text can be sensory or conceptual as in Springfield's writing objects (editions, copies, marginalia, and the page) that become drawing.

Finally, the (4) autonomy of text in its aesthetic dimension is present in its graphic form, capturing a unique, organic nature or technological process, and including idiosyncratic hand-writing or ambiguously autonomous gestures of drawing. Thereby, literacy is steeped in oral practice that surfaces in the letters of migration, and chirographically-typographically sculpted *calligrammes*. These unique forms prompt distanciation in offering themselves to a hermeneutic process, a close reading that uncovers thresholds of text in the examined examples. This is a return to the hermeneutic project as outlined by Hans-Georg Gadamer – the spirit and immanence of the acts of writing, the enabling factors and situative nature of writing, and meditation of writing by re-writing (1986 [1967]).

By presenting micrographies of threshold texts, i.e. the instances of text that exemplify writing at the limit of orality (via letters of migration); those that engage re-mediations and techno-text (digitized letters and digital poetry); and, meta-textual simulacra of writing, this hermeneutic project relies on material criticism. The readings of threshold texts have disclosed a number of text discourses and meta-textual forms that prompt an awareness of the materiality of text shaped by the metaphysics of writing.

References

Internet sources

Digitizing Immigrant Letters. Available from http://ihrca.dash.umn.edu/dil/
Emily Dickinson Electronic Archives. Available from http://www.emilydickinson.org

Literature

Aarseth, Espen J. 1997. *Cybertext: Perspectives on Ergodic Literature.* Baltimore: Johns Hopkins University Press.
Aarseth, Espen J. 2003. Nonlinearity and Literary Theory. In Noah Wardrip-Fruin & Nick Montfort (eds), *The New Media Reader.* Cambridge: The MIT Press, 761–780.
Altman, Janet Gurkin 1982. *Epistolarity: Approaches to a Form.* Columbus: Ohio State University. Available from https://ohiostatepress.org/books/Complete%20PDFs/Altman%20Epistolarity/Altman%20Epistolarity.htm

Apollinaire, Guillaume 2008. Il pleut. In Vincent St. Thomasino & Mary Ann Sullivan (eds), Apollinaire Museum at *E-Ratio*: Il pleut, *E-Ratio Poetry Journal*. Available from http://www.eratiopostmodernpoetry.com/editor_Il_Pleut.html

Bachelard, Gaston 1994 [1958]. *The Poetics of Space*. Boston: Beacon Press.

Broude, Ronald 2011. Performance and the Socialized Text. *Textual Cultures: Texts, Contexts, Interpretation* 6 (2): 23–47.

Burton, Antoinette 2005. Introduction: Archive Fever, Archive Stories. In Antoinette Burton (ed.), *Archive Stories: Facts, Fictions, and the Writing of History*. Durham: Duke University Press, 1–24.

Campbell, Marie 2003. Dorothy Smith and Knowing the World We Live In. *The Journal of Sociology & Social Welfare* 30 (1): 3–22.
Available from http://scholarworks.wmich.edu/jssw/vol30/iss1/2

Chandler, James, Arnold I. Davidson & Adrian Johns 2004. Arts of Transmission: An Introduction. *Critical Inquiry* 31 (1): 1–6.

Chaudhury, Sukanta 2010. *The Metaphysics of Text*. Cambridge: Cambridge University Press.

Dabkowski, Colin 2012. UB Exhibition Samples New Takes on Drawing. *The Buffalo News (NY)*. (12 October 2012). Available from https://web.archive.org/web/20160517224118/http://www.buffalonews.com/apps/pbcs.dll/article?aid=/20121012/gusto/121019761/1237

Dalbello, Marija 2011a. A Genealogy of Digital Humanities. *The Journal of Documentation* 67 (3): 480–506.

Dalbello, Marija 2011b. Micrographies and Microreadings – Writing at the Threshold of Movement, Sight, Sound. Paper presented at *Picture This: Postcards and Letters Beyond Text*, University of Sussex, 24–27 March 2011.

Dalbello, Marija 2013a. Digitality, Epistolarity and Reconstituted Letter Archives. *Information Research: An International Electronic Journal* 18 (3). Available from http://www.informationr.net/ir/18-3/colis/paperC26.html#.VTq0jV6AWIw

Dalbello, Marija 2013b. Molly Springfield: *Chapter IX* (2008). In *Art=Text=Art: Works by Contemporary Artists (4 September 2012 – 6 January 2013)*. Available from http://artequalstext.aboutdrawing.org/wp-content/uploads/2014/09/ArtTextArt_AudioGuide_Springfield_Dalbello.pdf

Davey, Nicholas 2006. *Unquiet Understanding: Gadamer's Philosophical Hermeneutics*. Albany, NY: SUNY Press.

Derrida, Jacques 1996. *Archive Fever: A Freudian Impression*. Translated by Eric Prenowitz. Chicago: Chicago University Press.

Derrida, Jacques 1997 [1967]. *Of Grammatology*. Translated by Gayatri Chakravorty Spivak. Baltimore: Johns Hopkins University Press.

Gadamer, Hans-Georg 1986 [1967]. *The Relevance of the Beautiful and Other Essays*. Edited by Robert Bernasconi. Cambridge: Cambridge University Press.

Gosetti-Ferencei, Jennifer Anna 2007. *The Ecstatic Quotidian: Phenomenological Sightings in Modern Art and Literature*. University Park, PA: Penn State University Press.

Hayles, Katherine N. 2002. *Writing Machines*. Cambridge: MIT Press.

Hayles, Katherine N. 2004. Print is Flat, Code is Deep: The Importance of Media Specific Analysis. *Poetics Today* 25 (1): 67–90.

Hirsch, Edward 2006. Winged Type. *Poetry Foundation*. (23 January 2006). Available from http://www.poetryfoundation.org/learning/article/177216

McKenzie, Don F. 1999. *Bibliography and the Sociology of Texts*. Cambridge: Cambridge University Press.

Mitchell, W.J.T. 1994. *Picture Theory*. Chicago: The University of Chicago Press.

Norris, Christopher 1988. *Derrida*. Boston: Harvard University Press.

Parkes, Malcolm 1993. *Pause and Effect: An Introduction to the History of Punctuation in the West*. Berkeley: University of California Press.

Phillips, Tom 2012 [1970]. *A Humument: A Treated Victorian Novel*. Fifth edition. London: Thames & Hudson.

Ricoeur, Paul 1976. *Interpretation Theory: Discourse and the Surplus of Meaning*. Fort Worth: Texas Christian University Press.

Saenger, Paul 1997. *Space Between Words: The Origins of Silent Reading*. Stanford: Stanford University Press.

Samoyault, Tiphaine 2011. Color Writings: On Three Polychrome Texts. In Marija Dalbello & Mary Shaw (eds), *Visible Writings: Cultures, Forms, Readings*. New Brunswick, NJ: Rutgers University Press, 237–253.

Shaw, Mary 2011. *Un coup de dés* and *La Prose du Transsibérien*: A Study in Contraries. In Marija Dalbello & Mary Shaw (eds), *Visible Writings: Cultures, Forms, Readings*. New Brunswick, NJ: Rutgers University Press, 135–150.

Shemek, Deanna 2015. Letter Writing and Epistolary Culture. In Margaret King (ed.), *Oxford Bibliographies in Renaissance and Reformation*. Last reviewed 29 June 2015. Available from http://www.oxfordbibliographies.com/view/document/obo-9780195399301/obo-9780195399301-0194.xml

Smith, Martha Nell 2002. Computing: What's American Literary Study Got to Do with IT? *American Literature* 74 (4): 833–857.

Springfield, Molly 2008. *Translation*. Drawings. 11x17 inches, graphite on paper. Available from http://mollyspringfield.com/section/38669_Translation.html

Van der Heiden, Gert-Jan 2010. *The Truth (and Untruth) of Language: Heidegger, Ricoeur and Derrida on Disclosure and Displacement*. Pittsburgh: Duquesne University Press.

Vieira, Kate 2016. *American by Paper: How Documents Matter in Immigrant Literacy*. Minneapolis: University of Minnesota Press.

Contributors

PERTTI ANTTONEN (⊙ http://orcid.org/0000-0003-4866-9910) is Professor of Cultural Studies, especially Folklore Studies at the University of Eastern Finland, Joensuu Campus (since 2014). His main interests in research and teaching include folklore and nationalism, politics of history, heritage and tradition, ethnopoetics and the textual representation of orality, and the rites of passage theory. He has published articles on these topics in both Finnish and international journals and research anthologies. His major publication so far is *Tradition Through Modernity: Postmodernism and the Nation-State in Folklore Scholarship* (2005), soon to be published in Greek and Chinese translation.

YURI COWAN is Professor in the Department of Language and Literature at the Norwegian University of Science and Technology (NTNU) in Trondheim, specializing in book history, 19th-century literature, and medievalism. He has published articles on topics including William Morris; the Aesthetic Movement; ballad anthologies and the history of editing; Victorian sporting periodicals; and the reprinting of Victorian fantasy in the 1970s. His current book project is entitled *William Morris and Medieval Material Culture*, and he is beginning to write about the portrayal of book technology in science fiction. He is also a founding editor of the online peer-reviewed open-access journal *Authorship*.

MARIJA DALBELLO is an associate professor of information studies at Rutgers, The State University of New Jersey. Her research and teaching focus on visual genres and epistemologies of the senses, the history of knowledge, and history of the book. Her recent edited books include *Visible Writings: Cultures, Forms, Readings* (2011) with Mary Shaw and *A History of Modern Librarianship: Constructing the Heritage of Western Cultures* with Wayne Wiegand and Pamela Spence Richards (2015).

MARGARET J.M. EZELL is Distinguished Professor of English and the John and Sara Lindsey Chair of Liberal Arts at Texas A&M University. She has been studying the texts of 17th-century English Quaker and other sectarian women writers from her early study, *Writing Women's Literary History* (1993) to her most recent publication *The Oxford English Literary History Volume V: 1645–1714: The Later Seventeenth Century* (2017).

CECILIA AF FORSELLES is Director of The Library of the Finnish Literature Society, PhD and Historian. Her recent research has dealt with literary culture and currents of thought, the cultural history of translations of the *Kalevala*, reading culture, changes in the academic community, and the rise of oral culture and the strengthening of natural history as topics of academic research in the 18th century. Her latest edited book *The Emergence of Finnish Book and Reading Culture in the 1700s* (2011) with Tuija Laine as well as her recent articles mainly deal with the history of the book and the press.

KYRRE KVERNDOKK is Professor of Cultural Studies at the Department of Archaeology, History, Cultural Studies and Religion, at the University of Bergen, Norway. He has published on the practice and politics of Second World War memory, the history of folklore studies in Norway and the cultural history of natural disasters. He is currently leading the research project "The Future is Now: Temporality and Exemplarity in Climate Change Discourse".

DIARMUID Ó GIOLLÁIN, Professor and Chair, Department of Irish Language and Literature; Concurrent Professor, Department of Anthropology; Fellow, Keough-Naughton Institute for Irish Studies, University of Notre Dame, USA. D. Litt. National University of Ireland (2006). Key publications: *Locating Irish Folklore: Tradition, Modernity, Identity* (2000); *An Dúchas agus an Domhan* (2005); *Léann an Dúchais: Aistí in Ómós do Ghearóid Ó Crualaoich* (2012, ed. with S. Ó Cadhla); *Irish Ethnologies* (2017, ed.).

KIRSTI SALMI-NIKLANDER (🔘 http://orcid.org/0000-0003-0552-1801) is University Lecturer in Folklore Studies at the Department of Cultures, University of Helsinki. She has published a monograph, articles, edited books and theme issues in the fields of oral history research, working-class culture, immigrant culture and history of youth. Her long-term research has focused on hand-written newspapers as an alternative medium in 19th- and early 20th-century Finland. One of her recent publications is the theme issue "International Influences in Finnish Working-Class Literature and its Research" in *Journal of Finnish Studies* 18 (2) 2015, co-edited with Kati Launis.

RIKARD WINGÅRD (🔘 http://orcid.org/0000-0003-4709-3761) is a PhD and senior lecturer in comparative literature at the University of Gothenburg, Sweden. His dissertation *Att sluta från början. Tidigmodern läsning och folkbokens receptionsestetik* ["To End from the Beginning. Early Modern Reading and the Reception Aesthetics of the Volksbuch"] was awarded by the Swedish Academy, and he has since continued his research on early modern bibliography and book history.

Abstract

Oral Tradition and Book Culture

Edited by Pertti Anttonen, Cecilia af Forselles and Kirsti Salmi-Niklander

Traditionally, oral traditions were considered to diffuse only orally, outside the influence of literature and other printed media. Eventually, more attention was given to interaction between literacy and orality, but it is only recently that oral tradition has come to be seen as a modern construct both conceptually and in terms of accessibility. Oral traditions cannot be studied independently from the culture of writing and reading.

Lately, a new interdisciplinary interest has risen to study interconnections between oral tradition and book culture. In addition to the use and dissemination of printed books, newspapers etc., book culture denotes manuscript media and the circulation of written documents of oral tradition in and through the archive, into published collections. Book culture also intertwines the process of framing and defining oral genres with literary interests and ideologies. In addition to writing and reading, the study of oral traditions must also take into consideration the culture of publishing.

The present volume highlights varied and selected aspects of the expanding field of research into oral tradition and book culture. The questions discussed include the following: How have printing and book publishing set terms for oral tradition scholarship? How have the practices of reading affected the circulation of oral traditions? Which books and publishing projects have played a key role in this and how? How have the written representations of oral traditions, as well as the roles of editors and publishers, introduced authorship to materials customarily regarded as anonymous and collective?

The editors represent some of the key institutions in the study of oral traditions in Finland: the University of Helsinki, the Finnish Literature Society, and the University of Eastern Finland. The authors are folklorists, anthropologists, historians and literary historians, and scholars in information studies from Finland, Sweden, Norway, Ireland, and the United States.

Name Index

Studia Fennica Historica

Modernisation in Russia since 1900
Edited by Markku Kangaspuro
& Jeremy Smith
Studia Fennica Historica 12
2006

Seija-Riitta Laakso
Across the Oceans
Development of Overseas
Business Information
Transmission 1815–1875
Studia Fennica Historica 13
2007

Industry and Modernism
Companies, Architecture and
Identity in the Nordic and Baltic
Countries during the High-
Industrial Period
Edited by Anja Kervanto
Nevanlinna
Studia Fennica Historica 14
2007

Charlotta Wolff
Noble conceptions of politics
in eighteenth-century Sweden
(ca 1740–1790)
Studia Fennica Historica 15
2008

Sport, Recreation and Green
Space in the European City
Edited by Peter Clark,
Marjaana Niemi & Jari Niemelä
Studia Fennica Historica 16
2009

Rhetorics of Nordic
Democracy
Edited by Jussi Kurunmäki &
Johan Strang
Studia Fennica Historica 17
2010

Fibula, Fabula, Fact
The Viking Age in Finland
Edited by Joonas Ahola & Frog
with Clive Tolley
Studia Fennica Historica 18
2014

Novels, Histories,
Novel Nations
Historical Fiction and Cultural
Memory in Finland and Estonia
Edited by Linda Kaljundi,
Eneken Laanes & Ilona
Pikkanen
Studia Fennica Historica 19
2015

Jukka Gronow & Sergey
Zhuravlev
Fashion Meets Socialism
Fashion industry in the Soviet
Union after the Second World
War
Studia Fennica Historica 20
2015

Sofia Kotilainen
Literacy Skills as Local
Intangible Capital
The History of a Rural Lending
Library c. 1860–1920
Studia Fennica Historica 21
2016

Continued Violence and
Troublesome Pasts
Post-war Europe between the
Victors after the Second World
War
Edited by Ville Kivimäki and
Petri Karonen
Studia Fennica Historica 22
2017

Personal Agency at the
Swedish Age of Greatness
1560–1720
Edited by Petri Karonen &
Marko Hakanen
Studia Fennica Historica 23
2017

Pasi Ihalainen
The Springs of Democracy
National and Transnational
Debates on Constitutional
Reform in the British,
German, Swedish and Finnish
Parliaments, 1917–19
Studia Fennica Historica 24
2017

Studia Fennica Anthropologica

On Foreign Ground
Moving between Countries and
Categories
Edited by Marie-Louise
Karttunen &
Minna Ruckenstein
Studia Fennica Anthropologica 1
2007

Beyond the Horizon
Essays on Myth, History, Travel
and Society
Edited by Clifford Sather &
Timo Kaartinen
Studia Fennica Anthropologica 2
2008

Timo Kallinen
Divine Rulers in a Secular
State
Studia Fennica Anthropologica 3
2016

www.ingramcontent.com/pod-product-compliance
Lightning Source LLC
Chambersburg PA
CBHW081739270326
41932CB00020B/3337